I0878489

Urban Social Movements in Jerusalem

SUNY Series in Israeli Studies

Russell Stone, Editor

Urban Social Movements in Jerusalem

The Protest of the Second Generation

Shlomo Hasson

STATE UNIVERSITY OF NEW YORK PRESS
in cooperation with
THE JERUSALEM INSTITUTE FOR ISRAEL STUDIES

Originally published in Hebrew, © Jerusalem Institute for Israel Studies, Research Series No. 26, 1987.

Production by Ruth Fisher
Marketing by Bernadette LaManna

Published by
State University of New York Press, Albany

© 1993 State University of New York

All rights reserved

Printed in the United States of America

No part of this book may be used or reproduced in any manner whatsoever without written permission except in the case of brief quotations embodied in critical articles and reviews.

For information, address the State University of New York Press, State University Plaza, Albany, NY 12246

Library of Congress Cataloging-in-Publication Data

Hasson, Shlomo.
[Meḥa'at ha-dor ha-sheni. English]
Urban social movements in Jerusalem : the protest of the second generation / Shlomo Hasson.
p. cm.—(SUNY series in Israeli studies)
New version of: Meḥa'at ha-dor ha-sheni.
Includes bibliographical references (p.) and index.
ISBN 0-7914-1427-2 (ch. : acid-free paper).— ISBN 0-7914-1428-0 (pbk. : acid-free paper)
1. Social movements—Jerusalem. 2. Civil rights movements—Jerusalem. 3. Radicalism—Jerusalem. 4. Jews, Oriental—Jerusalem—Politics and government. 5. Children of immigrants—Jerusalem—Political activity. 6. Jerusalem—Politics and government. I. Title. II. Series.
HN660.J47H3713 1993
303.48′4′09569442—dc20 92-15120
CIP

10 9 8 7 6 5 4 3 2 1

Contents

List of Map and Figures vii
List of Tables viii
Preface ix

1 Urban Social Movements—Theoretical Discussion 1

2 The Emergence of Urban Social Movements 15

3 The Varying Types of Urban Protest 53

4 Why Do Urban Movements Diverge? 87

5 The Relationships Between the State and the Urban Movements 113

6 Theoretical, Practical, and Ethical Reflections 153

Bibliography 179
Index 189

List of Map and Figures

Map 1. The Location of Urban Protest by Neighborhood in Jersualem 28

Figure 1. The Divergence of Protest According to Orientation and Strategy of Action 70

Figure 2. The Three Levels of Universal Orientation 71

Figure 3. Type of Organization According to Orientation and Interpretation 92

Figure 4. Internal Conflicts Within the Local Government 150

Figure 5. The Relationships Between Context and Human Agency 162

List of Tables

Table 1. Socioeconomic Disparities in Older Israeli Towns (1961–1972) 30

Table 2. Differences Between Three Types of Protest Movements 84

Table 3. Structural Conditions, Experiences, and Protest Tendencies 158

Preface

This book has its origins in 1979 in field research on the Ohalim movement. Since then I have studied all the urban social movements that appeared in the lower-class immigrant areas of Jerusalem during the 1970s and 1980s.

In field work I benefited from the thoughtful advice of Avner Amiel and Michael Paran, two distinguished community workers, from whom I gained a great deal of my practical knowledge concerning urban movements. The leaders of the organizations made every effort to help and shared their knowledge with me. The research was overseen by a professional committee, whose members were Alex Weingrod, Lotte Salzberger, Efraim Shiloh, Mordechai Lipman, and Uri Amedi. It is a pleasure to acknowledge their helpful contribution. I am also indebted to Baruch Kimmerling, who encouraged me to see the research published in English and who along with Shalom Reichman and Eyal Ben-Ari provided useful comments on an earlier version of the study. The research was funded by the Revson Foundation and by grants made by the Waldman family in Vancouver and the Shaine Center at the Hebrew University. The professional staff at The Jerusalem Institute for Israel Studies made every effort to facilitate the research, and turned the writing of the book to a pleasant experience. Needless to say, none of the people and institutions acknowledged here bears any responsibility for the findings and ideas expressed in the book.

1

Urban Social Movements— Theoretical Discussion

For many sociologists, community workers, urban geographers and planners, the rise of grass-roots organizations in the city, sometimes referred to as *urban social movements*, have come to signify the revival of everyday political life. They express social activity initiated spontaneously from below to produce innovations or resist change, either in the geographic surroundings or the social order (Pickvance, 1976; Castells, 1977; Dunleavy, 1981). Such organizations may be involved in a variety of activities affecting zoning regulations or the distribution of social and physical resources over space, as well as in activities associated with community development (Rothman, 1974). However, beyond seeking particular social and spatial outcomes, such as stopping construction of a freeway, resisting land use changes, or enhancing local cohesiveness, these organizations, as Castells (1983) observed, are frequently concerned with improving the delivery of social services, furthering citizen participation in decision making, and expressing an ethnic or historical-local heritage. When they articulate these economic, political, and cultural goals in their activity, they become, so Castells argues, genuine urban social movements. An urban social movement, then, is a concerted attempt of urban groups to further or secure a common interest either in the ecological, cultural or political sphere through collective action outside the sphere of established institutions.

This book clarifies the meaning of these organizations by examining the social protest of the second generation of immigrants in Israel. The issue of social deprivation in urban neighborhoods settled by immigrants has been well documented by sociologists, anthropologists, and urban geographers. However, only rarely has an attempt been made to explore in a systematic manner the transformation of social deprivation into organized patterns of activity. This book tries to fill the gap by exploring eight protest organizations that emerged in the lower-class, immigrant neighborhoods of Jerusalem. Like other grass-roots organizations, those that appeared in Jerusalem throughout the 1970s and 1980s marked a radical change in urban politics. Up until then the shaping of immigrant neighborhoods and housing projects, whether in social or spatial terms, was the responsibility of the state; that is, the prerogative of politicians, planners, and bureaucrats. The settlement and housing of the new immigrants was considered part of a national policy aimed at achieving three goals: immigrant absorption, asserting Israeli sovereignty over all parts of the country, and sociopolitical integration of the newcomers. With the exception of a few powerful local bosses who arose from among the ranks of the immigrants, the public remained quite apathetic and uninvolved. This pattern has been radically transformed with the rise of protest organizations. Members of the immigrants' second generation, people who came to Israel at a young age or were born in the housing projects, began to express their needs and take an active part in shaping their residential areas. They demanded to participate in determining the physical-social nature of the environment, identifying problems associated with local realities they themselves experienced: dilapidated housing, the lack of social services, the absence of an outlet for political expression as a result of manipulation and patronage, a sense of ethnocultural discrimination and frustration. They attempted to rectify these problems through collective action.

The rise of these movements took place within the framework of post 1967 Jerusalem; that is, after the unification of the city under Israeli rule. Since that time the city's urban pattern has turned into a microcosmos of the major ethnic and social divisions and conflicts that beset Israeli society. These divisions encompass the national conflict between Jews and Arabs, the cultural conflict between ultraorthodox and secular Jews, and the socioethnic cleavage between upper- and lower-class social groups.

In spite of their physical proximity, the Arab and Jewish communities remained largely segregated from each other. The Arab population, which amounted to 142,600 people in 1989 (that is, 28 percent of the city's population), occupies the eastern section of Jerusalem; the Jewish population, which amounted to 361,500 people in 1989 (that is, 72 percent of the city's population), occupies the western part of Jerusalem (the section of the city that has been Israeli since 1948) and several new neighborhoods in East Jerusalem (Jerusalem Institute for Israel Studies, 1991). The relations between the two communities have been characterized by outright conflict, which is rooted in the continuing Arab-Jewish struggle for control in the city. As Romann and Weingrod (1991)observed, "In a fundamental sense the dispute centers on the moral and legal basis of the city's political system and the mutual recognition of collective national identities, rights, and sovereignty" (p. 229). Within the Jewish population itself there has been some internal subdivisions; the ultraorthodox groups have formed their own enclaves, mainly along the northeastern section of the city. Within this section, which stretches from Mea-Shea'rim in the east to Romema and Kiriat Matersdorf in the west, lived about one-third of the city's population in 1989 (Shilhav and Friedman, 1989). Finally, along the pre-1967 cease fire line, from Ir Ganim in the southwest through the Katamon housing projects to the east and to Musrara and Shmuel Hanavi in the north, lie the immigrant neighborhoods and housing projects, wherein appeared the social movements of lower-class immigrant groups discussed in this book. The book therefore covers only one aspect of the social divisions and conflicts that characterize Jerusalem and relates to the role of lower-class immigrant groups in shaping urban life.

The theoretical questions concerning these movements are the following:

1. Why do urban movements develop?
2. How do types of urban movements differ in terms of ideological and political orientations and strategies of action?
3. Why do the movements diverge?
4. How does the government, either senior or local, respond to and interact with the movements?

The theme of the study, which is theoretically broad and general, is examined empirically by looking into the major urban-social movements arising in Israel in the 1970s and 1980s—most of them to be found in Jerusalem. In the following sections I will describe the main features of urban social movements, the units of analysis, the theoretical framework of the study, and the methodology.

Urban Social Movements

Urban social movements, from the 1960s onward, became a common phenomenon in the cities of developed and developing countries. These movements were eclectic in their goals, methods of organization, and the groups they represented. They included organizations that protested against threats to the environment, land use changes, and inappropriate educational policies, as well as organizations that protested against rent rises, inadequate housing, the distribution of resources, and the governing of municipalities. Socially, the movements encompassed different groups, including the entire range of social classes, from the middle and upper classes to tenants' associations and squatters' rights groups originating in the lower class. Despite the eclecticism of goals and social composition, they all focused on urban issues that were, in general, associated with collective consumption; that is, urban goods and services supplied by public agencies or consumed collectively, such as public housing projects, physical infrastructure, education, health care, and transportation.

The protest often went beyond urban affairs and expanded into partial or comprehensive criticism of the sociopolitical order. The expansion of protest stemmed in part from the cognitive link often made between concrete urban problems and wider social problems, such as the position of a given group in the political-economic system or its ethnic affiliation. In this way, problems of housing, transportation, or education affecting the lower class were linked on more than one occasion to their low position in the sociopolitical system. As a result, urban protest movements often transcended concrete urban issues and turned into a macrosocial protest.

Another reason for the expansion of urban movements beyond concrete urban issues was associated with the growth of the state's role in the provision of goods and services, especially those consumed collectively. This growing state intervention in the urban sphere enhanced the politicization of the urban space and, as a result, turned the state into a central object of sociopolitical criticism. In other words, problems of education, services, and housing were no longer seen as local but as macropolitical problems deriving from the functioning of the state—the policy that guides it and the principles and values that are at its foundation.

Urban protest appeared, therefore, at different levels—beginning with activity in response to concrete local issues and ending with debate and struggle over the nature of the existing political-economic order—that had reciprocal links between them. Although members of different classes took part in protests over concrete local issues, the relative weight of the members of the middle and upper classes was notably high. These forms of protest were discussed mainly by the literature on community organizations and organizations of limited liability. These studies indicated that the organizations were particularistic in nature, that is, they were oriented toward specific areas and well-defined problems, and had an instrumental-rational character. They had a voluntary membership quite often limited to those sectors of the population affected by the problem, tended to be uninstitutionalized and short range in character, and challenged the existing order in only a limited way (Suttles, 1972; Ben-Ari, 1984). Urban protest that expanded into universal criticism of the social structure was also made up of different classes, but the two ends of the social spectrum were most prominent: on one side, social elites, such as students and intellectuals; and on the other hand, members of the lower class. The literature on social and urban social movements deals mainly with this type of protest.

Despite the different character of the two types of urban protest, the particularistic and universal, both brought about social innovation in the urban political arena. The innovation ran against the prevailing tendency to concentrate political, bureaucratic, technological, and communications power in a few hands—those of politicians, producers, bureaucrats, and technocrats. Against this background, even when limited in its scope, the protest activity conveyed a clear message of discontent with the removal of political life from the public domain and its concentration in the hands of a political-technocratic elite.

The innovation was expressed not only in the struggle, but also in the ever-growing participation of members of the lower class in the protest activity. Because the protest movements of the lower classes is the central interest of this study, it is worth delving a bit further into this phenomenon. Since the 1960s the urban system has witnessed many indications of social protest on the part of the lower classes. Poor-people's movements protested against the quality of life in the neighborhood, against unjust state distribution of resources, and against their lack of participation in the decision-making process, and ethnic groups protested the absence of proper representation in the cultural field. In a comprehensive report on the politics of protest in the United States, Skolnick (1969) notes that the objectives of the protest of black organizations in the American city were obtaining resources, local control, and political autonomy. In the British city, the Asian and West Indian immigrant groups fought for greater political involvement and demanded reforms in the areas of housing, education, immigration policy, and cultural representation (Lewis, 1970, p. 86; Gilroy, 1987). In Paris and Barcelona the residents of public housing projects organized themselves into protest movements, seeking improvements in housing conditions (Castells, 1977; Borja, 1978). In Italy the newcomers who arrived in the cities of the north and south from rural areas demanded improvements in their living conditions and housing (Evers and Rodrigues, 1978). In Monterey, Mexico, and in Bogota, Columbia, for instance, squatters living on public land organized social movements and demanded that they be given ownership of the land, the necessary infrastructure, and housing aid (Lowe, 1986).

In many places the parties of the Left tried to ride the wave of urban protest and enlist its activists into their ranks. They succeeded only partially, however; in general the movements remained politically autonomous. The urban movements that appeared in this manner differed from conventional organizations and traditional interest groups in a number of ways. Their level of integration into the political system was low, the level of institutionalization of their organizations was low, and their strategies were based largely on conflict (demonstrations, squatting). The urban protest movements of the lower classes also differed from traditional social movements that functioned outside the mainstream; for example, the peace, ecological, feminist, and alternative communication movements. In contrast with these, the urban movements were characterized by a great measure of localism, and their existence was short lived and episodic. In general, they did not develop a coherent ideology of social change or a comprehensive economic, political, and cultural strategy; and their leadership tended to be absorbed into the established political system.

The Theoretical Framework

The study of urban movements triggered a heated theoretical dispute over the central topics of research and the methodological procedures for examining them. The dispute focused on the question of whether research should concentrate on the structural conditions that give rise to the movements or the process whereby the organization came into being (Touraine, 1985; Eder, 1985). This dispute is often presented as the dualism of structure and agency. For those adhered to the structuralist point of view, the social whole, whether conceptualized in economic, political, social or ecological terms, has a decisive influence over human subjects. On the other hand, for those adhered to the agency point of view, meaning and action are accorded primacy in shaping social conduct. The differences are both ontological and epistemological. Ontologically, what is at issue is whether reality is independent of the human agent's knowledge (realism) or whether it is a construct of human experience and thought (coventionalism or nominalism). The answer to the question has some important epistemological ramifications. Viewing reality as independent and objective suggests the employment of objective approaches of research associated with empirical-analytical procedures, whereas approaching reality as a construct of human mind has close affinity with subjective approaches associated with interpretative procedures. In the study of urban social movements, the dispute between sructuralism and human agency, realism and coventionalism, objectivism and subjectivism was given four different theoretical expressions.

1. The collective behavior theory focuses on the structural problems underlying the movements and their sociopsychological interpretation. The collective behavior approach also emphasizes absolute and relative deprivation and the system of beliefs and opinions and, in this way, combines social and psychological explanations (Killian, 1963; Gurr, 1970).
2. The resource mobilization theory deals with the organizational process and the role of the human agent in it (Olson, 1965; McCarthy and Zald, 1977). To account for the process of social mobilization, the theory turns to the role played by charismatic leadership, community workers, the media, and volunteers in fostering social mobilization. Folllowing Olson's (1965) seminal work, special emphasis is given to the agent's economic motive of profit maximization. This entails calculated assessment of risks and rewards on which a decision is made whether or not to take part in social action. For others, human agency is considered in more complex terms that take into consideration motives associated with pride, fear, and revenge (Perlman, 1982).
3. The structural-Marxist approach, postulated by the early writings of Castells (1977), elevates structure over human

agency and considers any reversal of this scheme, that is, any autonomous analysis of the human agent, to be psychological reductionism. It is contended that, in addition to the major conflict between the forces and relations of production in the workplace, a secondary arena of social exploitation emerged within the built environment itself. The capitalists' motive of profit accumulation, which results in a low level of physical development and poor housing conditions and social services, contradicts the citizens' will for a better and safer environment. The unavoidable result has been the rise of a series of social movements that conceive the environment not as an asset to be traded in the market, but rather as factor wherein biophysical and cultural reproduction is to be secured. Although Castells later renounced much of his earlier Marxist positions, and expanded his theoretical framework (see Chapter 3), he remained faithful to the claim that the structural, class conflict over the built environment forms one of the major axes around which urban movements develop.

4. The search for identity approach regards the social actor in the movement as a central force in shaping civil society within a specific framework of time and place (Touraine, 1981; 1985). Touraine is less interested in the deeper political-economic conditions underlying the movements than in their objectives and goals, hence his interest in the ideals and strategies of action pursued by the movements and their negotiations and exchange with other actors located in their "fields of action." For Touraine, social actors are animated by a search for identity and meaning. Such a search is defined by Touraine as a struggle "for the social control of historicity" (Touraine, 1981). Historicity implies the way in which the knowledge of social processes is used by social actors to reshape the social conditions of their existence. Criticizing the Marxist scheme, Touraine notes that the movements are not conveyors of certain teleological schemes, but represent social actors engaged in endless struggles and negotiations for an alternative society. In the course of their struggles and negotiations the movements may affect the system they wish to change, but may also be absorbed into the existing system, adopting some of its perspectives.

A temporal examination shows that the focus of the theoretical debate has moved from discussion of the deep structure in the 1960s to the human agent in the 1980s. The central debate today is between the resource mobilization approach, which is considered pragmatic and rational, and the search for identity approach, which contains some romantic elements concerning the nature of the good society. The contribution of recent studies of urban social movements to this debate is centered on the collective behavior and the search for identity approaches. Reviewing Castells's *The City and the Grassroots*, Pickvance (1985) pointed to four factors underlying the rise of urban social movements and shaping their character: (1) massive migration from rural areas to the cities, creating, among other things, squatters' movements; (2) state involvement in delivery of services, giving rise to consumption movements supporting or opposing state interference; (3) the inability of the establishment to absorb the protest; (4) the general economic and social situation, which may affect the rise and fall of the movement. As Pickvance explains, in a period of economic expansion there is a rise in expectations and a tendency for protest to grow, while in a period of recession the level of expectations goes down, and the tendency to protest fades. Referring to the situation in Europe, Pickvance pointed to the difference between British constitutionalism and continental pragmatism as a basic element in shaping the forms of urban protest (private communication). Other researchers, like Friedland (1982) and Lowe (1986), point to the unique historical and ecological conditions in shaping urban protest. Friedland emphasizes the place of corporations and labor unions in moderating the protest activity of blacks in American urban centers, whereas Lowe exposes the influence the British party system had on the protest movements, especially the activity of the Labour party. These explanations refine the structuralist approach, adding cultural-political content to it, and are without a doubt more fruitful than past structural approaches that claim universal validity. However, despite this contribution, thinking in the field of urban social movements remains structuralist in character. It is difficult to find any penetrating theorization concerning the construction of social action as mediated by structure and agency, and the relation of the movements with their environment at the neighborhood, urban, or national level. Likewise, there is almost no theoretical consideration of the search for identity; and in my opinion the messages of Touraine and Castells in this area were not properly received.

In summary, except for Touraine's and Castells's work, the forefront of research in the field of urban social movements is still stuck in a search for macrosocietal explanations and does not advance our understanding of the role of human actors and their reciprocal relations with the social structure. This is, precisely, one of the focuses of the present study. Inspired by Giddens's structuration theory, it is intended to show how human agency implicated in the social strucure make sense of their conditions, construct the meaning of the movements and their own identity, mobilize resources, and shape the nature of their social, political, and physical surroundings. Contrary to Giddens, however, the social structure, as conceived in this study, relates not only to rules (conventions and norms) and resources (allocative and authoritative), but also to the general political economic and the specific ecological (housing, services, communal norms, socialization mechanisms) conditions in which the actors find themselves. It is assumed that this structure both enables and constrains the human actor in ways not always entirely explicated by the subject. It is also assumed that some of the actions affect the structure in ways unintended by the human agent. And it is indeed one of the major tasks of the present study to expose through interpretative procedures those unacknowledged conditions of human action and to draw attention to the unintended consequences of action (Giddens, 1984).

My starting point in analyzing the relations between agency and structure will be the general socioeconomic and political structure and the specific social and ecological conditions in which the actors found themselves. Based on the analysis of this structure, I will address the following questions. How do the human actors interpret and respond to the general and specific sociospatial conditions in which they are located? How do they change their interpretations and orientations over time due to their sociopolitical interaction with neighborhood residents and with bureaucrats and politicians in the local and central state? What are the cultural-political orientations of the movements? How are these orientations structured by human actors? How does human action affect the sociopolitical structure, and what are the intended and unintended consequences of this action? These questions are rarely raised by the literature surveyed, although implicit in Touraine's general message and by the pioneering work of Castells in this field.

These theoretical questions may be rephrased through four theoretical arguments. First, the rise of urban social movements in

Jerusalem is rooted in ethnic disparities, the development of social classes (i.e., production classes in the Marxist sense) and housing classes (in the Weberian sense) and the translation of the ethnoclass gaps into spatial segregation through the state's housing policy. Moreover, to complete the explanation, one has to look at the human agents, that is, local leaders, activists and volunteers, community workers, and politicians, involved in turning social grievances and feelings of deprivation into organized social action.

Second, the social context in which the movements are rooted creates some similar broad tendencies for protest. My argument, however, is that in spite of the similar context shared by the participants in the movements, their protest tended to diverge in different directions. As a result, urban protest in Jerusalem took different forms and expressed itself in different strategies of social action.

Third, the divergence of protest is associated with different readings of the sociohistorical context by subgroups within the immigrants' second generation. In other words, the transformation from social context to organized action is not immediately given, because it is mediated by humanistic processes of interpretation and typification. It is also argued that the schemes of interpretation reflect some basic values, habits of mind, specific experiences, and processes of social learning characterizing the participants. These schemes are dynamic and tend to change due to social interaction with political institutions and with other social groups. As a result, patterns of action are not static and tend to change over time and space.

Finally, responding to the structural problems that underlay the movements and to the protestors' demands, the state assumed different strategies of action. These strategies varied across time: paternalism and control at the preliminary stages of absorption; confrontation-repression with the advent of protest and coproduction at present. It is contended that over time new modes of interaction were developed between the state and the urban movements through which political (legitimation), economic (material allocations), and social (cultural recognition) resources were exchanged.

The Units of Analysis

The protest movements of the disadvantaged neighborhoods and immigrant housing projects arose against the background of a social problem that developed in Israel from the 1950s onward. The 1959 riots in Wadi Salib, an Arab neighborhood in Haifa populated by Jews after the War of Independence in 1948, marked the first outbreak of social discontent in an immigrant neighborhood. The Ethnic Coalition of North African Immigrants, an organization created during the outbreak of protest, cited ethnic discrimination against North African immigrants as the main reason for the riots (Eisenstadt, 1967, p. 253).

At the beginning of the 1970s the Israeli Black Panthers appeared on the public scene. This movement was also born in a former Arab neighborhood, this time Musrara in Jerusalem, populated after the War of Independence (1948) by new immigrants, mostly from Morocco. In a series of violent demonstrations the movement demanded elimination of all discriminatory practices against Oriental Jews and supply of better housing, employment, and education for the Oriental community (Cohen, 1980, pp. 93–94). In 1973 the nucleus of the Ohalim movement—Ohel Yosef—consolidated in the immigrant housing project of Gonen (Katamon) Tet in Jerusalem. (The Hebrew word *ohel* [plural, *ohalim*] literally means "tent," but in this particular case indicates feelings of temporary residence.) The members of Ohel Yosef at first opposed the activities of the Black Panthers and looked for what they defined as positive activity to improve the life of their community by initiating self-help services from below. In the years 1977–1981 Ohel Yosef members and supporters worked to establish Ohel councils in other Jerusalem neighborhoods: Shmuel Hanavi, Nahla'ot, Baka, and on Stern Street in Kiryat Hayovel. In 1979 the governing councils of the different Ohel organizations merged into a citywide movement, the Ohalim movement, aimed at advancing the interests of disadvantaged neighborhoods and ethnic groups all over the country. The citywide movement was responsible for activity on the supraneighborhood level, while activity within each neighborhood remained in the hands of the individual Ohel councils.

The early 1980s saw the appearance of several other protest organizations in Jerusalem: the Dai (Enough) movement in Musrara, which made headlines by squatting in a neighborhood basement and establishing a 'settlement" there; Shahak (Improvement of Community Life, henceforth ICL) in Ir Ganim, which protested local housing conditions; Tsalash (Youth for the Neighborhood, henceforth YFN), also in Ir Ganim; and the Katamon Higher Committee, which represented residents in Katamon Gimel, Daled, Hey, Rashbag, and in the Pat housing project.

Methodology

The analysis works on both macro and micro scales. Thus, the general, theoretical issues are first explored, and then the specific features of the problem are clarified through detailed case studies. In this way I seek to integrate the specific findings into the already existing body of knowledge. My primary strategy relies on case studies that investigate contemporary phenomena (urban movements) within a real-life context through participant observation. The work has its origins in 1979 in research on the Ohalim movement and the Ohel councils in Katamon Tet and Shmuel Hanavi. In 1980, I observed the establishment of the Katamon Higher Committee and accompanied that movement until it was disbanded in 1982. During 1981 and 1982, I observed the activities of the local boss in Ir Ganim and the reaction of the young generation's grassroots organizations: Youth for the Neighborhood (YFN) and Improvement of Community Life. Simultaneously, an observation was carried out in Musrara, where the Dai movement appeared. The study, which is based on participant observation and interviews with leaders and volunteers, covers all the protest movements that emerged in Jerusalem in the 1970s and 1980s. The only exception is the Israeli Black Panthers movement, which by then existed only through the Heritage (Moreshet) project. The study has been complemented by the analysis of documents, correspondence, and minutes produced by the movements.

A major complaint against the case study approach is that it is difficult to generalize from one case study to another. The singularity of the case study findings is thus contrasted with the empirical generalization of the survey approach. But this problem can be overcome, as Yin suggests, not by generalizing to other case studies but by generalizing to theory (Yin, 1984, p. 39). By relating the particular set of findings of the specific case studies, examined in this book, to some broader theories it is possible to attain an analytical generalization. The study in other words is theoretically informed and the findings are interpreted through comparison with the existing theoretical knoledge. In so doing I sought to develop a comparative theoretical cum empirical framework, which transcends the details of any specific organization. In other words, it is not my intention to portray the specific ethnography of any protest movement, but rather to explore those details within general theoretical configurations.

The Structure of This Book

In light of the working framework just developed, Chapter 2 analyzes the constitutive conditions and the organizational processes that account for the rise of protest movements in Jerusalem. In this way it seeks to shed light on the transformation of social problem into social force. Chapter 3 examines the divergence of protest and elucidates the different meanings it takes. Chapter 4 analyzes why protest movements diverge in different directions. It examines the different interpretations attached by the social actors to the social conditions, and explores the factors that account for the different interpretations. Chapter 5 analyzes the state's response to urban movements and the ways in which these responses vary over time. The concluding chapter, Chapter 6, discusses the substantial, theoretical, practical, and ethical implications of this study.

2
The Emergence of Urban Social Movements

This chapter seeks to clarify why urban social movements emerge and develop. To this purpose, I examine the main theories existing in the field, analyze the empirical evidence accumulated in Jerusalem, and relate the empirical findings to the theoretical body of knowledge.

Theoretical Discussion

One of the most intriguing issues that besets the study of social movements is the question of why the movements appear. The question has received different answers, emphasizing the structural problem and the psychological interpretations at the root of the movements' appearances. The integration of a structural problem and pressures with a psychological interpretation, beliefs, or weak ideologies was considered a necessary, and sometimes even sufficient, condition for the appearance of the movements. This integration produced a comprehensive theoretical approach known as *collective behavior*, whose most prominent representatives are Smelser (1963), Gurr (1970), Turner and Killian (1972), and McCarthy and Zald (1977). According to these theoreticians, the structural problem may be caused by changes in the social or political system. The changes in the social system may be the result of large-scale immigration, of modernization processes, or of social mobility. They may be accompanied by the destabilization of social frameworks and of the rules and norms associated with them, which may lead to a rise in the level of social and political expectations. Raised expectations and pressures for social change may also be caused by structural modifications in the political system; for instance, adoption of a populist approach or moving from a centralized to a decentralized system. The growing demand for sociopolitical changes may find the political system unready and insufficiently flexible to respond to it (Huntington, 1968). The lack of a satisfactory response to political demands raised from the bottom might breed tension and frustration, especially when there is a gap between the level of expectations and the opportunities to realize them. For this reason, Turner and Killian (1972) attribute great significance to the psychology of individuals and groups in interpreting the problem and in shaping social protest.

The psychological interpretations of social problems is emphasized by disciples of the relative deprivation approach. Gurr (1970) argues that the structural problem itself does not cause people to organize and act collectively. The movement develops only when people analyze the problem in a critical way and interpret it as injustice and inequality. The emphasis here is transferred from inequality to relative inequality, as it is perceived by comparison of the situation of the group with the situation of another referent group. As a result of this comparison a feeling of discrimination and deprivation develops, as does a tendency to take action.

One of the most comprehensive accounts for the appearance of social movements is provided by Neil Smelser's explanatory scheme (1968). This scheme contains six conditions conceived of as necessary for the rise of an organization:

1. *Structural conduciveness* denotes the general social and political conditions that encourage or inhibit the formation of social movements of different types. Although such conditions, such as religious or political tolerance, may be favorable for the formation of the movements in themselves they do not bring them into being.

2. *Structural strains* implies tensions that may produce conflicting interests within society. The tensions may express general conditions such as ethnic or economic inequality or specific conditions associated with the nature of housing. In either case grievances, anxieties, and uncertainties lead to conflicting interests and clashes of goals.

3. *Generalized beliefs* refers to ideologies that crystallize grievances, anxieties, and uncertainties into a definite course of action.

4. *Precipitating factors* relates to events or incidents that may affect the participants in the movements to assume direct social action.

The combination of these four sets of factors does not necessarily breed social movements, Smelser argues. It may end up in social riots or sporadic urban disturbances unless a coordinated group is formed.

5. *Coordinated group* relates to those social conditions and processes that transform an unorganized group into a social organization. Such a transformation involves social mobilization of the participants by leaders, the existence of some kind of communication among the participants, and sustained supply of funding to secure the organization's existence.
6. *The application of social control* relates to governmental response, either to rectify the structural strains or to enforce law and order (Smelser, 1968, pp. 97–100).

Smelser thus provides a staged model wherein each stage serves as a precondition for the occurrence of the subsesquent ones, and together they account for the emergence of social movements. He fails, however, to theorize the social relations developed between the participants and other forces (social or political forces) at each stage, and the ways in which these relations affect social mobilization. These points were developed by the Marxist and Weberian theories.

Like Smelser the Marxists, and especially the structural-Marxists, tended also to see the social movements as the result of structural forces, but these forces were interpreted in the Marxist codex as a structural contradiction between the forces of production and the relations of production. This approach was especially common in Europe (in the United States it remained outside the mainstream and was represented primarily by Herberle [1968]), and received full expression in Manuel Castells's book *The Urban Question*. The book, written in 1972 in French and translated into English in 1977, served for a decade as the centerpiece for the study of urban social movements. As Castells himself acknowledges in the introduction to his book, he was influenced by the structuralist approach of Louis Althusser. In line with this approach, Castells does not put the psychology of the individual at the center of his study, but rather the structural problem that shapes, he argues, that psychology.

Despite the differences in theory and ideological-political outlook, Castells's structural explanation was very similar to those presented by the theory of collective behavior developed in the 1960s. In both cases there were deep structures that, according to the writers, transcended the human agent and affected the movement's action; hence the primary importance accorded to the analysis of these structures. To be sure, in both cases there was reference to the human agent, particularly as an interpreter of the underlying structures, but there was no analytic explication of the social process through which the social actor goes beyond interpretation, structuring the movement and shaping its goals and activities. The organization, in other words, was seen as derivative of something prior and deep rooted, and as less interesting as a subject for study.

The search for deep structures continues in Castells's book *The City and the Grassroots*, although this time in a much more subtle form. In this book, Castells seeks to theorize the rise of urban social movements by relating them to deeper societal structures: the capitalist mode of production (form of surplus appropriation in capitalist societies), the industrial mode of development (which concerns the increasing productivity of labor and capital through technological developments in the spheres of production, management, and control), the information mode of development (which concerns the increasing technological knowledge and its concentration in a small technocratic elite), and state power (which implies control over the means of violence). Each of these constitutive structures, Castells remarks, produces new dominant social oppressors—capitalists, managers, technocrats, and bureaucrats—who are to be challenged and confronted by the urban social movements.

The Marxist account for the rise of urban social movements has been sharply criticized by Weberian theorists. Relying on the works of neo-Weberians such as Rex and Moore (Rex and Moore, 1967; Rex, 1968), Pickvance pointed to internal divisions within the working class that prevented an overall class mobilization and offered a narrower basis for social organization. These lines of division were defined not in accordance with the social position in the production process, but according to the position in the goods market. As the neo-Weberian school claims, the existing distinctions within the working class as far as ownership levels of goods (housing or other durable goods) are concerned, and differences in life opportunities and social interests stemming from these distinctions, are the concrete factors that determine the development of urban social movements. In other words, the urban social movements do not express a struggle between social classes in the Marxist sense, but rather between different sectors of consumers that have different life opportunities and accordingly also different sociopolitical interests. The best-known example that comes from these studies is that of the mobilization of housing classes into urban movements—groups made up of individuals for whom the value of their housing is more or less equal, thus giving them common interests. These housing classes are often in conflict with each other: the residents of public housing projects with the residents of nearby disadvantaged neighborhoods or low-rent tenants with the owners of poor apartments who live nearby and who wish to preserve the value of housing in the area.

It is thus evident that the theory of collective behavior treated the organization as derivative of something prior and deep rooted, and less interesting as a subject for study. Against this background in the 1970s a comprehensive criticism developed of the various structural approaches and their different nuances. This criticism claimed that the focus of study ought to be the way in which the movement is organized and structured and accordingly wished to shift the central axis of research from the question of *why* the organization was created to the question of *how* it came into being. The theory that developed as a criticism of the collective behavior was the resource mobilization approach.

Advocates of the resource mobilization approach argued that structural problems, either absolute or relative, were not sufficient in themselves to bring about the creation of a movement. Beyond the existing problems there must be the intervention of a human agent to mobilize internal and external resources and create a link with the external environment—the media, pressure groups, and key figures—in order to obtain their support. Those who sided with this approach emphasized the social bases around which the movement was formed, the mobilization of resources, and the role of outside organizers and leaders in persuading individuals to join the movement, by highlighting the benefits and minimizing the costs of social activity (Olson, 1965; Gamson, 1975; Rich, 1980). As far as urban social movements are concerned, this approach was especially evident in the works of British urbanists such as Pickvance (1976; 1977), Saunders (1980), and Dunleavy (1977; 1981). Reviewing Castells's work, Pickvance (1977) argued that research should be diverted from exposition of structural elements to the processes whereby the social base is transformed into a social force. Without such an examination, Pickvance noted, the years-old Marxist problem of the transformation of the class-in-itself into a class-for-itself remained without an answer. Pickvance thus pointed to those factors that could enhance the mobilization process, like social networks that preceded the appearance of the movement or ethnic associations around which the organization might be formed. In addition to the social base, Pickvance noted, there is a need to compensate the participants in material or symbolic ways to secure their participation in the movement. The problem of compensation and persuasion to join the movement is the central factor in the resource mobilization theory and represents an ongoing attempt to deal with the problem of the free rider raised by Olson (1965). The main problem here lies with the assumption that an individual, acting rationally to maximize his or her benefits and aware of the movement's activity, would tend to abstain from participation and leave the work to others. The role of the leader is conceived, therefore, as one of encouraging and compensating the participants. Lipsky (1972), for example, pointed to the use of symbolic compensation, militant rhetoric, and the creation of true or imaginary identities to mobilize participants into American urban protest movements. Killian (1963) and Gouldner (1979) laud the role of intellectuals in rewriting historical narratives and developing social myths that serve as catalysts for social organization.

Main Arguments

In line with the theory of collective behavior, I will argue that it is impossible to understand *why* protest movements rise and develop without understanding the macrosocietal features of Israeli society. In analyzing these macrosocietal features, one has to reckon with those constitutive structures that may give rise to urban social protest: structural (sociodemographic) changes, ethno-class divisions, housing policy assumed by the state, spatial closure, and modernization and social mobility. However, as the theory of resource mobilization clearly demonstrates, the macrosocietal features are necessary yet insufficient to bring about social mobilization. To understand *how* the movements come into being one has to examine organizational processes associated with premovement organizational structures; that is, informal groupings predating the movement, social networks, and the role of local leadership and outside organizers in setting up the movements. This general argument may be broken into several specific arguments.

1. *Structural Changes.* Protest movements in the immigrant neighborhoods and housing projects of Jerusalem did not appear out of thin air. They arose against a general and supportive background of structural sociodemographic changes that took place in Israel during the 1950s and 1960s: mass immigration, the arrival of a large influx of poor people of Sephardic (Middle Eastern- and North African-born Jews) origin, housing shortage, and massive state intervention in the housing sphere.

2. *Structural Strains.* Concurrent with these changes, a deep *ethno-class division* emerged in Israel between the older Ashkenazic (European-born Jews) group and the Sephardic (sometimes referred to as *Orientals*) one. This division, primarily felt during the 1950s and 1960s and to a lesser extent in the following two decades, is characterized by socioeconomic inequality among Sephardic and Ashkenazic Jews and by unequal access to political power. The ethnoclass division was translated through *state housing policy* into geographic segregation and spatial enclosure of the Sephardic newcomers. *Spatial enclosure* denotes the geographic segregation of the lower strata of society in separate housing projects through a deliberate housing policy. Such a segregated pattern implied substandard housing conditions, a low level of social services, limited informal social contacts with the absorbing society, and the prominence of social inequality. These factors bred social resentment and facilitated territorial mobilization.

3. *Modernization, Social Mobility, and Relative Deprivation.* The terms *modernization* and *mobility* are laden with ideological and theoretical biases. What one group perceives as modernization according to a Western-rational or secular-humanistic system of values may be seen by another group as degeneration and reaction. Examples of this are the transition from a society with religious-traditional character to a secular society, the change in the authority of the rabbi and father, and so on. The term *mobility* is also ideologically and theoretically charged. To avoid misunderstandings, I will use the term *mobility* to refer to an absolute change in the social position of individuals and groups

and not to denote changes in the relative social gap. In certain situations, social mobility and the widening of the relative gap occur simultaneously, because the referent group has experienced absolute mobility at a greater rate. Such a situation characterizes, according to Nahon (1984), the situation of the second generation of Oriental origin in comparison with their fellows of European origin. Social mobility and modernization may be accompanied by a dramatic rise in the levels of demands and expectations and a growing critique and discontent with the practice and policy of the welfare state. The rise of social expectations and the difficulties incurred in realizing them may result in a growing gap between expectations and opportunities to realize them. It is this growing gap that accounts for feelings of deprivation, breeds social resentment, and encourages social protest.

4. *Precipitating Factors*. These factors are the immediate causes that lead to social protest. In Israel they might be associated with new waves of immigration, new economic and social programs, relaxation of the security tension, or growing social critique.
5. *Social Mobilization*. In themselves the social changes and precipitating events were insufficient to produce social movements. To enable such a change required social mobilization and coordination that could utilize existing social networks, transform existing grievances into coherent ideologies, and outline paths of action. Community workers with a liberal orientation and local leaders played a leading role in this process.

Structural Changes and Ethno-Class Division

Following the establishment of the state in May 1948, a large wave of Jewish immigrants arrived in the country. Between May 1948 and December 1951, some 690,000 Jews immigrated to Israel, almost doubling its Jewish population. During the whole decade of the 1950s, about 1 million immigrants entered the country. At the same time, there was an exodus of the Arab population. It is estimated that between 614,000 and 626,000 Arabs left the territory of Israel in 1948, leaving approximately 160,000 Arabs in the country in 1949 (Bachi, 1977, p. 54). For historical reasons associated with (1) the national-territorial conflict between Jews and Arabs in Palestine; (2) the differences in the socioeconomic systems of the two communities; and (3) the differences in their geographical distribution and settlement patterns, a social and spatial division existed between the two groups from the time the state was founded. Although that division is not the subject of this book it nevertheless affected significantly the social conflicts within Jewish society, and I will turn to it in due course.

The Jewish newcomers did not enter a social vacuum. Upon arrival they confronted an existing social structure that contained a variety of classes: petit bourgeoisie, small capitalists, managerial and intellectual social groups, and a large working class. The social relationships between these classes, shaped during the prestate period, were far from harmonious. Over the years, however, as the working class became less radical in its political orientation, a mixed economic structure emerged. This resulted in a sort of coexistence and collaboration, in the economic sphere, between the working class and the bourgeois-capitalist sector. Politically, however, most of the power positions at the national level were held by the political and cultural elite of the working class, which pursued a moderate socialist policy. Consequently, the power elite of the working class had gained control over the major power centers: the Jewish Agency, which attended to both domestic and foreign affairs; Hava'ad Hale'umi (The National Committee), which dealt with domestic matters; the Histadrut labor federation; and the Mapai (Labor) party. Later, when the state was established, the working class continued to maintain its political hegemony, with members of its power elite serving as prime minister and in the other top ministerial positions in the new government.

In this socioeconomic and political structure, the newcomers turned into a distinctive subworking class. Most of them lacked private economic resources, and their educational level and occupational skills were much lower than in the rest of the society. Moreover, in contrast to the prestate immigration of European Jews, known as Ashkenazim, a large portion of the state's new immigrants came from precapitalist countries in Asia and Africa. Accordingly, the proportion of Asian- and African-born Jews, known as *Sephardim*, or *Orientals*, increased from 10.4 percent in the 1919–1948 period to 51.2 percent in the 1948–1972 period (Bachi, 1977, p. 93).

As a result, the social structure of Israeli society became more heterogeneous, constituting three major social classes (the managerial and the intellectual groups are distributed among them): the emerging bourgeois-capitalist class, which owned private economic resources; the prestate working class (henceforth, the *old working class*), made up primarily of Ashkenazim who, by virtue of their knowledge, skills, and already established social networks, enjoyed easy access to social power, both public economic resources and organizational and political power positions; and a newly emerged fraction of the working class (henceforth, the *new working class*), made up largely of Sephardim (Oriental Jews) lacking both private and public economic resources and with no access to political power. The potentiality for social conflict latent in such a situation was evident to policy makers and high officials (Zaslavsky, 1954). And social scientists have often turned these socioethnic divisions into a necessary and even sufficient explanation for the rise of urban social movements in Israel (Cohen, 1980; Smooha and Peres, 1975).

These social inequalities were augmented by the cultural orientation of the Israeli power elite. Although there was an avowedly strong commitment to the ideal of gathering in the exiles, the dominant cultural orientation of the absorbing institutions, Eisenstadt notes, was to mold "immigrant social life as far as possible along the lines of existing social values and institutions, and to minimize their potentially disruptive effects" (Eisenstadt, 1967, pp. 196–197). Incorporating the immigrants into the cultural mainstream and treating them as a uniform whole implied, as Peres points out, a supremacy and dominance of the Jewish-European culture. This culture, with its history, literature, customs, and folklore, became the dominant one in the elementary schools, while the culture of Oriental Jewish communities, like those of the Kurds, the Yemenites, the Iraqis, and the Moroccans, was almost absent (Peres, 1976, p. 192).

This model of a melting pot, which absorbed but did not itself change as a result, was intended (according to a document quoted by Smooha) to avoid two "serious dangers for Israeli development." One "danger" was the pulling of society "toward Oriental rather than Western culture"; the other was polarization and ethnic division that could lead to "social conflict, tension, and unrest" (quoted in Smooha, 1978, p. 97). It should be noted, however, that this bias could not have been consolidated into an official (state) cultural policy had the old working class failed to ascend into social power, with which it could impose its cultural ideology.

The emergence of the protest movements is deeply rooted in

these ethnic, class, and housing-territorial divisions that were partly structured in the 1950s and partly developed throughout the 1960s and 1970s. However, any attempt to specify the link between the movements and the structure of Israeli society is ridden with ideological-theoretical difficulties, because of the deeper disagreements between different schools and approaches as to how Israeli society should be conceptualized. A perceptive examination of these approaches appears in Smooha (1984), where he distinguishes between three major schools: the cultural, the structural-pluralist, and the class approaches. Generally when accounting for the development of urban protest movements in Israeli society, the common explanation has been either cultural or structural-pluralist (Weingrod, 1980). Only rarely has an attempt been made to transcend these two approaches and link the emergence of the movements with the development of social and housing classes in Israel; such an attempt is presented in this study.

The cultural interpretation conceives of ethnic inequality as an objective outcome that stems from the late arrival of the Oriental Jews in the Jewish state and from their poor skills and inadequate experience of living in a modern democratic society (Eisenstadt, 1950, p. 215). Moreover, according to the historical-cultural approach, which is the dominant one in the Israeli literature, this gap is temporary and bound to fade away with the modernization of the Oriental Jews.

On the other hand, the structural explanation holds that the relationship between the two groups is characterized by institutionalized, relatively stable inequality along ethnic lines, with one overall group (the Ashkenazim) clearly dominant and a second overall group (the Sephardim) clearly subordinate (Smooha, 1978). Indeed, in the case of the Black Panthers, Ohel Yosef, the Ohalim movement, and Dai, ethnic deprivation was cited as one of the major causes for their emergence (see a detailed empirical study in Chapter 3). Subsequently, the movements demanded the preservation of Oriental culture and established an organizational link with the Moroccan Jewish Association and the International Sephardic Federation. From an ethnic point of view, seven out of eight organizations studied were headed by leaders of Moroccan origin. The only exception was the Katamon Higher Committee, which was headed by a group of leaders of Kurdish origin. This ethnic fact attests to the predominance of Moroccan Jewry among the new immigrants; this is indeed the largest ethnic group among Oriental Jewry in Israel. It has been shown that the more prosperous segments of Moroccan Jews chose not to come to Israel, while those who arrived in the country encountered harsh conditions; hence the general feelings of ethnic resentment within this group (Wiengrod, 1963).

One of the interesting facts about the movements in Jerusalem is that within the broader Oriental ethnic group, they were confined to the lower working class. This group was composed of a disadvantaged sector of Oriental immigrants and included people in the productive age groups who did not work and were not looking for a job (statistically defined as "not in the labor force"), unemployed (who are statistically included in the labor force), and low-wage workers. The founders of the Black Panthers were unattached and delinquent youth, who formed a local street corner group (Bernstein, 1972). According to a report provided by the employment officer in Katamon Tet, where Ohel Yosef appeared, 40 percent of the youth between the ages of 18 and 26 (excluding those serving in the army) were either unemployed or did not belong to the labor force. Indeed, many of them chose not to seek a job at all, preferring to live on social security grants and, for some, the underground economy (Report of the Employment Officer of the housing project in Gonen Het-Tet, 1981). The percentage of unemployed in the housing project was twice as high as the national average (Enosh, Shacham, and Laslow, 1981, p. 27; Israel Central Bureau of Statistics, 1981). The second generation Oriental youth who founded the Black Panthers, Ohel Yosef, the Ohalim movement, and Dai came, by and large, from this group.

Imbedded in this macrosocietal structure were the seeds of social conflict over cultural orientation and political hegemony. In particular, there was a potential threat to the ruling political force, Mapai, because the members of the new class, who came from traditional societies, found socialist ideology completely out of their ken. As Yishai writes:

> The concept of struggle between capitalist and the proletariat as well as the development of historical materialism were totally alien to them. In their native countries, where the Muslim ethos predominated, authority rested in an absolute ruler, and his sovereignty was sanctified by the religious establishment. (Yishai, 1982, p. 92)

There was nothing in the social culture of the new working class to grant legitimacy and political support to the Labor party that was founded by the members of the European-born working class. Hypothetically, the demographic change that occurred in the wake of the wave of immigration could have led to a cultural-political conflict, to changes in the social structure, and to a challenge to the status quo that had been established in prestate days. In the short run, however (and the emphasis is on the short run), the conflict remained latent and the system was preserved intact. The reasons for this are tied to the historical heritage the immigrants brought with them, and the central role the state played in preserving the system.

State Housing Policy and the Emergence of Housing Classes

From the outset the state assumed a leading role in internalizing the potential conflict. The state's role in stabilizing the system was made easier for a number of reasons. First, the Arab-Jewish conflict produced cohesive forces in Israeli society; second, the socialist ideology assumed by the Labor government and the basic commitment to the absorption of the new immigrants allowed the internalization of part of the conflict; and finally, massive transfers of capital from abroad prevented a zero-sum game among the social groupings and gave the state a leading role in immigrant absorption. The state thus intervened in almost every aspect of daily life: provision of housing, employment, social services, and last but not least, the nature of local politics.

Planning and housing were one of the central measures assumed by the state to internalize the conflict. Essentially, national planning was aimed at solving the immediate problems of the state, on the one hand, and those of the newcomers, on the other. The main problem of the state was to avoid a concentration of the population in the central areas of the country; the interests of the newcomers were, on the other hand, receiving shelter, employment, and public services. The historical conjunction between individual needs and state (collective) necessities enabled the state to pursue both goals. Over a short period of time, in accordance with its socialist policy, the state alleviated the housing shortage created by mass immigration. In addition, following its national necessities, the state succeeded in dispersing the newcomers to designated areas, most often on the periphery of the country or the periphery of the established towns (Gonen, 1972; Matras, 1973, pp. 3–14). Indeed, the housing projects in Jerusalem where the protest movements developed in the 1970s and 1980s are all located close to the 1948 cease-fire lines (see Map 1). Thus, due to deliberate political policy, the ethno-class division in Israel was transformed

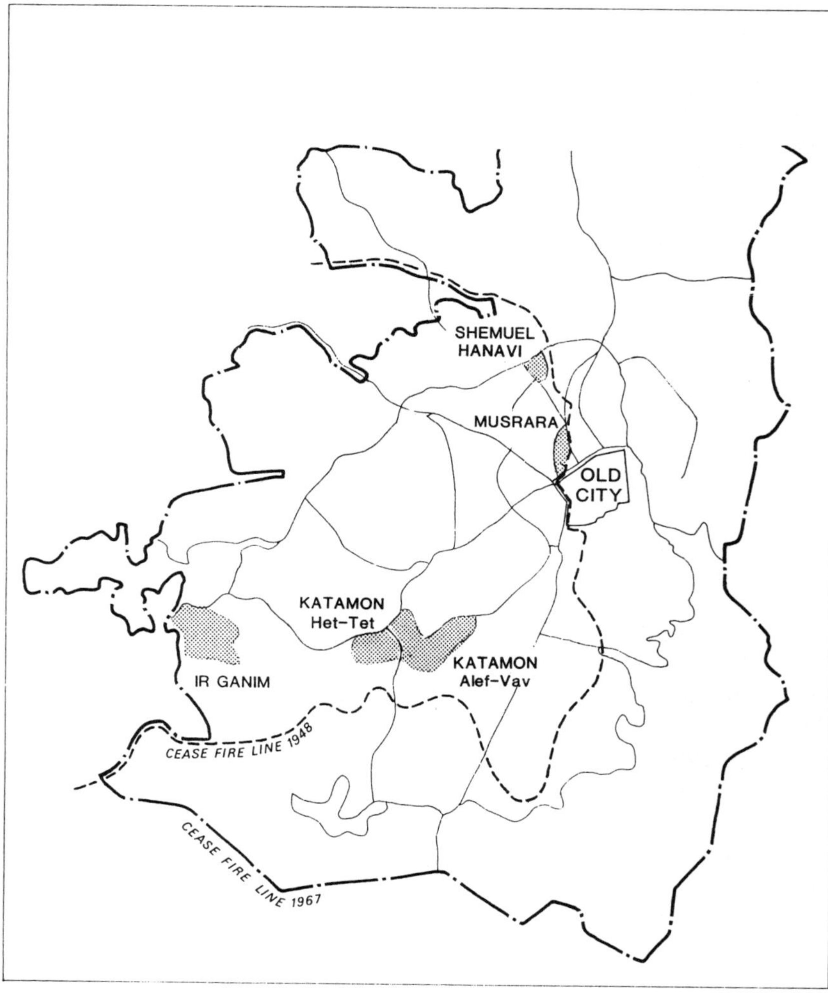

Map 1. The Location of Urban Protest by Neighborhood in Jerusalem

into an almost polarized spatial structure. The middle class and upper working class were spatially located in the core areas, both at the national and the intraurban levels, whereas the lower working class was relegated by state planning to the national and intraurban periphery. The housing projects of Ir Ganim, Katamon Tet, Katamonim Alef to Vav, Shmuel Hanavi, and the slum area of

Musrara, located at the outskirts of Jerusalem, were part of that periphery.

This spatial planning, however, was not accompanied by parallel social planning. In fact, both planning and housing were the domain of physical and spatial experts, whereas the social problem, and the question of how to cope with it in the long run, was largely neglected. Apparently, the housing process is one of the striking examples of the sociospatial relationship between the new immigrants of Oriental origin and the rest of society. Lacking adequate resources, the state tried in 1948–1949 to house 44,000 families in old neighborhoods and towns that had been evacuated by their Arab residents. There were such neighborhoods in Jaffa, Lod, and Ramla, in Ein-Kerem, Musrara, and southern Baka in Jerusalem, and Wadi Salib in Haifa. They were most often characterized by poor housing and infrastructure conditions, and some of them, like Wadi Salib and Musrara, became centers of social protest. Later on, between 1949 and 1954, the majority of the newcomers, some 61,000 families, were housed in transit camps, called *ma'abarot* in Hebrew (Ministry of Labor, 1959, p. 1). The majority of the *ma' abarot* were located at the periphery of existing cities and towns, and provided the latter with a cheap and, for the most part, unskilled labor force (Matras, 1973, p. 6). Daily life in the *ma'abarot* was controlled from the top by government agencies that provided employment, welfare, education, and other services.

By the mid-1950s, as the rate of immigration began to decrease, most of the *ma'abarot* were closed. Their residents, along with those who had just arrived in the country, were housed by government agencies on public land—either in the new towns at the country's periphery (such as Yeruham, Be'ersheva, Ofakim, and Dimona) or in immigrant housing projects located on the outskirts of established towns (such as Jerusalem's Ir Ganim, Katamonim, Shmuel Hanavi, and Baka neighborhoods). Because land and housing were provided almost free in these locations, the newcomers (who lacked private resources and were not provided with financial grants) became totally dependent on geographical decisions made at the top (Lavon, 1974; Weinshal, 1976). In this manner, the newcomers became geographically isolated from the absorbing society. In other words, during the 1950s and 1960s, due to massive state intervention in the housing sphere, political-economic and cultural divisions (and hence class divisions) were translated into core-periphery polarization. The old-timers occupied central locations either on the national or intraurban levels, whereas the newcomers were sent to the geographic edges.

It is beyond the scope of this study to describe such polarity in detail (see Hasson, 1981). Suffice it to say at this point that in the older towns and cities of Israel an enormous socioeconomic disparity has emerged between immigrant housing projects and central older neighborhoods. A study carried out in twenty-three immigrant housing projects, located in fourteen older towns and cities points to considerable socioeconomic differences between the two types of areas (see Table 1).

Both in 1962 and 1972, the population of inner residential areas ranked much higher than its counterpart in the immigrant housing projects. Examination of the social changes between 1961 and 1972 reveals that, although both areas witnessed absolute social mobility, the relative gap between them remained unchanged. To put it another way, the sociospatial system, when considered in

Table 1. Socioeconomic Disparities in Older Israeli Towns (1961–1972)

SOCIOECONOMIC CHARACTERISTICS	YEAR	IMMIGRANT HOUSING PROJECTS	INNER AREAS
Percent in labor force	1961	50.7	54.4
	1972	43.9	52.7
Median school years completed	1961	6.9	10.1
	1972	8.1	11.0
Median persons per room	1961	1.9	1.2
	1972	1.7	1.1
Percentage of households with 3 or more persons per room	1972	15.8	1.5
Percentage of households with no automobile available	1972	89.4	68.0
Median annual income per capita (Israeli lira)	1972	2,838.0	5,264.0
Median value of apartment (Israeli lira)	1972	34,051.0	61,448.0

Source: Hasson, 1977.

relative terms, tended to remain highly stagnant over time.

Parallel to these sociospatial disparities was the emergence of social apathy and uninvolvement in urban political life. The newcomers were settled on an individual basis; they shared no common social ideology and politically remained quite passive. In this manner, the dependency-paternalistic pattern developed in the *ma'abarot* was carried, through the housing policy, into the new towns and the immigrant housing projects. Consequently, neither social cohesiveness nor territorial commitment have developed in the new towns or in the housing projects.

Immigrant Housing Projects as the Cradle of Protest

Jerusalem is a miniature reflection of the polarized sociospatial structure in Israel. This polarized structure is clearly reflected in the social geography of Jerusalem. At the periphery of the city, adjoining the pre-1967 border areas lies a belt of housing projects and formerly settled Arab neighborhood inhabited by new immigrants (see Map 1).

Part of the belt stretches west to east along the city's southern rim; it includes Ir Ganim, the Katamonim, and southern Baka. The belt then turns to the northeast and includes Shmuel Hanavi and the formerly Arab neighborhood of Musrara. The proportion of Asian and North African immigrants in these areas in 1961 was between 70 and 90 percent, whereas the figure for the older neighborhoods was about 10 percent (Hasson, 1977, p. 70). A few examples may help in clarifying the nature of these neighborhoods.

Musrara, where the Black Panthers appeared in 1971, was until 1967 a frontier neighborhood, settled mainly by new immigrants of Morrocan origin. The neighborhood was built at the beginning of the twentieth century by affluent Arab families who sought to create a modern neighborhood outside the old city. During the War of Independence, the Arab families abandoned the area and Jewish families of North African origin were settled in the evacuated Arab houses. During the 1960s some multifamily houses, built to low housing standards, were added to provide cheap housing to the newcomers. Physical blight, overcrowded conditions, and poverty coalesced to transform Musrara into a poverty area. In the 1970s, when the Black Panthers appeared in the area, the neighborhood accommodated 610 families with a population of 2,200 people; 386 families lived in the Arab houses, which now suffered serious physical blight, and 224 families lived in the apartment houses. By that time about one-third of the families lived on welfare allowances, many of the youngsters did not attend school and were unemployed, and the neighborhood suffered a severe shortage in social services. One of the less advantaged areas in Musrara was the A'yin Chet street. This section, which accommodated large families with low income, was characterized by high residential density and suffered from severe physical blight. Most of the Black Panthers' members came from this street. In spite of the physical disadvantages and the harsh socioeconomic conditions, most of the residents of Musrara wished to stay in the area, as it offers them easy access to the city center. The proximity to the city center along with the vast potential associated with the old Arab houses in recent years turned Musrara into an attractive area for middle-class families. Confronted by a wave of gentrifiers, the members of the Dai organization set out to defend their neighborhood against the allegedly selling of Musrara to Ashkenazic middle-class families.

The entire area of the Katamonim (plural, singular *Katamon*) in the mid-1960s was considered one of the poorest in the city—65.7 percent of the local families were in the lowest income group as compared to 35.1 percent of the population of the country as a whole (Kimhi, 1970). The project's original six sections, bureaucratically named according to the Hebrew alphabet as Katamon Alef, Katamon Bet, and so on through Katamon Vav, were laid out during the 1950s at a relatively low density. They were made up of two-story buildings each containing four to ten flats, ranging in size from 28 to 45 square meters. Each building had a small garden plot in front. In the 1960s the four-story multifamily projects of Katamon Het and Tet were constructed, with the size of each flat ranging from 55 to 64 square meters. The different residential densities had an overwhelming affect on the future of the neighborhoods.

Over the years many of the residents of the low-density group of estates have been able to enlarge their apartments by expanding over the garden lots, while no such opportunity existed for the residents of the multistory buildings. As a result, the poverty belt over the years experienced an internal stratification manifested in relatively advantaged and less advantaged housing projects. In 1972, for instance, the market value of flats in the multifamily units of Katamon Het and Tet was 20 percent lower than those in the Katamonim Alef through Vav. The Katamon Higher Committee developed in the advantaged sections of the project. Being less attractive, the multifamily projects contained a far higher level of rented apartments—88 percent higher than in the rest of the Katamonim (Israel Central Bureau of Statistics, 1972).

To make matters worse, in a deliberate attempt to alleviate the housing problems of families living in overcrowded conditions, the state housing agency, Amidar, moved several hundred families to Bar-Yochai Street in Katamon Tet, where relatively large flats were built in the late 1960s. In blocks 101 and 102, where the Ohalim movement had its inception, in 1976, there were 207 families with about 1,000 children. Of these, some 90 percent were of Asian and North African origin and 10 percent were female single-parent families (The data are based on a survey carried out by the local residents in 1976). According to the local community worker, about one-third of the teenagers in the two buildings in the early 1970s had criminal records. Indeed, the entire area suffered from a high crime rate at the time: burglaries, rapes, drug trafficking, prostitution, and child abuse. It is apparent from these figures that residents of Katamon Het and Tet, and those on Bar Yochai Street in particular, belonged to the lower class and underclass and formed a distinct disadvantaged housing class. The Ohalim movement was largely confined to these subclasses.

Due to the concentration of the lowest stratum of the working class in Katamon Tet and the process of out-migration of those who moved upward, many housing units, particularly in Bar-Yochai Street, were administered by state agencies. The implication was that the housing space encouraged demands and social organization against the state, which ran the asset and therefore was held responsible for local problems. Such a process was mitigated to a large extent in the case of the privileged housing class located in Katamonim Alef through Vav, where many housing units were privately owned. Consequently, the demands of the two groups in the sphere of housing were not similar. They were directed toward the individual in the case of the privileged housing class and toward the state in the case of the underprivileged housing class.

Ir Ganim was built and populated in several stages during the 1950s and 1960s. The largest wave of population arrived in the 1960s, at the end of which the neighborhood numbered 8,730 inhabitants (not including Kiriat Menachem), most of whom (77 percent of the foreign born and 76.1 percent of the Israeli born) were of Oriental origin. The average income of a head of household in the housing project was about half that found in older parts of Jerusalem, and their educational level (median years of schooling) was about a third lower. Internal socioeconomic and housing stratification occurred over time within the project itself. Those parts of

Ir Ganim that contained one- and two-story buildings turned into attractive places for residents witnessing upward social mobility, while the large blocks became pockets of poverty. In the 1960s the housing project of Kiriat Menachem was built at the vicinity of Ir Ganim to accommodate old-timers and new immigrants together in better housing conditions. The YFN appeared in the less advantaged areas of Ir Ganim, whereas ICL developed in Kiriat Menachem (survey carried out by Project Renewal, 1982).

The housing project of Shmuel Hanavi is the final example in this presentation. It is made up of twenty-two multifamily buildings established in the 1960s at the northeastern outskirts of Jerusalem. In the late 1970s, when Ohel Shmuel emerged in the area, the neighborhood's population amounted to 4,000 people, most of them of North African origin. A survey carried on in the neighborhood at that time showed that many of the residential units suffered dampness; i.e., wet walls that required better isolation. Like Musrara the Shmuel Hanavi neighborhood contained a large group of youth who did not attend schools, were unemployed, and organized themselves into a local gang. However, unlike the unattached and delinquent youth of Musrara this group remained estranged from the local organization. Those who founded the organization represented the more established segments of the population in the housing project; they attended schools and were employed (survey carried out by Project Renewal, 1979).

The Black Panthers in Musrara, Ohel Yosef in Katamon Tet, Ohel Shmuel in Shmuel Hanavi, YFN in Ir Ganim, many of the supporters of ICL, Dai in Musrara and all the other neighborhoods affiliated with the Ohalim movement belonged to what Rex (1968) called the *underprivileged housing class*. Its appearance was often associated with the spatial concentration and the development of a lowest stratum of the working class in the slums and housing projects. The emergence of an underprivileged housing class affected the movements in several ways. Most of the movements' activities were geared to the consumption space; that is, toward housing, physical infrastructure, and social services. An attempt to draw in members of the privileged housing class living in adjacent immigrant housing projects, who organized themselves in the Katamon Higher Committee, was met with strong opposition. The leaders of Katamon Higher Committee argued that their interests and strategies were quite different from those of the Ohalim movement. Owning their houses, members of this group were concerned less with housing conditions and social services and more with zoning regulations and commercial services (Minutes of the Katamon Higher Committee, 1981).

The theoretical implication of this short survey is that at the roots of the movements was not only the ethno-class division but also, as the neo-Weberians may argue, the position of the groups in the goods (read, housing) market. The differences within the housing projects, in terms of housing values, level of ownership, and the differences in life opportunities and social interests associated with these differences, to a large extent affected the development of protest movements. In other words, the urban social movements do not crystallize along social classes in the Marxist sense, but rather along consumption interests. This point corroborates Rex's findings in Britain, where he shows how housing classes—groups made up of individuals for whom the value of their housing is more or less equal—were mobilized into urban movements (Rex, 1968).

Modernization and the Rise of Social Expectations

It would, however, be a mistake to assume that the ethno-class division and the housing gaps are permanent, and it is indeed questionable whether the first experience of disadvantage itself was sufficient for the creation of social protest. No less important for the development of protest were later experiences layered upon the first one; that is, the entire set of changes witnessed by the second generation. This set of changes, which defines the liminal situation of the younger generation, a broad field that itself deserves a separate study, expressed itself in a series of processes that may be labeled *modernization* and *social mobility*. Among these one could include the absolute rise in the level of education and income, the transition from a traditional society living in a precapitalist society to a society living in a modern society, the disintegration of social stabilizers (the system of social controls characterizing traditional Oriental societies) at the community and family levels, the tendency to reject the passive adaptation that characterized the first generation, and the moderation of political-economic dependence on the state. These changes were due partly to the welfare policy assumed by the Israeli state. In accordance with this policy the state enacted a series of laws that improved the socioeconomic conditions of the newcomers: the Compulsory Education Act (1953), the National Insurance Act (1953), and the Social Welfare Act (1958). When compared with the first generation, members of the second generation enjoyed better opportunities in the sphere of education and social welfare. To these changes, which took place with the transition from the older to the younger generation, may be added the growth of sociopolitical criticism, an almost institutionalized phenomenon in Israeli society, after the 1967 war, that also encouraged protest.

It is interesting to note that the mobility and modernization processes did not dull the sense of social disadvantage. Paradoxically, and in line with De Tocqueville's general argument (1955), they even contributed to making it more acute. Social mobility meant a dramatic rise in sociopolitical expectations and aspirations of the second generation that went beyond the basic needs that characterized the first generation. These needs, which may be placed on the higher rungs of Maslow's (1970) hierarchy of personal development, included social belonging, self-esteem, and self-fulfillment. This tendency was clearly expressed in the words of one of the leaders of the Katamon Higher Committee. "In the Katamonim," he argued, "vital needs have been met, and so we raise our eyes and think about the community: public institutions, a shopping center" (interview with a leader of the Katamon Higher Committee). Another expectation triggered by the modernization process was the demand for political control and citizen involvement. This political expectation was phrased by one organization as follows:

> We call for collective action by the residents in cooperation with their representatives and not residents who sit on their hands while the committee acts on its own. Our innovation, then, is productive cooperation between the residents and the committee, with the committee acting as a group; there cannot be a situation in which only one member of the committee functions. (Minutes of the YFN, 3 April 1982)

The innovation in ideals raised by the second generation was that some of them went beyond material well-being—ensuring basic necessities and security—that is, beyond the needs that were the focus of the first generation's leadership. But this statement has to be qualified. The creation of a sense of social belonging, local management, and participation in political life were ideals that characterized the elites that took part in the protest movements, but they were not necessarily the ideals of all residents of the neighborhoods. To what extent these ideals became a general demand, adopted by all the residents, and to what extent an effort was made to realize these ideals in reality, are complex problems that will have to be examined further.

A rise in the level of expectations does not necessarily imply a parallel rise in the ability to realize them. Expectations rose in the face of exposure to a modern cultural-historical situation, that is, different social values, modes of behavior, and life-styles that existed among other groups in the absorbing society outside the disadvantaged neighborhoods. However, within the social reality in which the movements developed, the realization of these expectations was difficult and required a struggle, precisely because of the existence of political, economic, and cultural constraints and barriers.

From a political point of view, the institutional system was not flexible enough (at least not at first) to respond to the demands and allow their realization in a nonmanipulative way. From the economic-cultural point of view, the organizations suffered from a dearth of resources, inexperience, and lack of the know-how and training required for ongoing organized activity. As one of the leaders of the Black Panthers pointed out:

> We didn't have many methods of action, because we had no backing and no resources. We were young and we didn't have a budget. The government had a wide field of action in which to fight us . . . the government of that time created a situation, in which we had to fight the establishment, and our path was demonstration–police–court. (Interview with a leader of the Black Panthers movement)

The absence of opportunities for realization of expectations—in other words, the lack of resources and guidance—led to a low level of institutionalization, a lack of sophistication, difficulty in defining a clear alternative, and a low level of social mobilization. The result was that the organizations had a brief existence and tended to disappear as fast as they had appeared. The gap between expectations and reality created a situation of relative deprivation that only grew worse in a large, old city like Jerusalem, where the ecological contrast between the poor immigrant neighborhoods and the well-to-do older neighborhoods is immediately evident. This gap intensified the second generation's feeling that it deserved more than it had, augmented the sense of injustice, and served as a catalyst for the development of protest.

Precipitating Factors

Structural demographic changes, social gaps, and the rise of social expectations formed the general and long-standing setting that nourished social resentment; but beyond these deep causes were more immediate circumstances that triggered social protest: the arrival of Soviet Jewry in the early 1970s and recently in 1990 and 1991, the undermining of political consensus in the aftermath of the 1973 (Yom Kippur) war, the ascendance of the right-wing Likud party to power in 1977, and the initiation of Project Renewal Program in 1978. All these events served, to use Smelser's terminology, as precipitating factors in arousing social protest.

The rise of the Black Panthers in 1971 took place at a time when a large wave of new immigrants from Eastern Europe (the U.S.S.R., Poland, Romania) arrived in the country. The European newcomers were received with enthusiasm by the Israeli public and the state and were entitled to the most advantageous conditions for their absorption. This treatment was interpreted by members of the second generation in Musrara as another indication to the state's discriminatory policy; a feeling that in this particular case was exacerbated by the establishment of new neighborhoods for new immigrants and old-timers in the vicinity of Musrara. As Cohen (1980) writes:

> The authorities, partly for political reasons, were anxious to give these newcomers every possible assistance. . . . The young Orientals objected particularly to the fact that small, relatively well-off, immigrant families were given large new flats and generous loans, while slum-dwellers were left in their overcrowded dwellings. It is not by chance that the Panther movement started in the slums of Western Jerusalem opposite the comfortable new Jewish quarters of the "Eastern city" being rapidly built by the authorities and where many of the new European immigrants are housed.

The rise of Ohel Yosef was associated with the intensification of political critique and protest in Israel in the aftermath of the 1973 war. The government failure to anticipate the war caused a tremendous shock in Israeli society and brought in its wake a plethora of protest movements, some of them headed by officers who took an active part in the war. Protest theaters organized by actors and students in poverty neighborhoods, including Katamon Tet where Ohel Yosef emerged, were part of this general critique.

The war also created a sense of social and political vacuum in the neighborhood. As one member of Ohel Yosef conceded:

> Those community workers responsible for the delivery of social services were mobilized by the army, and the neighborhood was left without any social services. Under these conditions we realized it was time for us to assume responsibility and to provide services to the local residents. (Interview with a leader of Ohel Yosef)

A different sort of events precipitated the protest movements in the 1980s. In 1977 the right-wing Likud party came to power, and one of its first social enterprises was to initiate the Project Renewal Program. The program aimed at improving the physical, social, economic, and educational conditions in poor neighborhoods. Moreover, the state, in a deliberate act, accorded local residents the authority to shape their surroundings in both physical and social terms and sought to involve the local residents in attaining these goals. Consequently, in each neighborhood a steering committee was established whose members were drawn equally from the local public and the providers of local services. The head of the committee had to be a resident, preferably the head of the local council. Under these circumstances local leadership became associated with access to political and social resources, and thus it turned into a desired position for the young generation. It is of no surprise, therefore, to note that the early 1980s have witnessed intensive organizational efforts in these areas. The YFN, ICL, Dai, and the Katamon Higher Committee were formed in the early 1980s and were all involved in local electoral campaigns trying to gain control over the new power positions inaugurated by the Project Renewal Program.

The last event that precipitated social protest in Israel is associated with the recent arrival of Soviet Jews in the country. One consequence of the new wave of immigration, which encompassed about 200,000 people in 1990, was a housing shortage and a sharp increase in rent. Mostly affected by these events were young couples in the slums and housing projects, who were left with no place to go. Consequently, in the last months of 1990 about 1,700 families squatted in forty-six improvised tent-protest encampments, demanding solutions to their housing problems. (The shortage of housing and the high rates of unemployment charecterizing the country at present may eventually lead to another wave of protest, which may comprise both the second generation and the new Soviet immigrants.)

It appears that social protest, although linked to deep social inequalities, tends to erupt in irregular cycles. These cycles are associated with precipitating historical events over which neither the state nor the residents in the poor neighborhoods seem to have any control. This is the unpredictable side of protest, which is quite often overlooked by those searching for structural regularities.

Human Agency

The context-oriented explanations discussed so far provide a certain insight into the nature of the ethnic, class, and housing-territorial problems underlying protest movements. In themselves, however, structural conditions are insufficient to account for the rise of urban movements. Structural problems of a similar kind prevail in other neighborhoods without developing into protest movements. It appears, therefore, that in addition to the underlying problems, humanist factors that transform these problems into organized activity have to be taken into account. These include such elements as informal groupings preceding the establishment of the movement and their orientations, local leadership, and intervention of social organizers—all of them acting as mediators between the underlying problems and action.

Informal Groupings

The whole set of social experiences described previously did not take place in a vacuum, but rather in a well-defined environment—housing project, street, section of street, or apartment building. The common experiences shared in a defined area sometimes created a group with a common social history and future aspirations, whose members had close social ties. In this manner, it created a local, social nucleus around which an organization could consolidate. In the case of the Black Panthers, the local nucleus was a street gang made up of young people from the neighborhood, who were either drop-outs or had a criminal record. Having a criminal record, many members of the group were not admitted to the army, and the others served for a short period. Describing the group Sa'adia Marciano, one of the leaders, said that they were unemployed, frustrated, and took drugs (Bernstein, 1972, p. 2). As Cohen writes:

> They were originally a neighborhood gang. There was an intense particularistic solidarity among their leaders which could not easily be extended to other groups; and other neighborhood groups, though essentially in agreement with the Panthers' goals, would not easily accept their leadership. (Cohen, 1980, p. 159)

The Ohel Yosef movement's nucleus was a group of delinquents and another mainstream-oriented group, both from buildings 101 and 102 on Bar-Yochai Street. The nucleus of the YFN movement was a group with a common religious-educational background: they had studied together at the local Habad school and thereafter continued to pray and meet at the local synagogue associated with the Habad Hassidic movement. Even after the movements were established they preserved their local character: a local leader, a local group with a common history of social experience, a close-knit nucleus with strong social ties, and decision making taking place within the nucleus group. Each group counted between ten and fifteen members, and these members were the dominant figures in the movements. Secondary circles of supporters formed around the nucleus, sometimes from the neighborhood and sometimes from other places, but these circles remained on the margins, the nucleus continuing to constitute the leading group.

All the organizations, both those that had a nucleus predating the organization and those that did not, were characterized by a strong sense of locality, identification with a certain place, and strong ties between members of the original group of organizers. The localism was expressed in a social consciousness of territorial uniqueness and by turning the area, be it Musrara, the Katamonim, or Ir Ganim, into a kind of symbol of local identification. Concurrently, the movements' names indicated and reinforced the specific territorial and communal distinctiveness: Panthers, Ohalim, Youth for the Neighborhood. A characteristic of the desire to maintain territorial distinctiveness is manifested by Ohel Yosef's attempt to widen its base from Katamon Tet to Shmuel Hanavi. The Katamon Tet youth who founded Ohel Yosef sought to export, in cooperation with a local community worker, the organizational model to the Shmuel Hanavi housing project, proposing to create a local Ohel Yosef organization there. The young people of Shmuel Hanavi adopted the idea of a grass-roots organization, but rejected the name and preferred to call their local organization Ohel Shmuel Hanavi, thus expressing their local identity (Minutes of Ohel Shmuel Hanavi). Later on, other embryonic Ohel councils were established, such as Ohel Nahla'ot, Ohel Stern, and Ohel Baka, in which local distinctiveness was also maintained.

The close ties between members of the founding groups, the symbolic importance of the territory, and the absence of organizational knowledge and resources made it difficult for the movements to expand or merge into urban coalitions. Movements that tried to establish branches in other neighborhoods and cities, like the Black Panthers and the Ohalim movement, found it very difficult to maintain ties outside their own turf, especially when it required large-scale organizational mobilization. Moreover, when the Black Panthers established such branches in Tel Aviv, Be'ersheva, and Ashdod, the founding group, which came from Musrara, remained the leading force, whereas others were left on the periphery. A similar process occurred in the Ohalim movement, where the leaders were the founders of Ohel Yosef in Katamon Tet. This territorial closure had a far-reaching influence on the organizations, leading to the geographic fragmentation of social protest.

To further explore the role of informal groupings in producing and shaping the protest movements, I will describe in some detail the case of the Ohalim movement. The birth of the movement in 1973 was associated with the existence of two informal groups in Bar-Yochai Street in the housing project of Katamon Tet. These two groups supplied the movement with the preliminary collectives, conventions (rules of behavior), resources, organizational energy, and leadership and thus shaped its activities and strategies. In themselves, the groups were a specific outcome of the underlying problems described earlier and might be explained by the "opportunity theory" developed by Cloward and Ohlin (1960). Culturally, residents of the housing project were exposed to the goals of achievement, success, and wealth that characterized the absorbing society. On the other hand, the historically specific ethnic, class, and housing conflicts denied many residents the attainment of these goals.

The incompatibility of expectations and the opportunities for realizing these expectations created frustration and feelings of deprivation. Such feelings were especially prevalent among second-generation youth in the housing project. Unlike their parents, they attended Israeli schools, were exposed much more to the prevailing social-democratic ideology, and were frustrated to find out that their social mobility was restricted by their social and housing conditions and the poor educational (formal and informal) services in their residential area. At the subjective level, these feelings of deprivation received an ethnopolitical expression. That is, the social problematic discussed previously was related to the ethnic deprivation of Oriental Jews by the so-called Ashkenazic establishment. This Ashkenazic group, in the residents' view, had dominated the Labor party (formerly Mapai) and therefore the state itself since 1948. Only rarely was a reference made to class structure and class conflict (interviews with members of the Ohalim movement).

Given the residents' feelings, it is hardly surprising that many assumed an anti-Labor political orientation. For example, in the 1981 electoral campaign for the Israeli parliament, the Knesset, the right-wing Likud party gained 57.8 percent of the votes in the southern outskirts of Jerusalem (where Ir Ganim, Katamon Tet, and Katamonim Alef through Vav are located) as against 13.7 percent for Labor (Gonen, 1982, p. 71). This pattern of voting behavior underwent an interesting change during the last two electoral campaigns of 1985 and 1989. In all the immigrant neighborhoods the Likud lost some of its power to the newly formed ethnic-religious party of Shas and to those parties positioned to the right of Likud. Shas, which is an ultraorthodox Sephardic party, a breed quite uncommon among the moderate Sephardic observants, used the issue of ethnic deprivation as a major slogan in its political agitation. The combination of religious revivalism and ethnic agitation in 1989 won the party about one-third of the votes in Shmuel Hanavi, 21 percent in Musrara, and between 10 percent and 14 percent in Ir Ganim, Katamon Tet, and Katamonim Alef through Vav. The urban average return for Shas was 8 percent (Choshen, 1990). It is also interesting to note that the rate of vote for those parties right of the Likud reached the 8 percent mark in many of these neighborhoods during the 1989 elections. Apparently, the population in the immigrant areas is inclined toward nationalism and involved in a process of religious revival.

The right-wing orientation of the residents, with its accompanying lack of reference to class structure and the predominance of feelings of ethnic deprivation, stem from several causes. First, many of the residents arrived from precapitalist societies in the Middle East and North Africa and thus lacked class consciousness. Second, a large number of the residents originated in religious communities that were far removed from socialist ideology. The fact that rightist political orientation and feelings of ethnic deprivation were also expressed by the young generation that founded the movement point to the influence of the community and family in reproducing cultural values and political orientations. Finally, the Labor party, together with leftist parties, failed to evoke an ideological adherence among the older immigrants and their offspring (Gonen and Hasson, 1983). Thus, at the ideological level, a vacuum was left that was filled with alternative ideologies to class consciousness; that is, with ethnic, religious, and nationalist ideologies.

At the practical level, the response of the younger generation went in two different directions, reflecting their specific social biographies and orientations. One group, which accepted the central values and orientations of the host society (henceforth, the *center-oriented group*, or COG) sought a "positive" way of coping with the opportunity gap. This group consisted of youth who attended primary and high school, participated in interest groups outside the housing project, and thus had an opportunity to socialize with higher-class groups. Members of the COG opposed violent activities like those used by the Black Panthers movement and conceived their role as working "not against the establishment but for the neighborhood" (interview with a leader of Ohel Yosef). Consequently, they emphasized such issues as personal creativity and independence, self-actualization, and innovation from below. They were willing to cooperate with radical forces coming from the outside to attain these goals. In 1973, they organized what later became the core of the movement, namely, the youth council of Ohel Yosef, which initially provided self-help services.

Contrary to the COG, the second group represented a radical rejection of the center values and the institutions representing them. (This group will henceforth be referred to as the *periphery-oriented group*, or POG.) As several community psychologists and community workers observed, this group reacted to the opportunity gap by turning to criminal activity, thus protesting their social conditions. Its members dropped out of school at an early age and established a gang of juvenile delinquents who specialized in burglary and drug trafficking. Unlike the COG, their relationships with the center were characterized by a continuous conflict, which was described by the leader of the POG as follows: "All we knew was that we were marginal people who could be arrested and released" (interview with the leader of the POG). Consequently, these youth opposed any cooperation with the so-called Ashkenazic establishment, which they held responsible for their social conditions, and were geared toward violent activity (interviews with community psychologists, community workers, and members of the periphery-oriented group).

The labeling used (COG and POG) follows Shils's (1975) conceptual distinction between center and periphery. The participants themselves referred to the two groups in a variety of ways. The POG described the COG as a *Yoram group*, which in underground slang denotes cowards who conform to society's values and norms. Members of the COG regarded themselves as a *positive group* or as a *semi-institutional group* and described the POG as a *marginal group*.

The fact that two different informal groups developed within the same social base points to the relative autonomy of orientations and intentional actions of the participants. In other words, within the structural constraints imposed by the system, the nature of the social response is relatively autonomous, reflecting the conventions (i.e., norms, values, and orientations) of the social actors.

The two groups, using social ties and friendship networks, were able to mobilize a social base. This was particularly effective in the case of the POG (the juvenile delinquent gang). Once its leader was mobilized to operate within the movement, his example was soon followed by the rest of the gang. The presence of the two groups in the first Ohel council facilitated the extension of the movement to groups with similar orientations, that is, peripheral or central orientations, in other neighborhoods. Their presence also provided the movement with a mix of cooperative and confrontation tactics rooted in their specific social biographies. In line with its sociohistorical background, the COG supplied the movement with what it termed *positive* activities, like self-help services, and was ready to cooperate with the establishment. On the other hand, the POG, though participating in the provision of self-help services, put an emphasis on confrontation tactics and was responsible for most of the movement's militant activities. Moreover, the mobilization of the POG into the movement provided it with leadership and organizational patterns developed previously within the gang. This meant strong leadership and a committed and obedient social core. Relying on this core and its obedience, the leader of the POG, who became a chairperson of the movement in 1975, was in a position to plan and carry out militant activities, which eventually put the movement on the national agenda. The rise of the movement reflected, to a large extent, organizational and behavioral patterns existing formerly within the POG. In the long run, however, these organizational and behavioral patterns had some severe implications for the movement. As Bernstein (1972) observed in the case of the Black Panthers movement, they were barriers to the extension of the movement to neighborhoods experiencing similar structural conditions (interviews with the chairperson of the Olswanger neighborhood and activists from the neighborhoods of Baka and Kiryat Yovel-Asbestonim).

Social Mobilization

The question arising at this point is how the informal groupings in the different neighborhoods were transformed from frustrated groups into the cores of urban social movements. Structural strains, feelings of social deprivation, either absolute or relative, and existing networks were not sufficient in themselves to bring about the creation of a movement. These factors might find an outlet in sporadic eruptions, as indeed actually happened in the Wadi Salib riots of 1959, or they may result, as Coser remarks, in deviant behavior and apathy, all of which bear no effect on the social system (Coser, 1957). How, then does a group *in* itself become a group *for* itself? Or, to invoke Pickvance's (1977) terminology, how does the transformation "from social base to social force" take place? To answer this question the focus of research has to be shifted from the question of *why* the organization was created to the question of *how* it came into being. In other words, the focus of research has to shift from the theory of collective behavior to the theory of resource mobilization.

Against the theoretical arguments made by the theory of resource mobilization, it is somewhat surprising to note the utter neglect in the Israeli literature of the role of leaders and organizers. The empirical evidence, portrayed in the following, clearly demonstrates that the initiative, encouragement, and support provided by social organizers, and especially by progressive community workers, played a crucial role in creating and shaping the protest movements in Jerusalem. All the movements that emerged in Jerusalem during the 1970s and 1980s were accompanied by community workers and in certain cases (i.e., the Israeli Black Panthers, the Ohalim Movement, Ohel Yosef, Dai, ICL) by sympathizers from the public as well. The following examples illustrate in some details the role of social organizers.

The Israeli Black Panthers

The transformation of the local gang in Musrara into the core of the Black Panthers movement was affected by the connections established with community workers and supporters from the Left. The beginning was modest, quite in line with the accepted and professional norms of community work. In the mid-1950s, Avner Amiel, the head of the Community Work Division in the Department of Social Work, set up a network of neighborhood clubs in poverty and immigrant areas with the purpose of treating unattached youth. In the mid-1960s, Amiel studied in the United States where he was exposed to liberal-radical social philosophies. Upon his return to Jerusalem, he went on to develop new programs that served not only the unattached but the juvenile delinquents as well; a group that until then had not participated in the local clubs and was even hostile to them. The Israeli Black Panthers movement appeared within this context of involving the unattached and juvenile delinquent groups in local-social activities. And it was the proximity of the events that led the deputy mayor and perhaps Mayor Teddy Kollek himself to draw a link between the activities of the community workers and the rise of the movement. In retrospect, it seems that the activity of the community workers was intended to socialize marginal groups in slum areas, such as Musrara, and improve their social and physical conditions. But things moved out of their control when a link was formed between the local group of unattached youth and members of the Left organizations of Matzpen and Siah (The Israeli New Left). Through the connection with these organizations the Panthers were exposed to the Marxist writings, and some of them even adopted a class-based approach in analyzing their social conditions (see Chapter 3). The community workers did not remain passive during this process. They continued to accompany the Black Panthers throughout the transformation from a local gang to a social movement, analyzed social problems with the group, outlined new patterns of action, and established connections between the movement and the media.

The Ohalim Movement

The organizers, who cooperated with the Ohalim movement, consisted of two groups: community workers, prominent among them Avner Amiel and Michael Paran, and sympathizers from the public, among them university and theater staff and students. The sympathizers were attracted by the area's problems or mobilized by the community workers. Such a mobilization was facilitated in Jerusalem because of the existence of liberal-radical groups in various cultural institutions throughout the city.

Interviews carried out with these organizers revealed that

their personal goals, although interacting with the movement, were of different kinds. Some, especially those associated with the Hebrew University, sought to enhance the personal creativity and self-confidence of others so that members of the movement would be able to cope with their problems. Some community workers, who were associated with mainstream social work, were interested in encouraging communal cohesion and social awareness and bringing about a shift from an alienated, apathetic community to an active one. This implied the revival of territorial-communal life and the strengthening of self-reliance on services organized from below. Another group of community workers regarded the movement as a means for producing a radical change in the ethnic, class, and housing structure. This group sought to transcend communal boundaries by exposing the structural forces underlying local problems. It attempted, in this way, to politicize local problems and subsequently to undermine the legitimacy of the existing system.

To attain these goals, which for some organizers were not mutually exclusive, they relied on the energies already existing in the two groups, around which the movement was formed, the POG and COG, and sought to divert them into new channels. In other words, they did not try to eliminate the existing energies (i.e., feelings of deprivation and hatred), but rather to give them a new form, another expression at the personal, communal, and structural levels. This was done through the use of both emotional and rational procedures. The emotional procedure was concerned with the motive of "taking revenge." As Michael Paran described it, "I told them you have suffered and you want society to pay for it. There is another way, a way of creating a social force, a social movement" (interview with Michael Paran). Such an agitation was echoed later in the way the movement justified the resources received from the state, regarding them as a sort of compensation for years of suffering. Contrary to the emotional procedure, the rational one sought to expose the basic conflicts and problems underlying the concrete situation of the two groups. Because the organizers grasped these conflicts and problems differently, various forms of theoretical interpretations (ideologies) were put forward: ethnic, housing-territorial, and class interpretations. Moreover, each of these theoretical interpretations or ideologies directed members of the groups to a different line of action. In this way the organizers played a dual role, which reflects the dual meaning of consciousness raising. On the one hand, they provided a theoretical insight into the nature of the problems; and on the other, they presented a line of action.

Practically, consciousness raising was carried out through a continuous dialogue, protest theater, and a self-survey. The dialogue between organizers and members of the groups was based on intensive interactions and long-standing commitment, which sometimes lasted for five or ten years. In the course of this interaction, the organizers established intimate social relations with key persons in the two groups and thus acquired their confidence. Further, a process of mutual learning took place in which both sides gained a new understanding of the social problems, radicalized their views, and developed a common perspective about proper strategies. Some of the organizers went on to write protest songs based on their experience with the two groups and became their spokesmen. Others became members of the movement. Another means of consciousness raising was the protest theater. This focused on the ethnic and class conflicts that characterized Israeli society, criticized the existing order, developed personal creativity through artistic protest, and enhanced communal cohesion, especially between the POG and COG, which collaborated in theater performances (Miller, 1973; Interviews with organizers and members of the POG and COG). The self-survey was used to produce social awareness and mobilize the social base. It ended up in a protest squat in a nearby, not yet settled housing project. The results of the survey, as well as reports on the squatting, were published in the media and stirred public interest in the movement (Dolev, 1976).

Not only did the organizers help raise the social consciousness; they also collaborated with members of the COG and POG in diffusing the movement to other areas. In addition, they mobilized financial resources from the outside and created alliances with other political and ethnic organizations. In this manner not only did they transform the marginal groups into a social force, but also secured the movement's survival for about ten years.

The ICL Movement

The ICL movement in Ir Ganim was developed by forces originating outside the neighborhood, among them community workers designated by the municipality and representatives of the Labor party and the United Labor party. The first step to initiate the movement was taken in September 1981 by Avner Amiel, who by now had a long record of grass-roots activity in Jerusalem. In a meeting he summoned with the local community workers in Ir Ganim, Amiel pointed to the growing discontent in the area among unattached youth and suggested utilizing this social unrest to advance social change and protest against the Likud's social and housing policy. As Amiel contends: "The idea is to knock out the government by inciting social unrest all over the city" (meeting with Ir Ganim's community workers on 21 September 1981). To attain this goal, which was favored by the Labor-oriented deputy mayor Yosef Gadish, a radical community worker was sent to Ir Ganim to help create the organization. Over a short period of time, the community worker and an academic associated with the Labor party managed to mobilize several well-to-do residents from the socially established section of Kiriat Menachem and turn them into the nucleus of the movemment. In line with Amiel's ideological beliefs, the group strived to transform personal and local problems into universal-political conflict. As the local community worker said: "Our duty is to show other neighborhoods the truth, the truth of an alternative possibility, a possibility of new rules, and along with them to struggle for a new social order." In line with this policy, the Ministry of Housing was singled out for practical critique and blamed for the dilapidated housing conditions in disadvantaged neighborhoods. Aided by the community worker as well as Hebrew University teachers and members of the Peace Now movement, the ICL launched a series of demonstrations against the government's settlement policy in the West Bank. Throughout the process the community worker strengthened his connections with the ICL, changed his place of residence to Ir Ganim, and finally joined the ICL as the movement's mouthpiece.

Conclusions

The theoretical question underlying this chapter is how to understand the rise of urban social movements. To answer this question I approached the empirical data on social protest in Jerusalem through the lenses of the collective behavior, resource mobilization, neo-Marxist, and neo-Weberian theories. Relying on these theories, I spelled out the structural conditions deemed as necessary (though not sufficient) for the rise of urban social movements in Jerusalem: massive demographic change, ethno-class division, spatial segregation and social enclosure, and specified the processes whereby structural problems could have been transformed into social forces.

The empirical evidence demonstrates that at the root of the

urban social movements in Israel are structural sociodemographic changes associated with mass immigration, the emergence of ethno-class divisions, spatial polarization between immigrants and old-timers due to deliberate governmental policy, and the development of social classes in the Marxist sense and housing classes in the Weberian sense. These developments brought about an internal stratification in the wide ethnic group of Oriental origin, and a lining-up of residents according to a more narrow social base. In other words, one cannot use a catch-all ethnic conflict, as has been often contended in Israeli literature, to account for the rise of urban protest.

The emergence of privileged and underprivileged housing classes not only created economic cleavage along the ethnic, social, and spatial dimensions; it also affected social consciousness. Essentially, it offered a housing-territorial interpretation of social reality and thus affected social alliances and activities.

The movements therefore reflected the intersection of the problems of Oriental immigrants belonging to the lower working class and underclass and of those who live in an area of low market value. They represented an urban activity on the part of the most deprived social and housing class within the Oriental ethnic group. Upper-class Oriental Jews and Orientals belonging to the privileged housing class remained estranged from the movements.

The objective problems rooted in the social structure produced different sorts of social groups: unattached youth, juvenile delinquents, and mainstream-oriented groups. These groups, with their social interactions, values, orientations, and power structure, provided the potential cores for the crystallization of the movements, but were insufficient to produce it themselves. To transform marginal groups living in substandard housing into social movements required, as the theory of resource mobilization shows, the intervention of a human agent. Indeed, the transformation from informal-marginal groups into a social movement took place through intervention of community workers, employed by the state, volunteers, and the movements' leaders. It is evident from the empirical data that state agents, that is, community workers, played a crucial role in creating and shaping the movements. They mobilized resources, established connections with the media, suggested interpretations to the existing social conditions, outlined paths of action, and developed local leadership. In this transformation, however, the social groups did not remain passive. They transferred their social orientations and behavioral patterns into the movement, thus affecting its activity and development. Prominent among those orientations was the tendency of the groups to social enclosure and their reliance on patterns of authority previously established within the gang or the local group. The social movements, which emerged out of this conjunction, reflected an integration between the structural problem rooted in the social context (ethnic, social, and housing-class problems), and social processes that are affected by the particular characteristics (beliefs, values, and intentional activity) of the social actors.

3
The Varying Types of Urban Protest

This chapter seeks to clarify the different forms urban protest takes through an analysis of the movements' orientations (messages or ideologies), strategies of action, and effects. The general question is whether there is only one type of protest or are there several others? I would argue that also there are certain generic features that run through the different movements; the interesting fact is that the movements diverge in different directions. The major goals, therefore, of this chapter are to elucidate the general features shared by the different movements that emerged in Jerusalem and to analyze the divergence of urban social movements in terms of their orientations and strategies of action. It commences with a theoretical discussion of the different types of urban movements, turns to the empirical evidence from Jerusalem, and finally relates the empirical findings to the theoretical corpus of knowledge.

Theoretical Background

Describing the general features of urban social movements, Castells argues in his early book, *The Urban Question*, that they express in the field of collective consumption (the urban system with all its services and products), a struggle over "social wage." As Castells and other structuralists (Olives, 1976; Lojkine, 1976) make clear, members of the working class aspire to receive goods and services of high quality and at the lowest possible price to ensure through their *use* their own biophysical and cultural continuity (reproduction) (whence the emphasis on the use-value of services and goods in the working class). In contrast, members of the capitalist class, engaged in the production of goods and services not for consumption but for *exchange*, aspire to minimize their investment as far as possible and obtain the highest possible price, thus maximizing their profit (whence the emphasis on exchange-value in this class). The urban structure, or more precisely the sphere of collective consumption, turns in this way into a secondary field of exploitation and class struggle, alongside the primary sphere of exploitation and struggle within the production process itself.

The struggle in the consumption sphere becomes more complex because of increasing state involvement in the provision of public goods and services. The low capital returns borne by public services caused the capitalist class to withdraw from the field, to be replaced by the state. As a result of the growing involvement of the state, the social struggle was partly diverted to the political level and tended to challenge state planning. The activity of social movements represents, Castells believes, the shift in the focus of the social struggle from production to consumption. The place of the labor unions, which were the vanguard of the social struggle in the past, has been taken by the urban social movements and their concern with consumption issues.

In spite of these general features, which characterize any social movement, Castells is sensitive enough to distinguish among different types of movements. He thus classified them into three types: *control movements* that serve the purposes of the state and help absorb social discontent rising from below; *reform movements* that make limited changes in urban elements, such as housing or transportation, without bringing about any fundamental changes in the social-political system, and *genuine urban social movements* that have as their purpose the creation of a qualitative change both in the system of ownership relations and in the political system (Castells, 1976; 1977).

Whereas Castells in his early writings defines the movements through their relations with the state, Alain Touraine defines their meaning by examining their role within civil society. He argues that the social movements represent a struggle over the "control of historicity in a concrete community" (Touraine, 1981, p. 77). By this he means a struggle over the set of rules and norms that govern relationships within society; that is, a struggle over forms of knowledge, patterns of economic activity, and moral principles. This is in essence a struggle to assert self-identity, which is revealed in different social movements: feminist, ecological, students, and urban movements. Even though these movements differ significantly one from the other, their common ground is the struggle over cultural norms and assertion of their own identity. In the course of this struggle, which for Touraine is fundamentally permanent and without any final purpose, the movements affect and reshape civil society. Touraine's central contribution, in my opinion, is in the innovative clarification of the cultural-symbolic meaning of social movements and the utopian vision they represent.

Touraine's interpretation seems to have a significant effect on Castells's work, as is apparent in the book *The City and the Grassroots*. No less than *The Urban Question*, this book, published in 1983, is a milestone in the study of urban movements, and it may be no coincidence that it is dedicated to Alain Touraine, whose influence is explicitly acknowledged (Castells, 1983, p. 301). One of the most interesting innovations in the book is Castells's explicit disavowal of the structural-Marxist arguments that appeared in his early work, and his attempt to create a kind of Tourainian interpretation of urban social movements. The movements are no longer seen as an expression of class struggle, but rather as an expression of a social struggle over the meaning of the city. This struggle takes place in three major spheres: the economic, the cultural, and the political. In the economic sphere it is expressed as a conflict between labor and the bourgeoisie, at the center of which are interests of the quality of life versus the accumulation of capital. In the cultural sphere it is expressed as a struggle over the preservation of unique social traditions and heterogeneity in the face of standardizing and conformist tendencies imposed by the mass media and the technocrats behind them. In the political sphere the struggle is expressed by the demands of citizens to be represented and participate in decision making versus centralizing and managerial tendencies of state politicians and bureaucrats (Castells, 1983, p. 321); hence, the conflicts pursued by the urban movements: use value against exchange value, self-management against state control, local-historical heritage against technocratic conformity.

According to Castells, these struggles no longer take place within the ruling political institutions, but within society itself. Unlike his argument in *The Urban Question*, the locus of social conflict is shifted here from the sphere of the state and its institutions to that of civil society, a sphere that is at the center of Touraine's social theory. Another similarity to Touraine's work can be seen in the movement's goal, which is no longer a radical change of the governing institutions, but rather a qualitative change in society.

In light of this view, Castells identifies three types of urban social movements: movements engaged in issues of collective consumption, which he calls *collective consumption trade unionism*; movements fighting for cultural autonomy, which he labels *community movements*; and movements fighting for increased political representation, which he calls *citizen movements*. He argues that a genuine urban social movement is one that unites all three struggles within it, and that its empirical archetypes are to be found in the urban movements that flourished in Madrid at the end of Franco's regime.

Main Arguments

1. In line with Castells's early and more recent theorization, I view the protest movements in Jerusalem as an expression of a deep social conflict characterizing Israeli society at large. This conflict, however, is represented by the participants not as a class conflict, but as a socioethnic one.

2. The struggles in which the movements are involved encompass the three major spheres indicated by Castells: the consumption sphere as revealed in housing struggles, the cultural sphere as revealed in struggles over the preservation of ethnic traditions and the assertion of self-identity by members of the immigrants' second generation, and political struggles as expressed in the demand for citizen participation in decision making. Consequently, there appears to be a large degree of similarity among the movements in terms of their protest tendencies. The various movements that sprang up in the city focused on consumption issues and especially on the issue of housing, challenged the somewhat stigmatized image associated with the residents in slum areas and public housing projects, and sought greater involvement in decision making concerning the social and physical layout of their own environments.

3. The interesting thing is that, despite the parallels among the movements in terms of the social problematic they expressed and the consumption, cultural, and political struggles they were involved in, they tended to branch off in various directions. This divergence produced distinct types

of urban movements that differ one from the other in their cultural-political orientations (political messages and cultural values) and strategies of action.

In this chapter I will depict the parallels and divergences of these different movements by way of a comparative study.

Parallels

The Shared Context

A basic characteristic of all these movements is their common location in the generational, social, and geographic context. To reiterate, the generation is that of people who were born in Israel or who came to the country at a young age and who at the time of their protest activity were in their twenties or early thirties. Their location in the social context is that of members of families who came to Israel from Oriental (Moslem) countries and who, upon arriving in Israel, constituted a well-defined social group at the lower levels of the class structure. From a geographic standpoint this group lived in immigrant neighborhoods and housing projects, built mostly to low standards at the city's periphery, characterized by a large measure of class and ethnic homogeneity. Every location in the various contexts had a great influence on the sociology of knowledge of the members of this generation. The generational context determines, according to Karl Mannheim (1965, p. 291), the range of experiences, and prepares the members of the young generation for a defined way of thinking and historical activity. The Marxist argument emphasizes the influence of the class context on social consciousness and on class interests, whereas Mannheim's theorization (1936) in this field elaborates on the emergence of a counterutopia that challenges the ruling ideology. As for the geographic context, Giddens argues that segregation of residential areas has a far-reaching impact in shaping the system of beliefs, attitudes, and ideas. In other words, the geographic enclosure affects social consciousness, life-style, and values (Giddens, 1980). Within these shared contexts, members of the movements developed certain progressive and conservative tendencies.

The Progressive Tendency: Social Liberation and Assertion of Self-Identity

Even though the distinction between the three contextual locations is important for analytic purposes, in reality all three collaborated to produce a common range of experiences, perceptions, and social responses. One of the experiences common to all participants in the urban movements was what sometimes has been referred to as *physical and social disadvantage*, or *ethnic discrimination and social deprivation*. This experience was the first and primary one on which other experiences, such as socioeconomic mobility, were later founded. As a first, childhood experience, it served as a central point of reference for the protest activities. A clear attempt was made, in every protest activity, to counter this first experience, and a somewhat vague attempt was made to produce an alternative social model. Over and over again members of the movements pointed to their marginal position within Israeli society. Leaflets of the Black Panthers asserted that Israel is "a state of Black and White people" (quoted in Bernstein, 1972, p. 31). Referring to the group's early experiences, the leader of the Ohalim movement said: "All we knew at that time was that we were marginal people that could be arrested and rearrested" (interview with the leader of the Ohalim movement).

It is not, however, only the experience that matters, but also, as Mannheim notes, the temporal order of the experiences. For the second generation, the first experience was a kind of trauma that hit them during childhood—in the beginning there was physical and social deprivation—and all the rest came afterward. The Black Panthers described the institutions of young delinquents where some of them matured and gained their first experiences. Others described in detail the history of broken families, unemployed parents, and the dependency of social welfare. "My father," claimed the leader of the Ohalim, "was a violent person who terrorized the neighborhood"; and reports of local community workers confirm this description (interview with the leader of the Ohalim movement and local community workers). Members of the YFN reported on poor level of schooling in the local school of Habad. In this sense members of the second generation differed from their parents, the immigrants of the first generation, for whom similar experiences came much later in life. Hence the unrelenting effort to negate the first experience, by protesting against the state identified with it, and the attempt to form a new socio-cultural situation and personal identity.

The negating tendencies were expressed on different levels of meaning and activity and reflected the second generation's different needs and conceptions. On the concrete level, the negation took the form of activity aimed at criticizing and modifying the existing material conditions—housing, employment, services—and replacing them with others. This concrete negation of physical-material disadvantage united different population groups around the leadership of the second generation and created the local base of support: activists, local resources, and local legitimacy for the activity of the movements. For instance, the demonstrations held by the Panthers in 1971 attracted from several hundreds to 7,000 people. The squat-in campaign at the Pat housing project in 1976, organized by Ohel Yosef, meant to protest against bad housing conditions in Gonen Tet, involved some 100 young couples, almost none of whom were members of the movement. The involvement of the young couples in such activities reflected their protest against substandard physical conditions, a protest to which the movement gave sociopolitical expression in the form of squatting. An Israeli army sergeant-major who took part in the operation testified that he had distanced himself from the movement because "unpleasant elements" (former criminals) had entered the organization. Yet he, like other squatters, joined the protest because its challenge was in line with his own personal protest, which was mainly material (interviews with participants in the protest).

Beyond the concrete negation of material disadvantage, was another form of negation, shared by all the movements, that expressed itself at the symbolic level. At its center was a sociocultural message, according to which a new generation emerged in the immigrant neighborhoods, a new entity different from the previous generation and from Israeli society's stereotyped image of them. This critique was leveled against what members of the movements perceived as something taken for granted by mainstream Israeli society—the existence of two cultures or societies: a higher culture outside the immigrant neighborhoods and a lower culture within them. In other words, the experience of physical and social disadvantage over time became associated with an experience of social stigmatization. It was precisely this stigmatized identity that the members of the second generation tried to reject and replace, by producing new social symbols or by reviving old ethnic traditions. Characteristic of this tendency is the claim made by one of the Ohalim leaders that "They never believed that power would emerge from this ghetto." The leader of the YFN addressed the same issue in more detail in a letter to the mayor:

> We tried to present a new approach that articulates ideology and innovation. We tried to prove that even in disadvantaged neighborhoods an intelligentsia can spring up, a second generation that tries to solve the problems rather than run away

> from them can emerge. We are not willing to be window dressing. We were not elected for that! The mentality of the young generation from which we come does not allow us to remain in our current state. (Letter of the chairperson of YFN to the mayor of Jerusalem, March 1984)

Apparently, the physical-social disadvantage was read and interpreted in different ways by various groups that rallied around the neighborhood movements. For simplicity's sake, we will talk about two groups: leadership and activists, on the one hand, and the supporting or receding periphery, on the other. The differing interpretations led to a variety of social actions in the physical, cultural, and political spheres and consequently to two types of sociopolitical discourse. One discourse, which expressed the desires of the movement's periphery, was entirely material and pragmatic, oriented toward immediate, individual solutions, and well-understood by the politicians. The second discourse, although not detached form the first, had additional components that went beyond the material sphere and aimed at defining social identity. By its very nature, the second discourse was an evasive one, pursued by local elites; often its very existence as an independent discourse evaded some of the leaders. It focused on postmaterial needs and was oriented toward ongoing collective and individual action, working for solutions on the personal and societal levels. The very existence of different and nuanced discourses, granting different meanings to the activity and purpose of the movements, points to internal tensions within the organizations between the leadership elite and the periphery. Theoretically, it also creates a problem with the conventional conception, which tries to classify urban social movements according to a single model of meaning and activity. In the current study, the classification of the movements' meaning is based largely on the interpretations of the elites that created and led the organizations, while noting the differences in conception and interpretation that exist in the peripheral environment.

The creation of a new identity at the sociocultural level, as was sought by the local elite, quite often collided with the existing local power structures and their supporters in the political parties. These power structures, known as the *local bosses*, see Chapter 5, were formed through cooperation between the state and the local leadership of the immigrants' first generation. This first generation leadership, which played the important role of mediating between the community and the state at the time of absorption, was seen by the younger generation as a network of party agents whose main interest was local control and voters enlistment. The socio-cultural change proposed by the members of the second generation required, in their view, the replacement of the older leadership with what the younger generation called *authentic leadership*, mass participation of residents in local affairs, and grass-roots activity. One of the leaders of the Katamon Higher Committee observed:

> It is hard to organize the people here. They [the parties and the local bosses] taught the people not to work together. They developed a myth of the leader who served as a vote contractor for a party. By the nature of his work he did not know how to work with a team—he gave orders. He had money. No genuine leadership developed. The neighborhood is striving for broad leadership.

In the Shmuel Hanavi housing project, the local boss took the form of an appointed committee whose power derived from the municipality and whose contribution to the neighborhood was minuscule. In Ir Ganim, the ICL organization published a leaflet calling on the people to organize against "a one-man neighborhood committee . . . a neighborhood dictatorship," a situation in which "a smart politician has succeeded in taking over the neighborhood." The leaflet concluded with a call to put an end to "party hacks from the period of the immigrant transit camps" and encouraged the residents to act to enable "greater public involvement in neighborhood affairs and the democratization of our life" (Declaration by the ICL movement to the residents of Ir Ganim-Kiriat Menachem, 1981).

A representative of the Dai movement in Musrara spoke in a like spirit: "The elections were approaching and we decided to fight the adults and Project Renewal" (Interviews with leaders of the Dai movement). The argument raised by members of the urban movements was that the second generation could develop a new approach that would make it possible to solve problems without intervention and manipulation by the parties, as the chairperson of the YFN movement in Ir Ganim said:

> I think that there's really something interesting about the second generation, even people who identify politically [with a particular party] . . . those people criticize their own parties much more stringently than the first generation did. . . . The

> first generation had a problem. . . . Sometimes political considerations and neighborhood considerations were opposed and there was a little leader in the neighborhood who was allowed by the party to put on airs . . . they gave him a few little incentives, and he felt that he had no choice but to do what the party told him to do . . . the party's interests took precedence over the neighborhood's interests.

The ideal, then, was to foster democratic values among the local residents and to enhance local management. In an appeal to the neighborhood residents the YFN said: "It is important to emphasize that everything noted here is in the form of goals and aspirations that we wish to realize, but without your help and cooperation with members of the committee nothing will happen. There is no other way except to work together! This is the true innovation."

The significance of these conceptions for the protest activity was that the search for a new meaning implied redefinition of sociocultural identity, improvements in the physical surroundings and a demand for change in the system of sociopolitical relations. There is much in this which resembles Touraine's and Castells's notions of search for identity and the creation of a new-liberated society. Like the movements discussed by Castells, the protest movements in Jerusalem had to confront several adversaries: the state, perceived as responsible for disadvantage and discrimination; the state's local representatives, that is the local leadership of the first generation; and the bureaucrats responsible for the provision of social and physical services.

The question that arises at this point is how to interpret these ideological-political changes. Do they suggest the birth of a new society in the womb of the old one? Castells's answer to the question, though posed in a different context, seems to be positive. In Castells's analysis, the urban social movement is depicted as an attempt to create a different urban reality. The main features of this reality are a high quality of life, authenticity and heterogeneity of culture, and self-management. This is, then, a city with an anarchist-communalist tinge, whose residents oppose economic exploitation, cultural coercion, and political oppression. But Castells is cautious to indicate the fragility of these movements. In response to the question of whether the urban social movement is an agent of social change or only a symptom of a deeper problem, he argues that the movement is indeed a symptom, but that it affects the sociopolitical system without itself being able to cross the limits set by the system. In this light, the movement, Castells observes, "cannot be proactive, only reactive, except in its utopian dimension" (Castells, 1983, p. 327). It remains a utopia because, to realize itself, it must transcend the urban domain and bring about a radical change in society, a change it is unable to cause. Castells argues explicitly that the urban social movements represent the frustration of the citizenry with the great political parties and ideologies, the return to a voluntary community, and an attempt to revive the communal utopia. There is in this a certain retreat, but also a moral criticism and a symbolic expression: a desperate cry against the barbarism of the existing system. "Urban movements," Castells concedes, "do address the real issues of our time, although neither on the scale nor terms that are adequate to the task. And yet they do not have any choice since they are the last reaction to the domination and renewed exploitation that submerges our world" (Castells, 1983, p. 331).

Castells's depiction of urban movements as contemporary utopia should be approached with some caution, especially when related to the Jerusalem case. There is no doubt that the localities, wherein the movements appeared, witnessed some fundamental changes. These places were transformed from alienated areas into places people care about and then into centers of power. From a social point of view, the local activity contributed to strengthening self-image and self-esteem, to increasing responsibility and creativity, as well as bringing about wider citizen participation in local affairs. From a political point of view, a sense of power was created in the area. This change, which by nature was vague, confronted the state with a charismatic force that challenged the bureaucratic-political system. A conflict thus came into being, between the rationality of the state and the formal ethics it proclaimed and the alternative-charismatic force. The alternative force aspired to revive territorial life; that is, to revive community interest in social and political issues that had hitherto been outside the neighborhood discourse, such as the organization of public services, participation in decision making, broad public management, and the role of the individual in shaping the environment.

Although I accept the kernel of Castells's argument, it seems to me that the role of the movements in producing social change is somewhat idealized, and the struggle between "communal utopia" and "the barbarism of the existing system," portrayed by Castells, appears to be a reminiscence of older-religious distinctions. Reality appears to be less dramatic, inasmuch as barbarism and even oppression might prevail within the social movements themselves. The empirical evidence from Jerusalem inasmuch as it is attuned not only to the progressive tendencies but also to the conservative tendencies within the movements, suggests a more realistic approach to their role in shaping society.

The Conservative Tendencies: Bossism and Underrepresentation of Women

The sociopolitical changes just outlined did not come about, however, without opposition and internal struggles; struggles that are quite often glossed over by advocates of urban social movement. In certain situations, and I will discuss only a few of them, the movements turned into an institution that repressed creativity, self-expression, freedom of action, and equal representation of social and gender groups. In other words, the liberating tendencies latent in the protest movements were not completely realized, at least not in the short run.

The reasons for this gap are complex, associated with political, organizational, and cultural processes. Politically, the massive state intervention in territorial life, through the Project Renewal Program (see Chapters 2 and 5), diverted local action toward bureaucratic operation of citizen participation in the supply of physical services. As a result, the independent and spontaneous activity of supplying of social services from below was cut short, and some of the local activists were absorbed as workers in the state-initiated project, thus putting an end to their voluntary activity. Organizationally, within the movements themselves no process of internal institutionalization occurred—that is, the development of a clear division of labor, establishment of procedures and work methods—and when the first enthusiasm dimmed, a certain winding-down of activity began. Culturally, at the core of the movement remained a small number of activists and organizers that controlled the centers of power. The core of the Black Panthers consisted of few key figures from Musrara, who previously belonged to a local gang. The core of the Ohalim movement and Ohel Yosef was made up of the former gang from Gonen Tet, headed by its leader. As a dominant force this group imposed its will on the movement's members. The emergence of internal bossism caused tensions and conflicts and led to some members leaving the movement. This bossism was expressed concretely in the attempt of the movement's leader to impose on the members of the Ohalim councils a joint national election campaign for the Knesset as a party representing the disadvantaged neighborhoods, the Ohalim party, and in decision making without consulting the other members of the movement (Minutes of the Ohalim movement).

In other words, the social power was concentrated in one person and a small group around him, thus negating the basic concept of broad citizen involvement, joint responsibility, and massive participation in decision making. In a letter (addrssed but never sent) to the chairperson of the Ohalim movement, the chairperson of the youth committee of Ohel Shmuel, who was the only woman active in the Ohalim movement, wrote as follows:

> Anyone who did not see Mussolini up close could have seen his double on 14 July 1980 at the meeting of the general council of "The Ohalim Movement Center." While the Ohalim movement pursued activities that aroused public opinion, such as "Ohel Moreh" and the squatting at the entrance to Jerusalem, and so on, there was no emphasis on the movement itself, but rather on one man. . . . My compliments to a man who was able to manipulate people so well and so forcefully (the media, among them) . . . he's against the establishment but behaves like the establishment. When the chairpersons of the Ohalim protested at not being consulted about the scheduled squatting settlements, he said: "the prime minister doesn't tell the other ministers everything." . . . I remind you that you are still not prime minister and that your movement is still not a government. Besides, if you are so opposed to the establishment why do you imitate it with such great precision? (Letter addressed to the chairperson of the Ohalim movement by the chairperson of the Youth committee of Ohel Shmuel, 14 July 1980)

It is evident, then, that within the movement itself, the conformity patterns and power structure transferred from the gang clashed with the norms and expectations of other members. Though the different groups in the movement shared a common goal of challenging the establishment authority through territorial activism, they differed radically in their conventional behavior patterns. Members of the COG, along with members of other Ohel councils, were unwilling to accept the power structure and conformity patterns introduced by the POG. These patterns of behavior were conceived of as replacing the establishment's external authority with a nondemocratic internal one. Consequently, this collision between opposing sets of values, norms, and group orientations created stress and tensions and contributed to the internal split.

A similar pattern of internal bossism was noted in the YFN,

where power tended to concentrate in the hands of one person. This tendency developed against the social constraints he faced while working within the framework of voluntary activity. The numerous applications by residents to the chairperson, mostly to solve material problems, threw him into a "game" in which a large number of the rules were not under his control. As a result, even though he supported a decentralization of authority, the expectations and demands he faced led to a situation in which, as he himself acknowledged, "a huge burden of 90 percent of the work falls on the chairperson of the neighborhood committee" (Interview with the chairperson of YFN). The unavoidable result was the concentration of activity and power at the apex of the organizational pyramid. What further contributed to the concentration of power in the hands of one person was, as the YFN chairperson explained, the natural evolution of volunteer activity:

> Sometimes you are disappointed at your best friends, I should have understood that not everyone has the same bug, and to tell the truth alongside the disappointment when you see it realistically, you understand that it really is hard for a person to push himself voluntarily and to keep up a certain level of excitement over many years.

This led to a change in his attitude toward the local boss who came from the first generation: "Today, in hindsight, I respect him much more, and maybe I'm the only one who can really appreciate what he did, as one who has gone through the same experience. To be a chairperson is not a simple job."

The change in outlook and interpretation given to the activity of the local boss led to contacts between YFN and the former local boss and cooperation between them. The YFN chairperson described the change as follows:

> Today, for instance, I cooperate very closely with him [the local boss]. It's not a secret that we've been cooperating for an entire year. . . . The relations have improved. There were crises, but today he helps me because he's accepted it. By the way, it was a difficult process because of the fact that he isn't chairperson, he isn't a member of the steering committee. I've changed a lot of things in my conception of him. . . . For instance, it's not fair only to criticize, sometimes you have to see the things from inside, the pressures that are on the chairperson. Only I or another chairperson can understand what the

> problems of a chairperson are, and I and he [the local boss] reached the point of talking. Sometimes I tell him about the shortcomings of the committee, too. Our level of trust is very high. He cares, in the end, about the neighborhood. I think it's an example of a political tragedy. (Interview with the chairperson of YFN)

These changes, which marked the rise of internal bossism within the movement, angered some of its members and led to a split and a crisis. The deputy chairperson of YFN claimed that the movement had lost the confidence of the public, abandoned its social commitment, and turned into a tool for a few people to pursue "totally questionable personal advancement" (Letter of the deputy chairperson of YFN to the movement's secretary, 19 July 1984).

Against this background of the emergence of internal bossism, the social struggles to create an alternative society, as described by Castells and analyzed in the present study, look like trends or tendencies that were not realized or, more delicately, that were only partially achieved.

The position of women in the movements sheds further light on the barriers to realize the democratic values of these organizations. The leaders of the eight movements analyzed here were men. In an embarrassing attempt to rectify the situation, members of the Ohalim movement decided that the deputy chairperson would be a woman (constitution of the Ohalim movement); but even this vindicating decision was never realized. Women played a secondary role in Ohel Yosef, Ohel Shmuel, ICL, and in the Ohalim movement, where they served as local representatives of the community. But they were not represented in the other movements; that is, in the Israeli Black Panthers, Dai, YFN, and in the Katamon Higher Committee.

In a striking contrast to the situation within the movements, women played an important role among the organizers and supporters who came from the outside. Thus, for instance, Dr. Naomi Kies, Professor Alice Shalvi, and Katherine Hirch were prominent figures among the volunteers who supported the movements and guided their activities. It is interesting to note that all these women were of Ashkenazic origin; that is, born either in Europe or in the United States. This, I would argue, is not mere coincidence. Originating in Oriental society, the protest movements of the second generation still retained some of its traditional features, not the least among them the patriarchal structure. Women were not expected to act as representatives of the community, therefore, and this attitude was never seriously challenged by the participants.

It is apparent from these detailed examples that the intention of creating a new type of society and space through the activity of urban movements was realized only partially. The local boss was removed, dependence on the state was reduced, the influence of political parties on local activity was mitigated, and there was an attempt to increase local democracy by decentralizing authority and broadening the involvement of the residents. Yet, when the dust settled, it became clear that the protest had produced an organization that, although it indeed had changed the former situation and strived to advance social democracy, still had preserved a large measure of conservative patterns.

Divergences

The movements' location in the generational, spatial and social contexts created an a priori tendency for protest activity, directed against the state, the leaders of the first generation, and the absorbing society. Alongside this activity, there was another tendency, somewhat vague, that sought to create a different environment and society. The interesting thing is that, when these a priori tendencies were translated into action, they tended to branch off in various directions that differed from each other in their orientations (political messages and cultural values) and strategies of action.

Urban theory, as shown in the introductory section of this chapter, points to the existence of different forms of social movements: "trade unionism," "community," and "citizen" (Castells, 1983). At a certain level of abstraction, it is possible, so I maintain, to classify these movements along an orientations axis with particular and instrumental messages and values on one extreme and universal and expressive messages and values on the other. The particular-instrumental orientation deals with rational profit-maximizing activity aimed at achieving a concrete physical or social change in the residential environment in which the movement functions and corresponds, to a large extent to trade union movements. The universal-expressive orientation has more to do with moral and political-economic critique as it aims to produce qualitative social, political, and cultural change. This orientation is associated with community and citizen movements. Essentially, the universal-expressive orientation is a kind of utopia, as Castells himself may be willing to concede, that goes beyond the narrow bounds of the neighborhood and wishes to lay the foundations for an alternative sociospatial structure, an ideal society seen as better than the existing one. (In developing the distinctions between universal-expressive and particular-instrumental orientations, I was inspired by Bernice Martin's book [1981]. She claims to draw her ideas directly from the thought of Talcott Parsons and Max Weber.)

Theoretically, whether universal or particular, the goals can be realized by assuming two different strategies of action. The first is based on activity within the established system and is characterized by negotiations with politicians, lobbying, use of the media to create supportive public opinion, and tactical protest that does not go beyond those limits considered legitimate by the state. These strategies may be associated with Castells's control and reform movement. The second approach is based on activity outside the established system and is characterized by social protest that may transcend the bounds of legitimacy (unauthorized demonstrations involving violent clashes and destruction of property), squatting in buildings or public areas as an act of protest or with the intention of taking control of them, and the development of alternative service systems to replace those supplied by the existing political system, as an expression of protest and creativity. This form of strategy may be associated with Castells's genuine urban social movement. (It seems to me that the classification of movements into those that function within the established system and those that function outside it is more exhaustive than one that relates to the conflict-consensus dichotomy, adopted more than once by researchers of neighborhood organizations. Organizations that function within the established system also may resort at times to confrontational strategies, but they do so only as pressure tactics, within well-defined limits.)

Crossing the orientation axis with the strategy axis creates four ideal types of urban social movements that may serve as a heuristic device: universalism and activity outside the system, particularism and activity outside the system, particularism and activity within the system, and universalism and activity within the system. As ideal types are rare in social reality, no movement fits neatly into any of these slots. Yet, with some distortions and reservations, common to any classification by ideal type, the Jerusalem movements may be sorted into three of these four categories (see Figure 1).

To reiterate, there are no ideal-type movements, as there are no pure dichotomies in the spheres of orientation and strategies of

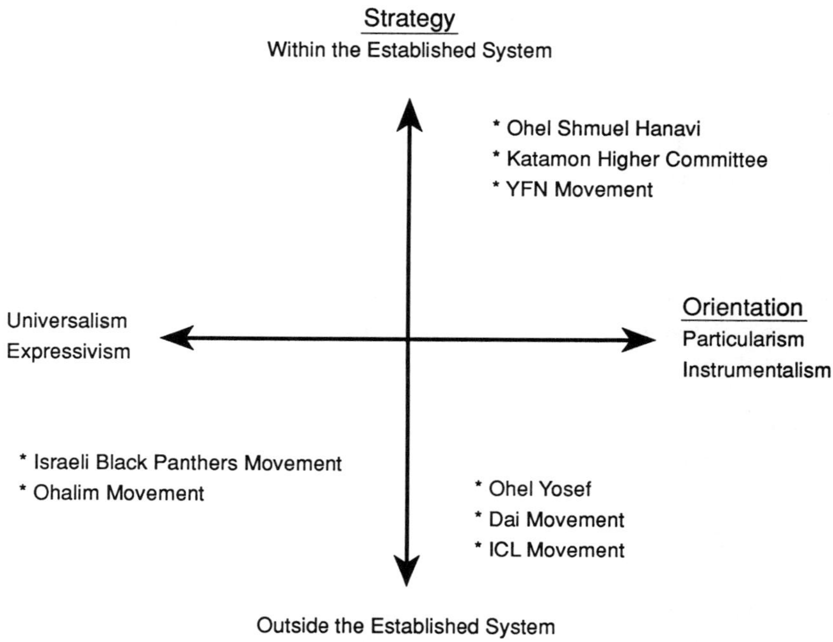

Figure 1. The Divergence of Protest According to Orientation and Strategy of Action

action. The classification is based, then, on my own interpretation of the movement's dominant orientation and strategy of action. When it registered as a nonprofit organization, the YFN movement, for instance, classified earlier as a particularist organization, nevertheless proclaimed a universalist message:

> The YFN movement wishes, both on the local and the national levels, to aid Israeli society with both physical and social concerns. The movement sees its purpose as explaining, all over the country, its goals and activities with the intention of serving as a model to be imitated—as a trail blazer for the social future of the State of Israel. (Original registration form of YFN as a nonprofit organization)

Reality, however, proved different. The movement concentrated on neighborhood matters, refrained from linking local problems with general sociopolitical problems, and even condemned such linkage.

The dichotomy in the sphere of strategies is also problematic and rare. Organizations generally develop multiple strategies, some of which are based on coproduction with the state and some on conflict with it. The Israeli Black Panthers and the Ohalim movement, for instance, adopted strategies based on discussions, meetings, and negotiations with bureaucrats and politicians and on participation in joint committees. But the most common or dominant activity that set these movements apart were demonstrations (in the case of the Black Panthers) and squatters' protests (in the case of the Ohalim movement). The distinction between different orientations or between different strategies is not, therefore, clear-cut: it is based on the dominance of a specific orientation or strategy. The following section describes in some detail the orientations and strategies of action of the varying movements.

Type 1. Universalism and Activity Outside the Established System

The message of the Black Panthers and the Ohalim movement about comprehensive change was aimed primarily at the existing reality of everyday life and the policy that stood at its base, whereas the proposed changes in deep social-moral values were embryonic and incoherent (see Figure 2). On the level of existing social reality, the Black Panthers and the Ohalim movement pro-

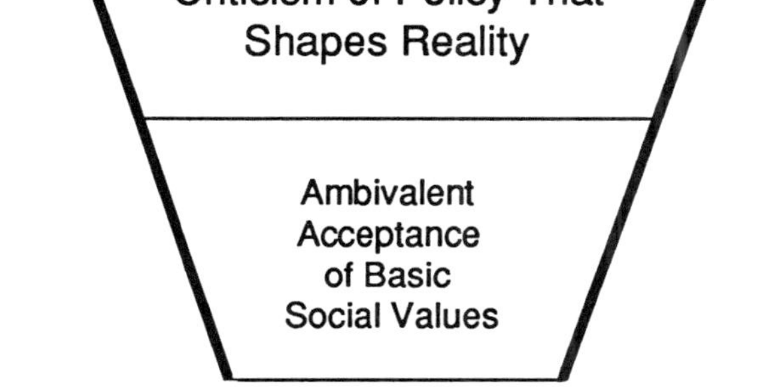

Figure 2. The Three Levels of Universal Orientation

posed a set of socioeconomic reforms concerning housing problems, employment, juvenile delinquency, and the ethnic-social gap. In accordance with this, they demanded reorientation of sociopolitical policy, further redistribution of resources to disadvantaged socio-ethnic groups, recognition of the cultural richness of the Oriental community, and participation in decision-making processes. The Black Panthers made the following demand: "We demand the repeal of ethnic discrimination and disadvantage . . . equal rights for all ethnic groups, [provision of] education, work, and housing. Equal rights will bring about the liquidation of the social gap" (Speech at a Black Panther demonstration, 5 July 1971, quoted by Bernstein, 1972, p. 38). The Ohalim movement demanded building a new society and called for, among other things,

> 1. A revolution in the field of education and culture . . .
> 2. . . . a turnabout in housing policy that will enable every family in Israel, and every young couple, acceptable human shelter and that will enable proper social and health development.
> 3. A guarantee of free health care.
> 4. Recognition that we have equal rights in the formulation of policy and the content and goals of the social services.
> 5. While toppling the ghetto walls, to enable us to develop our original cultural uniqueness.
> 6. To offer a hand to all those who were victims of disadvantage in order to bring them back into society.
> 7. To ensure proper living conditions for children, the elderly, the pensioner, and the ill . . . we strive towards a progressive and egalitarian society without social gaps. We demand to be at the center of social reform that will be carried out immediately under the direction of the Ohalim Councils. ("The Declaration of Independence of the Ohalim Movement," June 1979)

The call for a comprehensive reform of social policy did not imply a rejection of the basic system of social values underlying the existing policy. It was argued that the basic system of social values on which the State of Israel was founded had been repudiated and distorted while the state moved from the normative-declarative to the political-concrete level. This point was put forward by the Ohalim movement, which argued:

> The basic charter of our country, written on May 14, 1948, contains the following language: "The State of Israel will labor to develop the country for the general welfare of its inhabitants, will be based on the principles of justice, freedom, and peace, in keeping with the vision of the prophets of Israel, will establish social equality. . . ." You have turned your backs on the Declaration of Independence . . . and instead of a democratic, egalitarian state you have divided the nation into two parts . . . therefore we, the young people of the Ohalim councils in Jerusalem's disadvantaged neighborhoods, the second generation in the neighborhood ghettoes, have decided to bring this situation to an end and to fight for a new society. ("The Declaration of Independence of the Ohalim Movement," June 1979)

Despite the criticism of the existing social reality and the policy on which it was founded, the fundamental values of Israeli society were largely accepted by both movements.

Committed to the central value system, the movements, as Cohen (1980) noted, failed to develop any alternative ideology or social myth that would lead people to abandon their previous commitments and attitudes and put them on the track of a radical change in the structure of society. On this level, members of the movements remained attached to the basic assumptions of the unity of the nation and did not go beyond the framework of the existing system of values. At base, then, these movements aspired mainly to change the ways in which the accepted values were being realized, to reform policy, and thus to create a change in social reality.

The messages in these three areas—that is, the change in reality, the reform of policy, and the endorsement of the basic values—were aimed not only at the neighborhoods in which the organizations arose, but also at other areas with similar socio-economic and housing conditions. The Black Panthers went to neighborhoods in Tel Aviv, Ashdod, Be'ersheva, and Hadera; and the Ohalim movement turned mainly to neighborhoods in Jerusalem. Likewise, both movements turned to the members of other social classes in an effort to win over public opinion and mobilize supporters, especially among intellectuals.

The dominant strategy in raising the social messages on the

public agenda was that of activity outside the system, with the use of demonstrations and squatters' campaigns as a way of exerting pressure on the state. In the period between March 1971 and January 1972, the Black Panthers held fourteen demonstrations, some of them violent, involving clashes with the police. The Ohalim movement also held demonstrations. One of them, in November 1980, protested the rise in prices of subsidized food products and took place simultaneously in several Jerusalem neighborhoods. The central confrontational strategy of this movement, however, was protest squat on public land or in public institutions to call attention to the dilapidated housing conditions in poor neighborhoods or to put problems associated with a low level of public services and education on the public agenda. In 1976 the Ohalim movement led a protest squat at the Pat housing project to protest against the housing problems of young couples. In 1979, it organized an occupation of abandoned buildings belonging to the Talpiot educational institution at the entrance to Jerusalem to make the public conscious of the shortage of public services in the neighborhoods. In 1980 came the Ohel Moreh and Lifta squatters' "settlements," which publicized the housing problems of young couples in disadvantaged neighborhoods. In 1981 the members of the movement occupied the Beit Hanoar Ha'ivri community center in protest against the way neighborhood community centers were operated. It seems, then, that the Ohalim movement saw the entire issue of service provision by the state as problematic and turned it into a struggle for political power.

The activity outside the state system was also expressed in an effort to initiate and operate a grass-roots system of social services that would reflect the needs of the residents, with only meager, if any, assistance from the state. This activity, which expressed deep criticism of the existing social services, was especially common in the Ohalim movement, whereas the Black Panthers preferred the development of political links with supraneighborhood organizations such as ethnic groups and political parties. In 1973, the Black Panthers proposed their own candidates both in the Histadrut elections and in the general elections to the Knesset, and they secured 1.6 percent of the votes in the former, and 0.7 percent in the latter (Etzioni-Halevy, 1980, p. 240). As a result, the Black Panthers, in their attempt to develop vertical links, tended to abandon their territorial base, whereas the Ohalim movement invested most of its efforts in reshaping its locale and developing horizontal links between the neighborhoods.

The horizontal activity of the Ohalim movement carried out

through an urban headquarters known as The Tent (Ha'ohel) Neighborhood and Community Center, made up of representatives of the neighborhood Ohel councils. In this urban framework information was shared between neighborhoods, policy was formed, and activity on the interneighborhood level was coordinated. From a geographical-political point of view, this urban framework was meant to achieve two central ends: first, to combine forces in a larger space than what is generally accepted among neighborhood organizations, with the intention of increasing the movement's bargaining power on the city level; and second, to create a model of urban activity that would be of interest, and might even contribute, not only to those areas linked to the movement, but also to other areas and groups. To this end, the Ohalim movement tried to raise from the neighborhood reality economic, social and political problems that contained a citywide or even national message (Constitution of the Ohalim movement, 1979; "A Proposal for Activity in the Public Council of Katamon Tet," 6 December 1981). The activity on the urban level focused on issues such as the housing problems of young couples, price rises of basic commodities, the allocation of resources to settlements in the occupied territories, and the affect this had on the disadvantaged neighborhoods. Thus, for instance, the Ohel Moreh "settlement," set up on public land in West Jerusalem, was meant to draw attention to the housing problems of young couples all over the country and point to the link between the housing problem and the allocation of resources to the settlements in the occupied territories. As the leader of the Ohalim movement argued at that time:

> Then came the matter of Ohel Moreh. I saw the government's policy as encouraging construction outside the Green Line [the border between the State of Israel and the territories]. The Likud's policy was to send young couples to the other side of the Green Line. I don't accept that ideological line . . . we said let's put the government to the test. The idea was to set up a settlement inside the city, to do what Gush Emunim [the movement that initiated illegal settlements in the West Bank] did, but in the city.

In this way the housing problems of young couples who were members of the movement was grounded in the context of a more general problem of young couples all over the country and linked to the public debate over the goals of national foreign and defense policy. From the point of view of the urban physical effect, the movement was allotted land at the edge of the city, upon which it was to establish a cooperative neighborhood (*Kol Ha'ir*, 24 April 1981). In fact, the plan was not carried out, mostly because the movement failed to pursue it. This may indicate that the physical achievement was not the major interest of the movement, whose main purpose was to protest, put the subject on the public agenda, and change political attitudes.

Other activities included the creation of citywide projects, like the community theater, participation in activities initiated by the establishment, such as the "18+" project that looked for employment for young people, and aiding other neighborhoods when they encountered physical and social problems. For example, the movement acted against the closing of the Musak House (a children's shelter) in Baka and used all its influence to prevent a change in the zoning of land in Mekor Haim from residential to industrial (*Ohalim*, the movement's periodical, one-time publication, March 1980; Minutes of neighborhood councils, activists, and Ohel councils, 1 March 1981 and 5 April 1981).

Whereas the Black Panthers sought to promote social change through protest and vertical links with the political system, the Ohalim did it through protest and horizontal links with other neighborhoods. The effects of the Black Panthers appear in retrospective more comprehensive than those of Ohalim. Following their protest, the government allocated funds to clear slums and construct low-priced housing projects. In addition, various committees were set up to look into the problems of underprivileged groups. Chief among these was the Prime Minister's Committee for Youth in Distress. Yet the Panthers's protest seems to suggest old patterns of pressure politics, whereas the Ohalim tended to develop new modes of organization from below, whereby the neighborhoods become a vital force in shaping their life. It is not surprising therefore to note that the leaders of the Black Panthers became Knesset members, whereas the leaders of the Ohalim pursued their activity at the local level.

Type 2. Particularism and Activity Outside the Established System

The Ohel Yosef, Dai, and ICL movements functioned in narrow residential spaces (Katamon Tet, Musrara, and Ir Ganim), their goals being an improvement of the housing conditions of local residents, raising the level of local services, and strengthening local political representation. These particular messages were on occasion accompanied by universal tones, for instance when arguing against "throwing away billions on settlements in the occupied territories instead of investing them in disadvantaged neighborhoods" (ICL announcement No. 2, 1981), or when Dai claimed that money promised to Musrara was being used by the Ministry of Housing to build Ma'aleh Adumim and other settlements in the occupied territories (Dai information sheet No. 1, 1981). But the message was meant principally for neighborhood residents and dealt with local subjects. The Ohel Yosef council was interested in developing local services in Katamon Tet, in the development of local creative talent, in the education of youth and turning it from crime into what was described as positive protest, and in the improvement of housing conditions, especially in buildings 101 and 102. Ohel Yosef thus went on to develop the following services: a student house, where local schoolchildren received help with their lessons; clubhouses for children from the ages 8–13; a clubhouse for 14–18 year-olds; a club for teenage girls; a women's club; a bakery; a babysitting service; a community theater; and a summer camp for 200 young people (Budget proposals for Ohel Yosef in various years). All these activities were planned at the grass-roots level by members of the organization, community workers, and volunteers who worked with the organization.

The financial resources were mobilized in part by state bodies (Project Renewal, the municipality, the World Sephardic Federation) and partly by bodies outside the state (such as the "Katamon France" organization founded at the Sorbonne by Jewish scholars). In mobilizing the resources there was an effort to transfer the money, including that received from the state, through Ohel Yosef and thus to achieve local control. These processes marked a radical break with dependence on services allocated from above. They indicated a tendency to break free of dependence and achieve a situation in which social services would be initiated from below in accordance with local needs and the aspirations and values of the residents. One of the founders of the Ohel Yosef described these processes as follows:

> It was decided to open clubhouses for children, and we would be the counselors, one secretary and one chairperson. This helped us to form a definite identity, to define our roles and purposes. . . . All the young people in the neighborhood and its adjoining constituent groups grew up with Ohel Yosef . . . boys who were 12 when we were their counselors today see us as their teachers. We educated them, we have influence over them.

A community worker who accompanied the process noted: "It taught the residents how to present a subject, to confront problems in a democratic society . . . there are youth counselors, public figures, actors, and political leaders who have come from among those boys." The leader of the former gang of delinquents reinforced this claim: "We learned what services are needed. . . . I took a course to be a counselor, and worked as a counselor in the local club, and then I conducted negotiations with Prazot [a public housing company] over housing."

This activity in the neighborhood, and its results suggest a significant change in the social and political relations between local residents and the state. For one thing, the involvement in the provision of social services created some links between the marginal groups involved in the organizations and the state apparatus. A Hebrew University professor, who served for a long period as treasurer of the movement, noted:

> The major contribution of the Ohel was to turn the boys at the margins of society into an integral part of the neighborhood and society. Their entire self-image changed, the movement developed a neighborhood leadership, the character of the neighborhood changed and people cared, felt that they themselves could do something.

The grass-roots activity in the framework of the movements thus had a contradictory effect. On the one hand, the participants learned how to challenge the state apparatus, to confront the bureaucracy and the politicians, to identify their problems and confront them in a creative way, to shape the area and so change the sociopsychological and cultural nature of the territory. On the other hand, the grass-roots activity contributed to the socialization of the participants into mainstream. Thus although engaged in protest and confrontation, members of the groups learned new rules and norms and consequently moved toward the cultural core. These findings may suggest that the triadic struggles identified by Castells are only part of a much broader process; one that comprises both challenge of the system and its acceptance. I will pursue this point further in Chapter 5.

The Dai movement was interested in self-help construction in Musrara; in preventing older families from leaving the neighborhood, which members of the movement thought was the result of a deliberate policy undertaken by the state through the Project Renewal Program; and in solving the housing problems of young couples in the neighborhood. Local patriotism was a notable characteristic of the Dai movement, revealed in expressions like "The residents of the neighborhood will not allow the neighborhood to be destroyed under the guise of Project Renewal" (Dai information sheet No. 2, 1981) and "Will the residents of Musrara or people from Rehavia [an affluent neighborhood] live on the most valuable land in the city?" (Dai information sheet No. 1, 1981). These principles of localism and attachment to place were also apparent in the movement's platform, which proclaimed:

> 1. The movement will act to change the distortions of housing, rehabilitation, and social policy in Musrara and other neighborhoods. 2. The Dai movement will act to halt the liquidation of the Musrara neighborhood. (Principles of the Dai Movement—Residents for Musrara, 20 September 1982)

The ICL movement in Ir Ganim also focused on local housing problems. In a call for the residents of Ir Ganim to attend a demonstration against Housing Ministry policy, it stated:

> Enough of horrible overcrowding, enough leaky buildings. . . . One thousand two hundred apartments in the neighborhood are damp and leaky. Six hundred apartments are not fit for human habitation, 1,700 are overcrowded so that people live on top of each other . . . in the case of a small number of families in Yakir [a settlement in the West Bank] the Ministry of Housing spends $200,000 on thirty families. In Ir Ganim and Kiriat Menachem, the same Ministry is spending only $70,000 over four years of Project Renewal, why? (Leaflet calling for residents to participate in an ICL demonstration, 1982)

The ICL platform contained a list of demands for the improvement of living conditions in the neighborhood. Alongside improvements in housing conditions were the following demands: political representation for the neighborhood in accordance with its size, that is, to treat it as a small town and not as a neighborhood; raising the local standard of living; the establishment of medical clinics and a pharmacy, the improvement of public transportation; the installation of telephones; and an improvement in public lighting.

The three movements functioned on the local level to replace the leadership of the older generation, but they had different measures of success. Ohel Yosef gained local control in 1975 through neighborhood elections. The Dai movement succeeded in elections in 1982, but after a short period lost power because of its inability and lack of desire to take over local positions of power; and the ICL movement failed in the 1982 elections and did not win a single one of the fifteen seats on the local council.

Even though the strategy adopted by these three movements included negotiations with state authorities, the most prominent feature of their activities was protest and conflict. In 1983 the Dai movement initiated the occupation of a basement in the Musrara neighborhood and declared the establishment of a "Musrara settlement" to focus attention on the housing problems of local young couples. A similar squatters' protest was organized by ICL in June 1983 at Givat Masuah near Ir Ganim. Occasionally, members of the movements participated in demonstrations against the settlement policy of the Ministry of Housing. Yet, despite these universal aspects of their activity, they remained essentially local, emphasizing activity within the neighborhood.

Type 3. Particularism and Activity Within the Established System

Ohel Shmuel Hanavi, the YFN movement, and the Katamon Higher Committee dealt with concrete local problems in a pragmatic and efficient manner, engaging mainly in peaceful activity in cooperation with the state. Ohel Shmuel, the archetype of this kind of movement, organized neighborhood clean-up campaigns, helped rid one of the buildings of prostitutes, organized cultural activities and holiday celebrations, initiated activities for the elderly, helped involve marginal youth in productive activity by setting up a lighting fixture factory for them, and organized learning centers for children and youth. The major issues dealt with by the Katamon Higher Committee were the installation of traffic lights at the Pat intersection, where there had been a number of traffic accidents, and the initiation of negotiations to establish a shopping center to serve the Katamonim neighborhoods. In addition the committee dealt with the problem of dampness in apartments in the Nicanor neighborhood and the repair of development faults in the new Rashbag neighborhood: laying a path to the store, completing the development of kindergarten classes, tarring roofs, putting up fences, gardening, and constructing pedestrian walkways (Katamon Higher Committee plan of action, 29 September 1982; Summary of tour by representatives of the Ministry of Construction and Housing and the municipality in the new Rashbag neighborhood, 26 April 1982). The YFN, an organization that aspired at first to develop a universal model of social action, dealt with local problems like housing, transportation, cleanliness, and lighting (reports of the YFN chairperson from various dates in the 1983–1985 period).

These three movements based their activity on coproduction with the state. True, Ohel Shmuel had to pay dues to the Ohalim movement and occasionally participated in squatters' campaigns and demonstrations, but despite its participation in these activities the organization signaled the state that it preferred coproductive relations to conflict and confrontation. Coproduction was manifest in participation in leadership seminars organized by the municipality, in developing working relations with politicians and with senior administrators, and in sending representatives to joint committees with the city government. Confrontational strategy was rare in Ohel Shmuel and was used only in exceptional cases. Thus, for instance, when members of the local organization learned that their neighborhood would not be included in the Project Renewal Program, which in Israel involved renovation without any population displacement, they staged a demonstration during which they blocked intersections and disrupted traffic. The demonstrators called on the mayor to come talk to them; eventually he came and promised to use his influence to include the neighborhood in the program. Three weeks later, the neighborhood was included in Project Renewal. The use of confrontation strategies was rare, however, and relations with the state were described by an activist in the movement as "wonderful. . . the city's policy is not to pressure the Ohel, always to leave an opening and to be good. The deputy mayor is acceptable even though he's a snake . . . today Ohel Shmuel Hanavi is something intermediate—not establishment, not anti-establishment." The Katamon Higher Committee and YFN also preferred cooperation and good relations with state authorities. They explicitly rejected the confrontational strategy adopted by the Black Panthers and the Ohalim movement and ruled out any possibility of cooperation with a movement like the Ohalim (Minutes of the Katamon Higher Committee, 23–24 April 1982). From the start, members of the Katamon Higher Committee agreed to pursue coproductive activity with the state and avoid demonstrations and militant activities. The strategy of action included writing letters, holding meetings with administrators at the local and central government, and the use of social contacts. This strategy, which had the nature of lobbying, relied on personal connections of members of the committee with senior administrators and politicians. One member of the organization, for instance, was a district sanitation inspector in the municipality and openly admitted that, due to his connections with key figures in the local government, he was able to obtain a budget to improve housing conditions in Katamon Gimel.

Similar activity was pursued by YFN. The movement condemned the confrontational strategy practiced by the Black Panthers and the Ohalim movement and declared explicitly: "We naturally took a solid, drab, and quiet approach (letter from the chairperson of YFN to the mayor, March 1984). The emphasis on "solid, drab, and quiet" activity and the tendency to focus on neighborhood matters set these organizations apart from other groups and added to the protest of the second generation a shade of moderation, in which criticism and acceptance were mixed.

Conclusions

Urban social movements, Touraine and Castells argue, are expressions of deep conflicts that take place within civil society. In the course of these conflicts, new social forces, which arise on the urban scene, seek to define and redefine the meaning of society and space. The protest movements, which originated in the immigrant housing projects and slums of Jerusalem, fit quite well into these definitions. They arose, as noted in Chapter 2, against a background of social and ethnic inequality, substandard housing, poor supply of public services, absence of cultural expression, and lack of political representation. The general tendency of the movements was social liberation in the two senses posited by Berlin (1969): negative, that is, negation of the current economic, political, and cultural conditions, and positive, the creation of an alternative model in which residents become involved in shaping their social and physical conditions. I agree with Castells that on the purely theoretical level the urban social movements, including those emerging in Jerusalem, represented a utopian force aiming at social change. But unlike Castells, I have tried to show that this utopia underwent significant alterations and distortions in the process of institutionalization and activity. Despite the message of qualitative change in the nature of society and space, new oligarchies have consolidated in the movements, replacing the old boss system. Under these conditions it is difficult to accept at face value the claim that there was a qualitative change in the sociopolitical nature of the neighborhood. But a deeper examination of social trends shows that one must avoid oversimplification and an interpretation of the process described as a return to the starting point. A number of factors militate against returning to the old model. Among these are the lessening of dependence on the state, the decline in the influence of political parties on local action, and the relatively democratic ideals of the movements' elite. In the large gap between the local reality as shaped by the state and the local boss and the idealist or utopian messages presented by the protest organizations, a new space was created containing both old and new elements.

One of the most intriguing features of the protest movements in Jerusalem is that despite their similar socioeconomic origin, they tended to diverge in their orientation and activity. This chapter identified three major types of urban protest movements: movements with a universal orientation and activity outside the established system, movements with a particular orientation and activity outside the established system, and movements with particular orientation and activity within the established system. The first type represented social protest that went beyond the boundaries of the neighborhood and proposed an alternative society and alternative space; it is called an *urban social movement.* The second type challenged the system but functioned only on the neighborhood level, especially in the area of the supply of collective means of consumption; this type is called *neighborhood protest.* The third type, although born out of protest, acted in coordination with the state; it is called a *coproductive organization.* Following Castells's early (Marxist) writings, the first type of movement may be called a genuine urban social movement; the second type, a reform movement; and the third type, a control movement. Table 2 summarizes the differences between the three types of organizations.

The data show that the protest of the second generation went in different directions, as is expressed in the orientations, strategies, and degree of legitimacy accorded to the political system. The differences in orientation become apparent in the spheres of language and action. Whereas in the particular-instrumental sphere, represented mainly by the coproductive organization, the goals are clearly stated and the relationship between means and ends is straightforward, in the universal-expressive field, represented by the urban social movements, the goals are vaguely defined, quite often stated in poetic, artistic language, or as slogans and the means of achieving them are even less clear. In Cohen's view, it is precisely this vague message that accounts for the failure of the Israeli Black Panthers movement to develop into a nationwide ur-

Table 2. Differences Between Three Types of Protest Movements

	COPRODUCTIVE ORGANIZATION	NEIGHBORHOOD PROTEST	URBAN SOCIAL MOVEMENT
Orientation	Solution of concrete and immediate problems		Dealing with deep problems in the sphere of political, economic, and cultural relations
Area of activity	Neighborhood	Mainly neighborhood, but occasionally urban and national	Neighborhood, city, nation
Dominant strategy	Consensus	Conflict	Conflict
Matching means with ends	High	High to low	Low
Participants	Organization members and community workers	Movement members, intellectual groups, and radical community workers	
Prospect of achieving solution	High	Low to high	Low
Social meaning	Pragmatism	Pragmatism and moral criticism	Moral criticism
Public interest	Low	Moderate	High

ban social movement (Cohen, 1980). In other words, the instrumental sphere denotes a pragmatic activity leading toward a well-defined and tangible goal. In contrast, the expressive sphere is one of critical activity. It relates to deep layers of culture, economics, and politics and seeks to advance alternative ideals that are generally represented in an unclear and dim way.

From a theoretical and practical point of view one should refrain, then, from confusing concepts and grouping all kinds of movements under a single heading. The general family resemblance among protest organizations should by no means obscure the differences among them. An urban social movement can act in a way similar to a neighborhood protest movement, but its world-view is entirely different, and this is of great importance in setting the movement's agenda and affects relations with society, state, and space.

4
Why Do Urban Movements Diverge?

Empirical and theoretical studies, such as those examined in the previous chapter, clearly indicate that urban social movements may assume different forms: "trade unionism," "community," and "citizen" in Castells's terminology; or "coproductive organization," "neighborhood protest," and "urban social movement" in mine. Yet only rarely has an attempt been made to account for this variation. The general question underlying this chapter is, Why do protest movements diverge? This question becomes particularly perplexing in the Israeli case, because all the movements discussed so far developed within the same generational, social, and environmental context.

The existing theories on urban social movements hold no clue to this question. They provide, as shown in Chapter 2, a theoretical framework to analyze the rise of these movements but do not explicate the specific conditions under which varying sorts of movements may spring up. Relying on Mannheim's theory of "the sociology of knowledge" and Geertz's interpretative theory, I would like to suggest that, to answer this question, one must look at the fundamentally different interpretations given by members of the second generation and the social organizers accompanying them to the social dilemma in which they find themselves (Mannheim, 1965; Geertz, 1973).

According to Mannheim, members of the same generation process the data they encounter along their life trajectories in different forms, depending on their specific experiences, and they consequently develop different forms of social action. Invoking Geertz's theory, it may be argued that members of the movements decode their experiences within different cultural horizons; that is, they use varying types of codes in order to make sense of their experiences. The study of the meaning of protest movements has therefore to address, as Thompson remarks in a different context, the images and messages conveyed by the participants, the specific sociohistorical conditions in which the images are constructed and received, the interpretations attached to these conditions and images, and the strategies of action assumed by the movements (Thompson, 1984).

But what exactly are these codes and images, and how are we supposed to relate them to social action? Peter Marris makes a valuable theoretical contribution at this point by clarifying the interrelationships between meaning and action. According to Marris "the choice of language affects the choice of action" inasmuch as metaphors may shape the strategies of social action (Marris, 1980, p. 6). Marris's observation is important in that it relates orientations and strategies of action, discussed in the previous chapter, not only to material conditions and social relationships, but also to the metaphors through which people represent these conditions and relationships to themselves. Specifically, Marris draws a distinction between two types of metaphors: "the structural" and "the reproduction of relationships" metaphors and analyzes how they affect social action.

The structural metaphor, as Marris contends, "was introduced by the Left, and insisted upon, because it represented the interconnections between neighborhood, city, nation and the international economy as an indivisible set of relationships." Consequently, it is asserted that "neighborhood problems could only be solved by a national or even international strategy for controlling the process of capital accumulation" (Marris, 1980, p. 229).

By sharp contrast, the reproduction of social relationships metaphor assumes a pragmatic position. Whereas the structural metaphor takes social conformity to the rules of the material context for granted, the reproduction of relationships assumes that social relations and social action are affected by the specific interpretations attached to the material context and the choices made by human agents. "However constrained these choices are," Marris claims, "we rarely perceive them as the inevitable outcome of our situation. On the contrary, we characteristically feel the need to justify them, to assert their moral and rational superiority. . . . These rationalizations are too idiosyncratic, subtle and various to be treated merely as the internalization of a dominant ideology" (Marris, 1980, pp. 236–237).

It is not hard to see at this point how the two metaphors

shape the nature of social action. The structural metaphors, Marris claims, "by their very nature, make radical changes appear impossible. . . . If instead we think in terms of the reproduction of relationships rather than their structure, this image of powerlessness becomes transformed" (Marris, 1980, p. 245).

It is precisely such schemes of meaning that this chapter sets out to decipher. In addition, I will try to identify these social and biographical factors that shaped the schemes of meanings characterizing the social actors. In so doing I will not try to put the social actor outside the social context of action but, along with Marris, to demonstrate the idiosyncracy of the interpretations and how they affect social action.

Main Arguments

1. Members of the second generation did not represent a monolithic cultural group, but rather were divided into generational subunits that read the sociohistorical context in different ways. That is, these generational subunits gave different interpretations to the generational, social, and geographic problems, grounded them in different contexts of meaning and, on the basis of this differential reading, created varied types of protest.
2. The different contexts of meaning were of two major types, empirical and structural, each reflecting specific social experiences of the individuals and groups involved in the movements.
3. This implies that, to understand the sphere of social action and divergence of protest, one must proceed in two steps: first to identify the different contexts or schemes of meaning developed by the movements; and second to explain how these different contexts came into being.

Contexts of Meaning

Interpreting the sociogeographic conditions, members of the second generation took two significantly different approaches. One located these conditions within a deep, invisible context—that is, gave them a structural interpretation that went beyond the empirical facts—whereas the second relied on an empirical interpretation that was confined to tangible and concrete objects within the neighborhood.

Deep Invisible Structure

The Black Panthers, the Ohalim movement, Ohel Yosef, and the Dai and ICL movements had a tendency to place their local problems in a deep context out of which the meaning of the problems was derived. For example, a concrete local problem, such as overcrowded housing, was associated with a deeper sociopolitical context, presented as an outcome of basic social conflicts (the ethnic gap or class conflict) and thus turned into a universal problem. The Black Panthers, for instance, argued:

> You're screwed not because you were born, God forbid, screwed, but because they screw you. Let's assume that you are an Iraqi, Yemenite, or Moroccan-born manual laborer and father of a large family. It's easy to guess, more or less, your past. When you came to the Land of Israel—they threw you into a transit camp. You received exploitation wages, and more serious—the fruits of your labor were eaten by them—the work managers, the factory owners, the bosses. To this day they pride themselves on building the country, paving the roads. . . . Today they hold senior positions in the country you built. And you—the real worker, the real builder—were screwed in the end, because you didn't come to Israel from Moscow or Leningrad. So why should you get a decent apartment? (Placard, August 1971)

The Black Panthers and the Ohalim movement grounded their local problems in the context of ethnic and class conflict and tied the two inseparably. Both movements had a tendency to emphasize ethnic discrimination as a factor that determined class position, and the class conflict had an ethnic tinge. This conception caused some confusion in the movements as regards those Oriental Jews who had experienced upward social mobility. These were sometimes described as *Mishtaknezim* (assimilationists into the Ashkenazic community), secure economically, standing outside the camp represented by the two organizations.

Movements with particular orientations, such as Ohel Yosef, Dai, and ICL, also tended to develop universal interpretations linked to deep structure. At a demonstration against settlements in the West Bank the leader of ICL argued:

> The struggle for peace is primarily the struggle of the exploited groups in the country. . . . The ICL movement is a movement of disadvantaged Sephardim and Ashkenazim who see the connection between foreign and defense policy and the economic and social situation in the disadvantaged neighborhoods. (Speech by the chairperson of the ICL movement at the disadvantaged neighborhoods demonstration in the West Bank, 5 January 1983)

The local problems in Gonen Tet, Ir Ganim, and Musrara were thus linked by the leaders with deeper societal problems, such as class conflict and the allocation of resources for settlements in the occupied territories.

Visible Empirical Structure

In the Katamon Higher Committee and the YFN movements there was a notable absence of an interpretation based on ethnicity or class conflict. The minutes, correspondence, and statements to the press of these movements are interesting not only for what they contain, but also, especially, for what they do not contain. These organizations made no attempt to explain the problems they faced in terms of prejudice or ethnic discrimination, or in terms of class conflict. They made no attempt to ideologize or theorize about local problems by looking to deeper levels. Their interpretation had an empirical character and was limited to surface phenomena. Lack of reference to ethnicity, even for tactical purposes of exerting political pressure, indicates that one should be very cautious when dealing with the ethnic category. Objectively, protest might be linked to the ethno-class positions of individuals and groups (and such a link was indeed made in Chapter 2), but subjectively one should avoid careless reduction of every struggle and protest movement in the disadvantaged neighborhoods to an ethnic or class context. Combining a general context that includes ethnic and class elements with a specific interpretation that relates in a variety of ways to these elements is essential, without them (the objective position and subjective interpretation) necessarily being coincident.

Crossing the interpretations and orientations axes allows an additional classification of organizations, which in eight cases coincides with the strategy-orientation classification (see Figure 3). The interpretations that relate to the deep structure point to its weaknesses and call for a fundamental change in the system of

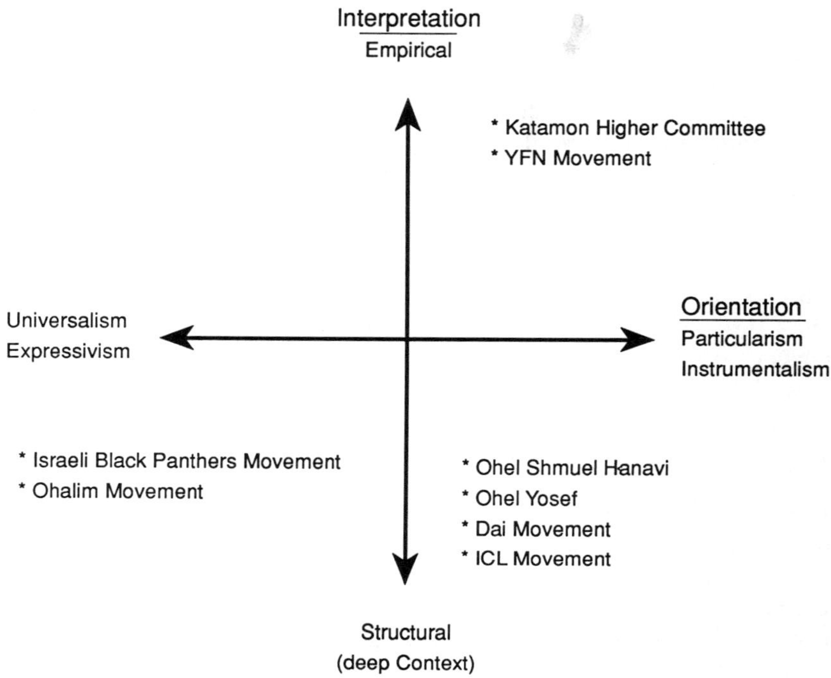

Figure 3. Type of Organization According to Orientation and Interpretation

social, cultural, and political relations. Advancing such changes would obviously lead to conflict and confrontation with the state. On the other hand, the empirical interpretations, which focus on surface phenomena, identify problems on the visible physical and geographic level. These problems can be solved peacefully through a coproductive action taken within the geographical area in which they were discovered; hence, the basic difference in the essence of the social action undertaken by the various movements. What makes the classification more problematic is the issue of orientation. Rationally and a priori, one may presume that organizations that developed a structural interpretation would tend to expand beyond the boundaries of the neighborhood, and sometimes even to ignore some of its problems, to bring about a general, comprehensive change. On the other hand, organizations with an empirical interpretation would tend to focus on local problems and would remain indifferent toward broader and deeper problems. It is likely, of course, that they would find other frameworks, such as political parties, in which to express their universal concerns.

This presumption is confirmed at the two extremes: the Ohalim movement and the Black Panthers at one end, and YFN and the Katamon Higher Committee at the other. The problematic case is that of organizations that develop a structural criticism and nevertheless tend to develop particular orientations, such as Dai, ICL, and Ohel Yosef. The explanation for this contradiction is complex and differs from one organization to another. In Ohel Yosef and Ohel Shmuel particular-local work was seen as a necessary condition for further socioterritorial expansion. Put in another way, activity on the local level was meant to consolidate power, enlist residents, and raise local consciousness, thus serving as a base for the next step, of creating a movement whose message transcended the confines of the neighborhood. Indeed, Ohel Yosef and Ohel Shmuel together created the Ohalim movement.

A similar pattern of development could probably have been expected of Dai and ICL had they not lost their hold on their neighborhoods in the early stages of their development. The participation of representatives of these movements in demonstrations against the Ministry of Housing in the West Bank seems to indicate that behind the particular orientation, which may well have been essentially tactical and aimed at enlisting the support of neighborhood residents, hid a different orientation, much more in tune with the universal interpretation of the two movements. In other words, it would seem that the particular orientation was one component of a broader program developed by these organizations. That this has been the case can be inferred from a meeting held by representatives of Dai and ICL with the leaders of the Black Panthers and the Ohalim movement in April 1983, in which discussion was held on possibilities for cooperation among the movements, participation in Peace Now activities, and the formation of a joint disadvantaged neighborhood slate for the municipal election campaign. These large plans never came to fruition because of the failure of Dai and ICL to win the support of their neighborhoods and enlist residents into their ranks.

The different interpretations that shaped the orientations and strategies of the organizations are still not sufficient in and of themselves to explain the way these interpretations came into being. Here one must go one step further and tackle the question of how the interpretations were created. The answer to this question is complex and requires a simultaneous and nonreductive examination of a number of factors: the social position and biography of groups and individuals around whom the movements were formed; the interrelationships between the groups and their environment, whether the neighborhood environment or the wider sociopolitical environment outside the neighborhood; the learning processes within the organizations, and the interaction with the state over time.

The Factors Shaping the Context of Meaning

The Character of the Groups Involved

The interpretation of the sociogeographic conditions encountered by the movements' participants was influenced by the sociocultural characteristics of individuals and social groups involved in the organizations. Among the urban social movements of the Black Panthers and the Ohalim (i.e., organizations with a universal orientation and a strategy of acting outside the established system), the presence of criminals and the unemployed was most conspicuous. The group that founded the Black Panthers had originally been a street gang, and the members of the dominant group in the Ohalim movement had in the past belonged to a criminal network. Members of the groups had been unemployed for a long period and had difficulty adjusting to work and accepting authority. Thus, for example, between 1980 and 1982 the three chairpersons of the movement were either unemployed or sporadically unemployed. (For more details on the two groups, see Chapter 2.)

A completely different social background characterized the groups that founded the coproductive organizations of Ohel Shmuel, YFN, and the Katamon Higher Committee (i.e., organizations with a particular orientation and a strategy of working within the established system). Ohel Shmuel was established in 1978 by a group made up mostly of high school students, some of whom studied in day schools and some in night programs. They brought in a group of adults, from the older generation, and along with them identified local problems and suggested possible solutions. Most members of YFN had high school educations and were professionally established. The chairperson of the movement, who has lived in the neighborhood since coming to Israel from Morocco as a young boy, completed his studies for a masters degree in Jewish philosophy, worked as a youth counselor, and was appointed social affairs adviser to the prime minister. His two deputies also have college educations; one teaches at an elementary school and the other is a lecturer at the Bezalel Art Academy. The movement's secretary has a high school education and works as a bookkeeper at the district health clinic. Other representatives of the movement on the neighborhood council include two electrical engineers, a former army captain who completed a college degree after his tour of duty, five service workers with high school educations, a police officer, and a student at a religious seminary (yeshiva). The leaders of the Katamon Higher Committee were all gainfully employed, some of them in senior positions, such as a district sanitation inspector and an assistant television producer.

Members of the neighborhood protest organizations of Ohel Yosef, Dai, and ICL (i.e., organizations with a particular orientation and a strategy of acting outside the established system) represented two radically different social extremes. Some of the leaders of Ohel Yosef, for instance, had high school educations whereas others had been members of a criminal gang. Dai was made up in part of remnants of the Black Panthers, whereas other members, such as the movement's leader, a student at the Bezalel Art Academy, were socially established and had university degrees. Most members of the ICL leadership came from the relatively well-off area of Kiriat Menachem and none of them suffered any basic disadvantage, be it housing, income, or employment. The leader of the group was a laboratory technician at the university, and others were teachers or service workers.

It would seem that, in the specific case under study here, the social background had some influence on the tendency to adopt certain orientations and strategies of action. Groups of criminals and unemployed, members of the underclass who played a central role in the urban social movements (i.e., in the Black Panthers and in the Ohalim movement) dismissed even in the premovement stage, to use Shils's (1975) terms, the center's authority and the values and norms it represented. This dismissal made it easy, once the movement was formed, to adopt a critical orientation that denied the legitimacy of the center, and it later brought about the adoption of confrontational strategies. At the other extreme were groups that created the coproductive organizations, like Ohel Shmuel, YFN, and the Katamon Higher Committee. The education, employment, and social ties of their leaders brought these groups closer to the center, and they tended to adopt its values and norms. This tendency blocked the development of a critical interpretation and a strategy of confrontation. (One should be cautious, however, not to extend these findings to other places, as they merit further exploration and substantiation.)

The situation of the neighborhood protest organizations, that is, Ohel Yosef, Dai, and ICL, was different. These groups were not only socially heterogeneous, with two social extremes represented in them; even the socially established group within these movements adopted a critical stance toward the state. Some of the established members of these groups felt alienated from the start, despite their education and economic position, as happened in Ohel Yosef; another group was influenced by radical intellectuals from the outside, and consequently tended to develop structural interpretations, as happened with ICL and Dai.

The social background, then, provides a partial explanation of the interpretations and forms of protest that were adopted. This is especially true of the two extremes, the urban social movements on the one hand and the coproductive organizations on the other. The deep interpretations and expressivist protest were associated with the lower social groups, whereas the empirical interpretations and the instrumental protest originated in the relatively upper social groups, apparently reflecting these groups' different attitudes toward the center and the values it represented. The exceptions were the neighborhood protest organizations, where even the upper social groups adopted a critical position toward the center.

Personal Biographies

The interpretations and forms of protest adopted by the organizations were partially rooted in the historical experiences of individuals and groups within the organizations. This subject will be presented here by the personal profiles of three leaders of the three different types of organizations identified: the leaders of the Ohalim movement, YFN, and Dai.

The leader of the Ohalim movement was born in 1955, one of eleven children. His father served in the border police and later became permanently unemployed. His mother worked as a cleaning lady and seamstress, but her salary was not enough to feed the family, which needed welfare support. Home life was tense and violent, and the children united around the mother. According to the local community workers, the instability of the family had an enormous effect on the development of the children, especially of the eldest and future movement leader, who was an active participant in home affairs (Interviews with local community workers). In third grade he began displaying signs of aggression and was transferred to a special class and later to a special school, which he in practice did not attend. At the age of 11 he was first put on trial and was sent to a special educational institution, where he studied for three years and finished eighth grade. By the age of 14 he had several entries in his police record and was put under the supervision of the juvenile rehabilitation service. After a year in the army he was discharged because of adjustment difficulties. On Bar-Yochai Street in the Katamon Tet neighborhood a group of young men of similar background gathered around him, and he became the leader of a local gang. In his words: "I was the leader of a crime gang. I was a thief and terrorized the neighborhood." In 1975, a local community worker succeeded in persuading him to join Ohel Yosef, which up until then had been run by a mainstream-oriented group. This was the turning point in both his life and that of Ohel Yosef, because until 1975 he and his gang had interfered with the work of the local organization. His involvement gave the organization a charismatic leader with a predilection for activity outside the established system. A community worker described him as follows:

> Sharper and more violent young men give into him silently, he does not speak well but he controls. He hates the establishment and is ready to kill them all. All his violence and criminality are an attempt to destroy society. He learned that he can be more destructive in this [urban social movement] new way. (Interview with local community worker)

Coinciding with his activity in the local organization, which reached its climax in 1979 and 1980, when he became the leader of the Ohalim movement, he continued his criminal career, although less actively; as a result he was tried and imprisoned. In other words, in these years he was simultaneously involved in anti-establishment social activity and criminal activity, the two seeming to have joint roots in his early history. Community workers and psychologists who worked with him suggested that his family background, the problematic home environment, and his father's violence had pushed him toward criminal activity and protest against the establishment, because he saw the latter as responsible for the social problems he had witnessed. Against this background, the community workers and psychologists suggested, he developed a hostile interpretation of the role of the state, an interpretation that was fostered later on by outside agents. Nevertheless, as several community workers emphasized, his activity in the movement led to socialization and his moving closer to the central value system.

The biography of the leader of YFN, a movement at the opposite extreme from the Ohalim movement, is entirely different. The leader was born in 1958 in Casablanca, and in 1962 his family moved to Israel and was sent to live in the asbestos houses in Ir Ganim. He studied for eight years in the local Habad (a Hassidic group) school, completed his studies at the prestigious Himmelfarb High School, and served three years in the army's tank corps. Upon completing his military service he entered the Hebrew University and completed his masters degree in Jewish philosophy. During his university studies he began taking part in public affairs: he was a member of the student council for three years, ran the university's training program for public activists, and served as a consul-intermediary between the university and the neighborhood. His public activity at the university, his education, and his personal criticism of the local boss system in Ir Ganim motivated him in June 1981 to found YFN.

His sociopolitical criticism focused on the patronage system that characterized the rule of the local boss and the political-economic support of this system granted by the parties. This criticism, however, lacked the hostility and resentment that characterized the leader of the Ohalim movement. It would seem that his exposure to the social system outside his neighborhood aided him in learning the dominant rules and procedures, contributed to the development of a favorable view of the existing system, and consequently fostered a tendency to function within the existing sociopolitical framework. This may explain his call for "solid, drab, and quiet activity" and cooperation with the state.

It appears that the biographies of these two leaders and the interaction that developed with the center (the institutional system, the prevailing rules, norms, and procedures of society) served as important factors in shaping their personal interpretations. The leader of the Ohalim movement, for instance, demonstrates an interaction that rejects the existing system and its rules, whereas the leader of the YFN movement demonstrates an interaction that accepts this system. The internalization of the prevailing social rules led the latter to a positive interpretation of the system, and in return the YFN was accorded legitimacy and resources by the state. In contrast, the rejection of the rules by the leader of the Ohalim movement, a rejection rooted, among other things, in his social trajectory, led him to a hostile interpretation of the system and made it difficult for him to receive legitimacy and to mobilize state resources.

The biography of the leader of the Dai movement and his interaction with the center has elements of both previous profiles.

The Dai leader was a resident of Musrara and had experienced upward social mobility. During the period of his activity in the movement he was a student at the Bezalel Art Academy, where he had received a scholarship. This trajectory is somewhat similar to that of the YFN leader.

However, in the case of Dai's leader, it did not lead him to adopt the existing rules. On the contrary, it sharpened his criticism, his indignation, and his resentment of the existing system. Like the leader of the Ohalim movement, his resentment of the system had personal roots. When he returned to Musrara after a long absence he tried to buy an apartment and was not able to do so, because, he claimed, the Project Renewal Program did not let him. It was only after a long struggle that, he claimed, "they threw up their hands and gave in." This incident exacerbated his sense that Project Renewal was not designed for the benefit of local residents but for people with connections and resources who could pay the prices being charged. His antiestablishment activity, which focused at first on Project Renewal, therefore had a motif of personal revenge against the bureaucracy he had to endure. But the personal motif in the shaping of his world-view sprang from a wider, hostile view of the state, a system he identified with what he termed *the Ashkenazim.*

> I use the term *Ashkenazim* in order to push my point to the extreme. I don't hate Ashkenazim. You have to let your anger out at something, at a group. . . . I feel good that I am able to gore those miserable assholes who always see these people [neighborhood residents] as people who don't know how to read and write, who can be screwed, who can be fooled. (Interview with the leader of Dai)

The Project Renewal Program, identified by the Dai leader with "its Ashkenazic director," served, in his opinion, as a front for this system and so, in his words, "it has to be thrown out of here."

Two central activists and founders of Ohel Yosef have profiles similar to that of the Dai leader. Both completed elementary and high school, served in army entertainment groups, and were exposed, in the course of visits to youth clubs and stays at kibbutzim, to mainstream social groups. They became drama teachers and directors and engaged in educational activity among youth in disadvantaged neighborhoods. Their encounter with mainstream culture led to only a partial internalization of the dominant rules, values, and procedures of society. Fundamentally, their conception of the center remained hostile, and the encounter with the outside environment only heightened their hostility. One of the founders of Ohel Yosef spent some time on a kibbutz and discovered, he said, that "there is racism in the kibbutz. At the kibbutz they treated the group I came from like unfortunates, and we did not feel equal to the kibbutz children." He claims that the battle being fought today in Israel is between those who came from Europe and those who came from Asia and Africa, since the Orient, in his words, is based on emotion and looks to the past, whereas the West is based on reason and looks to the future. He believes that the meeting of the two cultures in Israel created ambivalence, a society that is Oriental at base but with Western accouterments. In Ohel Yosef this ambivalence was expressed, he said, in a feeling of discrimination, but also in a desire to use positive-Western means (improvement of neighborhood services) to improve the standard of living (intervews with the deputy chairperson of the Ohalim movement).

It appears, then, that the difference in interpretation and forms of protest are associated with class positions and social experiences, personal biographies, and nearness to the center. The closer the group is to the center in its conceptions, values, norms, and tendency to accept the authority of the center—features that in themselves are linked to class and previous social experience—the greater is the tendency for an empirical interpretation, particularism, and activity within the established system.

The differences in interpretation reflect, then, the fundamental differences between the groups in the extent to which they accept the central values and their recognition of the center's authority. In Israel there is a strong tendency for consensus, which is associated with the ideals of building the nation and gathering the exiles and with the external threat. The socially unattached and delinquent groups at the root of the expressivist-universalist movements, like the Black Panthers and the Ohalim movement, challenge the consensus and existing order and sometimes unconsciously advance an alternative order. Such a challenge under certain conditions may serve as a social magnet for another group—made up of radical intellectuals—that has its own alternative utopia.

Yet, on the other hand, this challenge may distance from the expressivist-universalist movements those traditional elements within the neighborhood and outside it that would prefer a particularist orientation and activity within the established system. In other words, the interpretation and patterns of activity that grow out of class background and social experience may trigger a negative or positive response in accordance with the kind of cultural interaction that develops between the organization and its environment.

Cultural Interaction with the Environment

In general it is possible to distinguish between two types of environment with which the organizations had social interaction and by which they were influenced in terms of the interpretation, symbols, and forms of protest they developed. One environment was the internal one, composed of neighborhood elements, which held traditional values, and the other environment was the outside one composed of community workers, street gang counselors, intellectuals, and politicians who held radical values.

The neighborhood environment, which represented to a large extent a tradition that consolidated partly before the immigration to Israel and partly while coping with conditions in Israel, encouraged the creation of a particularist orientation. The culture of this environment may be likened to a kind of heritage from the past that was adopted unconsciously and uncritically. It was a kind of ideological hegemony, to use Gramsci's (1971) terms, that shaped the interpretation of, and attitude toward, society. In an abstract and general way one could argue that this cultural-political tradition was characterized by the following: ethnic enclosure, a traditional-religious spirit, a tendency to support the right wing on the national level, a sense of community, adjustment, conformism, dependence on a local figure who represented the community to the authorities, and avoidance of conflict. The nature of this tradition was opposed to radical protest, which assumed a radical-leftist orientation and tended to support what it saw as pragmatic activity of an apolitical nature, directed at improving the neighborhood. It was strengthened indirectly, and to some extent unconsciously, by community workers who took an apolitical stance and who aspired to identify concrete local problems and encourage the residents to find solutions to them. On the basis of these traditional values and the contribution of apolitical community workers, a set of expectations emerged that saw the neighborhood organization as an instrument for dealing pragmatically with local problems. In other words, the internal tradition in conjunction with professional-pragmatic and apolitical input created a system of expectations and demands, and this system served as a filter through which reality and possibilities for action were reflected. An example of this is a letter sent to the leader of YFN by a local resident, containing between the lines a pragmatic-local conception as regards the role of the organization:

> I write to you with a great request as chairperson of the neighborhood council that you help me find the most efficient possible solution for a loan to complete construction. I turn to you with this request since I am a resident of the neighborhood and have a right to assistance from the head of the neighborhood council. (Letter of a resident to the chairperson of YFN, 12 December 1984)

The YFN organization strove, in its initial stages, to develop a universal orientation and to become an organization that would, according to its founders, serve as a model to be imitated by the entire society. The local traditions and expectations were different and demanded activity within the neighborhood in concrete consumption spheres: housing, transportation, lighting, and services. The response to the environment required giving a different interpretation to the problems, to developing a local orientation and a pragmatic approach in coordination and cooperation with the state.

The traditional cultural framework that was based on patron-client relations, a sense of community, and conformism was broken to a certain extent in the case of the socially unattached groups (the Black Panthers and the Ohalim movement, for example) due to social associations established with liberal-radical groups who came from the outside. The articulation of the challenge to accepted social norms, presented by the marginal groups, with the political-moral criticism carried by liberal-radical agents, who came from outside the neighborhood, was common to the Black Panthers, the Ohalim movement, Ohel Yosef, Dai, and ICL, and it had considerable influence on the interpretation and orientation of these organizations. Working among the Panthers were people from Matzpen (a Trotskyist faction), Oded (a left-wing organization of Oriental intellectuals), high school students, leftist university students, community workers with a progressive orientation, and politicians from the periphery of the establishment. In the Ohalim movement and Ohel Yosef there was a similar coalition: the activists here were in particular South and North American students with a Marxist approach and radical community workers. The ICL movement was joined by the following elements: a community worker who defined himself as an anarchist, an activist from the 77 Circle, associated with the Labor party, activists from the local chapter and central committee of

Mapam (a left-wing socialist party), and members of Peace Now.

These groups had a considerable influence on the interpretation adopted, because they tried to explain to the members of the organizations that the problems characteristic of disadvantaged neighborhoods were part of a larger set of deep contradictions and conflicts that affected broad sections of the public. Leftist elements from Siah (the Israeli New Left), for instance, spurred the Black Panthers into raising the class problem. A placard written by Siah activists, or with their help, before the demonstration of 18 May 1971, stated: "We call on you, residents of the poor neighborhoods, factory workers, and all the exploited people of the country to join a consistent, uncompromising struggle" (quoted by Bernstein, 1972, p. 47). The contact between ICL and Peace Now and with Mapam led to the creation of a political-universal message that confronted the government's settlement policy in the occupied territories. Consequently, members of the movement took part in Peace Now demonstrations and went on to establish a "tent settlement" as an act of protest. One of the placards displayed at the "settlement" read:

> We have called our settlement "ICL Elit" (upper ICL, in a hint to the new settlements established on upper-strategic points in the West Bank) in order to protest the government's policy of spending billions on settlements like Shechem (Nablus) Elit, and pennies on solutions to the problems of the disadvantaged neighborhoods. (Placard at "ICL Elit")

The intellectuals and organizers arriving from outside thus gave a broader interpretation to local problems, passed on messages, directed activity, and in this way raised local consciousness. An examination of the placards, poems, texts of plays, and slogans adopted by the organizations with a structural interpretation shows that their protest was a kind of "political art," that is, an articulation of communication-artistic sophistication and political activity, brought in different ways from outside to the local elites. This applies especially to the first stage of the protest of the Black Panthers and the Ohalim movement and to the entire period of activity of the Dai and ICL movements.

It would be overly simplistic to label the interaction between the cultural elite from outside and the members of the movements as manipulation or to see in this interaction an expression of emotionalism or sentimentalism on the part of intellectuals from the outside, even though these elements did exist. Fundamentally, this interaction marked an attempt to deliver to the social movements in disadvantaged neighborhoods messages that originated in high culture, while adapting and translating them into the language of popular culture prevailing in the local environment.

The mediation between the two cultures was carried out through a medium that, with LaCapra, may be called the *carnival* (LaCapra, 1983, pp. 52–54). The carnival, in the framework of which come the demonstration, the squatters' protest, the provocative play, and the furious placard, served as a means of attracting attention, of overdramatization, of criticism and mockery of the social system, and sometimes of the participants themselves. The activity turned into a sort of show that displayed the complex messages associated with resource allocation, social and class divisions, and a sense of discrimination. The classic expressions of the carnival were the simplistic placard with a humorous slant, the dramatic, showlike activity, and poetry. As one of the community workers who participated in the organization of Ohel Yosef's squatters' campaign at the Pat housing project explained, the central idea behind the placards was the use of concise slogans so that the message would penetrate and be accepted. For example, "Families had children to get housing points, but then they changed the point system." The system of points for housing (by which young couples accumulated points toward a mortgage based on income, number of children, housing density, and other factors) became an object of criticism and was widely and sharply attacked by community workers, one of whom wrote the following poem:

> Poor neighborhood resident remember!
> In the housing company the point system operates!
> For a sick heart or leg problems
> They give you a pair of points
> And a man in a sleeping bag
> Gets another point.
> And for each and every soul
> And for cracks in the walls
> And for most diseases
> You might even get double.
> The point system operates
> The miseries grow;
> Overcrowding buries us,
> And the neighborhood asks
> To hell with it! How must you look
> To get two thousand points?! (Ross, undated, p. 49)

This protest poem was very popular among the residents of the disadvantaged neighborhoods, and in the first (and last) issue of the newspaper put out by the Ohalim movement, it appeared at the top of the page as a sort of anthem. Alongside the artistic-political criticism, the carnival also focused on glorifying the past in the country of origin while giving expression to values and behavioral patterns that, in the opinion of the intellectuals, signified positive and attractive aspects of Oriental culture in Diaspora. A poem written for the play *Marokanos*, which was presented by the Black Panthers and Dai, nostalgically embraced the past and in doing so communicated a series of messages.

> Of Morocco in the Exile
> And of Massuda my mother
> Whose house was a light to all members of the community
> And of my father who was a real father . . .
> And we children
> Loved to sit in his shadow . . .
> And we offered our hand to everyone
> Not under spotlights . . .
> And of one street that had a great heart
> As if it were the heart of the whole world . . .
> And Jews and Arabs lived there like brothers.

The poem, which portrays a kind of naive picture of a real and imagined past in Morocco, centers on a series of values that were rooted, according to the poet, in the Jewish community of Morocco and were lost after the migration to Israel. Among these values are honor for the mother and father, mutual help given "not under spotlights," and brotherly relations between Jews and Arabs.

Modern culture, according to the poet, is characterized by modernization, individualization, alienation, and the retreat of communal values in the face of material values. The role of the intellectual, he believes, is to revive the values of the past by developing symbols and myths, thereby fostering ethnic pride among the members of the movement. Relying on the Oriental heritage and its linguistic-cultural contacts with the Arab world, he also sought to reopen the dialogue between Jews and Arabs through the mediation of Oriental members of the movements. Accordingly, the outside intellectuals, aided by members of the Peace Now movement, helped to organize several meetings between members of the movements and Palestinian and Israeli Arabs. The meetings, however, were sporadic in nature and did not result in an ongoing dialogue between the two groups.

The cultural elite that came from outside the neighborhood played, then, an important role in shaping the protest, developing criticism, creating ethnic-cultural myths, and in establishing links with other groups. It reinterpreted the past, singled out objects for criticism, created symbols of group identification, and indicated directions of activity. The question that arises is, then, To what extent were the movements with structural interpretation autonomous in creating their messages and activities and to what extent were they directed from backstage, sometimes without being aware of it, by the outside environment? A hint of this situation, in which the leading force comes from outside, may be found in the "tent settlement" initiated by ICL on Givat Masuah, when it entered its fourth day (26 June 1983). Most of those present on the hill were members of the Peace Now movement who came to identify with ICL, and there was only a small group of residents from Ir Ganim and Kiriat Menachem. The hill was crowned with placards from Peace Now, the student faction Ofek (associated with the Labor party), and one large placard that carried the legend "ICL Elit." At the foot of the hill, in the house of one of the residents, the radical community worker who had initiated the settlement and who was wanted by the police met with a number of members of Kibbutz Negba who had brought tents and mattresses for the "settlers." The community worker claimed angrily that he had been abandoned by the residents, and said "Dede (the chairperson of ICL) and I were the only ones who spent the night there, so I'm not surprised that the police saw us." He struck out at the local residents: "They're worthless, they want me to sit in jail for them." All this did not prevent several Knesset members (including Shem-Tov, Aloni, and Zakai) from visiting and expressing their support for the residents. In this way the squatters' protest on Givat Masuah appeared not necessarily as a physical invasion, but more as a cultural invasion of liberal-radical intellectuals into a social space that remained foreign and alienated.

The interaction with the external environment and the adoption of radical interpretations often created a deep rift between the organizations with structural interpretations and their neighborhoods. The radical tradition associated with the structural interpretation and the orientation and types of activity that derive from this tradition to a great extent contradicted the traditional conceptions of the local community. This created a conflict in which, generally, the neighborhood's traditional view won. As a result, the movements that adopted deep structure interpretations and expressive orientations, such as the Black Panthers and the Ohalim movement, did not put down roots in the neighborhood and were conceived, by those who adhered to the local traditional conception, as a stain on the neighborhood. In contrast, there was greater correspondence between the local tradition and the movements that adopted the empirical interpretation and instrumental orientation and that acted within the system. As a result, they won broader support in the neighborhood. This phenomenon was evident in the 1982 elections to the local council in Ir Ganim. The YFN, which had a strong link with the local culture (religious observance, a right-wing leaning, apoliticization on the neighborhood level, avoidance of conflict, an instrumental orientation, and respect for the authority of the local rabbis) won fourteen of the fifteen seats on the council, while ICL, which had close contact with the external-radical environment and remained foreign to the neighborhood won not a single seat. In other words, the interpretations and symbols shaped by ICL were not accepted by the residents, whereas those of YFN won much favor. The rift between the urban movements and the neighborhoods' residents came into the open dramatically in the attitudes toward the Palestinian Arabs. Whereas the leaders of the movements sought to build some connections with Palestinians, local residents were involved in sporadic riots and took an active part in violent attacks against this group.

Learning from the Experience of Previous Movements

The various protest organizations consciously related to patterns of activity developed by previous organizations, derived lessons, and consequently created new interpretations and patterns of activity. This learning process was carried out through a critical examination of previous experiences, which involved a partial adoption of already existing knowledge and the development of new layers based on the organization's specific experience. In the light of their examination of past experiences, they adopted conceptions, expressions, and approaches in a selective way, made selective use of previous symbols and categories, and rejected other symbols and approaches.

The founders of Ohel Yosef in 1973 related in a critical manner to the militant and political activity of the Black Panthers, which in their opinion did not contribute to improving conditions in Musrara. Relying on this critical evaluation, the Ohel Yosef activists defined their goal as diametrically opposite to that of the Black Panthers—constructive activity within the neighborhood in order to develop the local community. As the then leader of Ohel Yosef put it: "The movement was in some sense a reaction to the Black Panthers. The active part did not favor violent activity . . . we wanted positive activities." Later, in 1975, Ohel Yosef was radicalized by the entrance of a group of criminals. This radicalization culminated in the establishment of the Ohalim movement in 1979 and was criticized by the leader of YFN, a movement that appeared in 1982: "I'm very critical of Yamin Suissa [the leader of the Ohalim movement] . . . they're the most radical on the map," and in a letter to the mayor he said:

> This should make it clear that our way was not that of the demonstrations and violence so characteristic, unfortunately, of our city. The damage they cause is almost irreparable, at least as far as self-image is concerned. We naturally acted in a solid, drab, and quiet manner. (Letter by the head of YFN to the mayor, March 1984)

The social critique of previous organizations does not mean a total rejection of the patterns they developed. The chairperson of YFN did not hesitate to adopt symbols and approaches from the past:

> Unfortunately, our members gradually began realizing that in the atmosphere that has been created in Jerusalem there is no practical possibility of serving as a conventional council. The only way to get things moving is still the way we have not chosen, the way that is so opposed to our principles and to our central idea—the way of violence and demonstrations and turning tables over etc.—the way with which our predecessors succeeded . . . we are not interested in continuing to be window dressing . . . the mentality of the younger generation from which we come does not allow us to remain in our present situation, we have come to act and there are other possibilities for action outside of the system in which we now function. (Letter from the chairperson of YFN to the mayor, March 1984)

There seems to be a clear reference here to precedents characterizing the militant movements that turned to activity outside the system. The militant approach adopted by these organizations serves here as a source of power, as a political resource that can be used to put pressure on the state.

At times, the conceptual categories developed by previous organizations were replaced by new ones, thus indicating a different conceptualization of the social problem. For instance, the members of ICL argued: "We are not another protest organization. The difference between us and the Black Panthers is that the Panthers were an ethnic movement and we are a class movement (interview in *Ma'ariv*, 18 March 1983). In both cases the context was interpreted structurally but the categories of the interpretation were modified and social orientations changed along with them from activity with an ethnic orientation to activity with a class orientation.

The interpretation and the following action did not, then, emerge in a historical-organizational vacuum. Symbols, conceptual categories, and ways of thinking developed by previous organizations were examined by the new organizations and subsequently adopted, rejected, or revised. In other words, there was a continuous process of interorganizational learning, based on prior experiences and adjustment to the changing sociocultural environment.

Conclusions

This chapter analyzed the causes for the divergence of social protest. Relying on Mannheim's theory of sociology of knowledge and Geertz's interpretative theory, it has been suggested that this divergence stems from the different meanings attached to the social context by the participants in the movement. It has been argued that, although members of the second generation share similar social, housing, and generational conditions, they view these conditions in different ways and give them different meanings. Relating Marris's insights, as illustrated in his study of Neighbourhood Development in London, to my empirical observations in Jerusalem, I suggested two major forms of interpretation: a deep or structural form and an empirical one. The structural interpretation, prominent among the urban social movements of the Black Panthers and the Ohalim movement, located the local problems (housing deficiencies, lack of social services, dilapidated physical infrastructure, social detachment, and juvenile delinquency) within a deeper or structural context of socioethnic inequality. Hence, the conception that any serious response to these problems presupposed a radical change in the relations of power within the city and the state. The empirical interpretation, on the other hand, which characterized the coproductive organizations of YFN, the Katamon Higher Committee, and Ohel Shmuel, viewed the same problems as concrete issues that should be pragmatically confronted through negotiations and exchange with the state. The meaning associated with the social conditions thus affected the position toward the state and shaped to a large extent the strategies of action. (For a detailed discussion of these positions and strategies of action, see Chapter 5.)

The theoretical question that still requires an answer is how these varying forms of interpretation come into being. The interpretative approach tends to leave this kind of question without an answer. Geertz, for instance, in his article "Thick Description," provides penetrative insight into the modes of interpretation of different cultural groups, but does not explain the specific contingencies within which these interpretations were formed. And this has been precisely one of my major theoretical goals in this chapter. Based on the empirical evidence from Jerusalem, I have tried to demonstrate that the schemes of interpretation were produced by the joint impact of multiplicity of factors: social characteristics of the groups that formed the movements, personal biographies of the leaders and key activists, social interaction with the internal and external environment, and social learning from the experience of previous organizations.

Meaning (read, interpretation) and action, as argued by Marris, and demonstrated by this chapter, are inseparable. But meaning itself, as demonstrated in this chapter cannot be detached from the specific historical circumstances encountered by the social actors. This conclusion suggests a certain qualification of earlier statements made in Chapter 2. I would argue now that the different forms through which social protest expresses itself cannot be directly inferred from the constitutive context, but rather is mediated through the actors' experiences and interpretations. In other words, the context in which the protest grew up is not conceived in terms of creating, demanding, and shaping, but is treated as filled with potentialities that might be realized in different ways, by different agents who live in different places. In encountering the sociohistorical context, the social actors do not face it directly. They confront it through specific experiences in specific places, through local knowledge accumulated in the course of daily life experience and through disparate forms of interactions with different environments. Values and norms gained through these specific processes coalesce to shape specific schemes of interpretation; through these schemes of interpretation local experiences and the broader context become meaningful, and diversified types of social protest are formed.

Yet the social process does not stop at this point. Power relations and social exchange between the movement members and state agents affect both parties by remolding their norms and developing common conventions. These forms of interaction and their effects on socialization and integration of the participants in the movements are discussed in the following chapter.

5

The Relationships Between the State and the Urban Movements

The purpose of this chapter is to analyze the relationships between the state and the urban social movements. This theme has triggered a heated debate among social scientists. Smelser (1963) argues that the state may respond to the movements and the problems they raise by either rectifying the structural strains or by enforcing law and order.

According to the neo-Marxian school, as represented, for example, in the works of Castells (1976; 1977; 1978), and Olives (1976), there exists an unresolved conflict between the state and its planning apparatus on the one hand and the movements on the other. The purpose of the state and its planning extensions, so they contain, is to ensure the interests of the ruling class and reproduce the social relations of production. In contrast, true urban social movements, which have not become tools of the establishment, seek to bring about a qualitative change in the political-economic structure (Castells, 1976, pp. 151, 155). In other words, there is an antagonistic, class-based conflict between the two: state planning from above, by its very nature, strives to suppress social change initiated by urban social movements originating from below. Although this class-oriented position was explicitly abandoned in Castells's later writings, he still maintained that state control over information and its centralist supervision sharply clash with the aspirations of residents to advance self-management and local control (Castells, 1983).

The Marxist theory is rejected by the neo-Weberians, who contend that there is sociopolitical pluralism and separation among the various centers of power (political, economic, cultural, and territorial). According to Giddens's interpretation of Weber, this theory implies that politicians would not assume such policies, which are designed to enhance their social class's or status group's interests (1971, p. 68). As Harloe (1977, p. 8) writes, "Weber maintained a distinction (contrary to Marx) between the economic and the political (and the legal) aspects of society; although developments in each sphere had an influence on the others, they are autonomous rather than relatively autonomous." It follows from the neo-Weberian theory that the state is not a monolithic body that invariably strives to restrict and suppress urban social movements.

This point has been accentuated by Saunders (1987), who draws an ideal type distinction that sets apart the politics of production and wealth creation, associated primarily with the central state, from the politics of consumption and wealth distribution, associated primarily with the local state. Such contradictory projects arising within the state may well enable political expression by urban social movements operating from below, provided that they are represented by and affiliated with local state agents. Reforms in the urban system are therefore likely to stem from implementation of a welfare policy, especially when linked with urban social movements (Cox, 1976; Pickvance, 1976; Saunders, 1980).

Approaching the relationships between the state and the grass roots from an historical perspective, Susskind and Elliot (1984) identify three types of strategies assumed by the state: paternalism, conflict, and coproduction. Paternalism marks the politics of control in which decisions are made in a highly centralized manner. Conflict appears when decisions made at the top are challenged by residents and consumer groups, who seek to attain control over certain resource allocation or policy decisions. Coproduction is a strategy based on face-to-face negotiation between decision makers and residents.

Relating to the Israeli case, Etzioni-Halevy describes the relationships between the state and the grass roots as one marked by conflict absorption. She argues that the state neither suppressed the grass roots movement nor did it provide genuine solution to the structural strains. What followed then, was a set of responses that "have been fashioned in such a manner as to introduce little change in the basic allocative patterns of Israeli society" (Etzioni-Halevy, 1980, p. 252). Although I tend to accept the main kernel of Etzioni-Halevy's argument, it seems to me that a more complete analysis of the relations between the state and the protest movements requires a consideration of the following: the specific socio-historical conditions within which the state operates; the principal categories of social actors; the relationships between these actors in terms of the resources, strategies, and tactics employed; and the outcomes of interaction among the actors. In this chapter I will examine from a sociohistorical perspective the relationships between the state and the movements, the actors involved on each side, the strategies employed by the actors, and the sociopolitical outcomes.

Main Arguments

1. The relationships between the state and local organizations arising in immigrant lower-class areas are inseparable from the specific historical conditions of which they are part. At the preliminary stages of immigration, due to the socioeconomic-political weakness of the immigrants their dependence on the state and the aspiration of a political elite to preserve the status quo, paternalistic forms of relationships tend to develop that are associated with local bossism. This is indeed a general tendency noted in several other immigration countries, such as the United States, Canada, and Britain. At base, the immigrants arriving in these countries settled in slum areas, well segregated from the host society. They lived in deficient housing, had limited access to power positions, and found themselves socially and economically inferior to the host society. With time, however, social mobility and modernization, exposure to new social values, and the rise of universal systems of services provision attenuates state control and the power of its local agent; protest movements do emerge, and the state tends to develop new strategies of action, ranging from confrontation-repression to cooptation and coproduction. It follows, then, that the relationships between the state and urban social movements may vary across time, depending on specific sociohistorical conditions. Within this historical context social actors, whether from the state or the grass roots, met each other; power relations between the state and the newcomers developed; and strategies of action were assumed.
2. The power relations and strategies of action may vary not only across time but also across space depending on the actors involved and their orientations. One, thus, may expect the coexistence in time of a multiplicity of rela-

tionships, such as paternalism, confrontation-repression, coproduction, and exchange. The interaction between the state and the grass roots involved three types of actors: community leaders of the immigrants' first generation and second generation; elected politicians of the central and local government; and appointed officials of the central and local government. Each group merits a further elaboration.

The community leaders are leaders of the first and second generation of immigrants. There has been a remarkable difference between the leaders of the immigrants' first generation and those of the second generation in terms of their relationships with the state. Whereas the leaders of the first generation served as state agents and sought to maintain the sociopolitical status quo, the leaders of the second generation, who headed the protest movements, challenged the status quo, were very critical of their predecessors, and did not hesitate to assume confrontational strategies while interacting with the state.

The elected politicians include politicians at the central and local government, such as leaders of national parties and senior municipal politicians who strive to enlist the immigrants' votes. This group controls the authoritative and allocative resources and thus is in a position to affect the residents' quality of life.

The appointed officials serve as a mediator between the state and the community. Due to their positions they may affect the distribution of resources, the processes of socialization, and the relationships between state and society.

3. The coexistence of different relationships between the state and the movements reflects and encourages internal divisions and conflicts within the state. It is argued that state responses cannot be reduced to an uncompromising class struggle between state planning and urban social movements. Rather, they reflect a wide variety of attitudes stemming from the structure of the political system, the internal power struggles taking place therein, the interests of various groups (central and local governments, political parties, and departments involved in the process), and the sets of values upheld by politicians, administrators, and professionals.

In the following sections these arguments will be applied to the local organizations that developed in Jerusalem during the last forty years. In line with the first argument, I will commence with the strategy of control and paternalism, then present the strategy of confrontation-repression, and finally describe the coproduction relations.

Paternalistic Relationships

The political response of the state to the social strains of the new immigrants preceded the emergence of protest movements. With the inception of the state in 1948, the government, headed by the Mapai (Labor) party, assumed a leading role in immigrant absorption. This was due partly to the moderate socialist policy assumed by the government and partly to a deliberate attempt to socialize the newcomers, to enlist their vote for the leading party, thus to maintain the status quo. The appearance of paternalistic relations was also associated with the socioeconomic-political weakness of the immigrants and their dependence on the state. Consequently, during the problematic stage of absorption when the immigrants, just arrived, needed frequent and close contact with those decision makers and bureaucrats responsible for allocating resources, this contact was extremely limited. Such conditions created the need for a mediator within the community itself to provide a link between the residents and government agencies and to help find solutions in the spheres of production (employment) and consumption (housing and social services). To further explore the nature of state paternalism and local bossism, I carried out an empirical study in the immigrant housing project of Ir Ganim.

The local boss in Ir Ganim was born in Casablanca, Morocco, to a wealthy family with a long tradition of involvement in community affairs; his father served as a representative of the Jewish community. In accordance with his family tradition, he himself had entered public life at a young age, and before coming to Israel had served for six years as a representative of the Jewish Agency in Marseilles and helped organize the immigration of Moroccan Jewry to Israel. In 1962 he arrived in Ir Ganim and settled in a transit camp (*ma'abara*). During his stay there he personally experienced the housing problem and the absence of services, was elected chairperson of the local committee, and began to act as a representative of the residents of the *ma'abara* to the institutions responsible for housing. Such a local link was vital for the politicians as well, because it could render them a number of services:

enlistment of voters, political presence and control over neighborhood affairs, and legitimacy. Hence a local figure emerged, entrusted with many power positions, who served as a mediator between the government and the community.

Yet it would be inaccurate to ascribe the paternalistic relations and the strategy of control that developed only to these structural needs. The complementary argument is that this pattern of relations was also triggered by the biography of the individual and his personal traits and by the cultural-communal tradition. To his personal experience in public activity was added a pronounced will for power. As the local boss testified of himself, "Sometimes, when I meet people who say that thanks to you we were able to expand our house, thanks to you we could do this, thanks to you we could do that . . . that gives me a lot of strength, a lot of motivation." What could be seen on the surface as altruism is revealed on deeper examination as a combination of willingness to help and a hunger for power, with the helper enjoying the gratitude and the sense of power no less than the person assisted enjoyed a material benefit. The will for power that appears in the local boss's case has two components: the sociopolitical, that is, the need to achieve power in order to apply pressure and realize concrete goals (loyalty and votes), and the psychological-aesthetic, which is primarily personal gratification and benefit without a material interest, its significance being existential. It would seem that the existentialist component becomes more important over time, especially as the power of the parties declines. It can, therefore, cast light on the boss phenomenon from a psychological perspective that is quite often missed by sociopolitical research, and thus indicate the personal conditions that assist in the creation of bossism of a new type in the neighborhoods (see Chapter 3).

The cultural tradition that stood at the foundation of the model of the local boss was not foreign to the new immigrants from Oriental countries, nor to those older residents who had been involved in the life of the Oriental community before the establishment of the State of Israel. This tradition, with certain variations deriving from differences of time and place, was common among North African communities, expressing itself in the *Naggid* (local governor) system. Among the Jewish communities of North Africa, the *Naggid* functioned as a secular authority alongside the traditional-religious authority of the rabbi and served as a mediator between the government and the community. A similar system, that of the *mukhtar*, was the practice among Oriental Jews in Palestine. The *mukhtar* of the Kurdish community during the prestate period, for instance, was appointed by the government and served as a representative of his community and as a liaison between it and the state. It would seem that the patterns of patron-client relations that formed among Oriental Jewish communities in their countries of origin and in Palestine continued also after independence. These traditions, together with the biographical background, personal traits, and structural necessities, created a hierarchy of patron-client relations: the local boss with his clients in the community; and the government with the local boss.

It was only natural, then, that under these historical conditions and in the struggle that developed between the various parties to win the votes of the immigrants, the local mediators became the agents of the parties at the neighborhood level. The local boss from Ir Ganim described it as follows:

> Of course, it was highway robbery by the parties. All the parties chased after the new immigrants in order to coopt them. . . . Each party wanted to acquire the largest public here in the neighborhoods, so we, the activists, who wanted, really, what was good for the residents, turned into vote contractors to bring people to the parties. Of course, it's true that they used us for their political interests because we were green then, we didn't know anything about politics or parties, that was something that belonged to European Jews, and we certainly didn't have anything like that in the Arab countries, in Morocco, and we became their political slaves. Of course, I won't hide that we learned their methods, their whole social and party system. We had no choice but to enter the public political realm. . . . Without a doubt, the people I met then in the establishment were close to Mapai. It was impossible to get anything done without having connections with those people, and I'll mention Akiva Azulai, deputy mayor and chairman of the Moroccan community in Jerusalem, when I went to him he asked me to become associated with the Labor party [sic]. Of course, I had no socialist ideological background, I didn't know what socialism was before I came here, I didn't know the difference between Right and Left and all those things. But we had to be partners with the people who were our friends, who helped us when they were, then, in the establishment—members of the city council, of the Histadrut, of all those institutions. Of course, that was the ruling party in the country and we had to be with them and we helped them and became part of the same party, and then we picked up the

> ideology of the Labor party, too. (Interview with the local boss in Ir Ganim)

The social exchange described—material allocations to the neighborhoods for political party support—was accompanied by an additional deal, centered on the local mediator. Being the channel to the local community he became a political asset in great demand. As a result he was offered, quite often by the ruling Mapai party, a wide variety of power positions. These positions, which included a long list of functions linked to the allocation of resources and services on the local level, made it possible to achieve a number of goals: to ensure the local boss's support for and loyalty to the party; to increase his power among the residents of the neighborhood; and, to apply direct and indirect political pressure on the voting public in the neighborhood through the agency of a local resident. In this way, the local mediator was absorbed into the political-bureaucratic system and became a local boss.

The reciprocal dependency, which characterized the relationships between the state and the local boss, was not unique to Israeli society; indeed a similar pattern emerged in other immigration countries. One of the most studied instances is that of neighborhood bossism in the American city, where it evolved in the nineteenth century by the political machine (Sait, 1963; Cornwell, 1964; Banfield and Wilson, 1967). The neighborhood boss in the American city was an outcome of the immigrants' social conditions and of the way the political machine worked within the municipal system. The emergence of ethnic neighborhoods populated by immigrants from the lower class, the existence of an electoral system based on geographical districts (the ward system), which turned the immigrant neighborhood into the basic unit of political organization, and the structural need of the political machine to control the voters gave the ward boss an important status in urban politics. In general, the local bosses were themselves immigrants. They spoke the language, knew the culture, were aware of the needs of the immigrants, and so could function as a cultural-political bridge between the political machine and the immigrants. The local boss served the ethnic community as a sort of patron who supplied personal benefits and thus assisted the immigrants and provided their immediate needs. As Cornwell notes:

> They had at least three kinds of needs which the ward heeler could fill on behalf the party leadership. Above all, they needed the means of physical existence: jobs, loans, rent,

> money, contributions of food or fuel to tide them over, and the like. Secondly, they needed a buffer against an unfamiliar state and its legal minions: help when they or their offspring got into trouble with the police, help in dealing with inspectors, in seeking pushcart licenses, or in other relations with the public bureaucracy. Finally, they needed the intangibles of friendship, sympathy, and social intercourse. These were available, variously through contact with the precinct captain, the hospitality of the organization into a local political clubhouse, the attendance of the neighborhood boss at wakes and weddings, and the annual ward outing. (Cornwell, 1964, p. 28)

In this way the political machine fostered, through its local agents, far-flung networks of personal relationships whose goal was to ensure political support. As Sait (1963) noted, the boss kept his job as long as he kept up his ties with his clients and proved his loyalty, efficiency, and ability to deal with people and get the vote out on election day.

From a sociogeographic point of view, the political machine played the role of preservation and oversight of the existing order, refrained from changing the economic and political environment of the immigrant; only a few politicians in the system proposed progressive ideas about creating a new social order. From this point of view there is a certain similarity between the political machine in American cities and the political machine in Israeli cities. Both systems, implicitly or explicitly, maintained that local politics was determined by a small number of individuals and not by the general public, and both used local agents to preserve the status quo.

The neighborhood organization that developed in this way was characterized by the control of one person over a long list of local power positions and contacts with power centers outside the neighborhood. In Ir Ganim the local boss held, along with his role of chairperson of the neighborhood committee, the following posts: director of the neighborhood Histadrut club, where he had an office and the service of a secretary; secretary of the Labor party chapter in the neighborhood; and member of the directorate of the municipal religious council, a post with great importance in a neighborhood where there were twenty-eight synagogues. He also served two terms as a member of the city council and was a member of the Labor party executive committee. Through these and other positions he developed a wide network of contacts with the mayor, his deputies, with the chairperson of the Labor party district committee, and with members of the Knesset from Jerusalem.

The Project Renewal program, launched in 1978, aimed to enhance citizen participation, but in practice helped only to strengthen the boss's grip over the neighborhood. At the end of the 1970s, the local boss was appointed by the mayor and by an administrator in the Ministry of Housing to be chairperson of the Project Renewal Steering Committee, a post that brought control over local budgets; to these roles were added the following positions: chairperson of the housing subcommittee of Project Renewal, a body that provided solutions for the housing problems of young couples in the neighborhood; director of the local center for vocational training, a position that involved providing information on employment possibilities and organizing vocational training courses; and a member of the directorate of the community center. Yet, because the project sought to encourage broad citizen participation in local activity, involve them in decision making, and advance the political democratization of the neighborhoods, the local boss had an ambivalent attitude toward the program. On the one hand, the project and its budget were seen as a source of power and control; on the other hand, it caused the boss endless anxiety over the possibility that it would bring about the formation of local alternative organizations with the encouragement of the state. To minimize what the local boss saw as a threat to his position, he tried to put his own people in central positions in the project, and so to establish his hold over it. The first director of the project indicated, in an interview, that he was "the chairperson's man." The position was offered to him by the boss, and as he claimed: "I decided from the start to work only with him [because] it was easier to work with him than against him . . . if he had wanted to, he could have destroyed the entire project. So I always saw to it that I reached an agreement with him before bringing matters before the steering committee." These facts of life were also well known to the second director of the project. In giving instructions to the staff that had been hired to do physical and social planning in the neighborhood, the director made it clear that the staff had no mandate to interfere with the responsibilities of the local organization, "even when the neighborhood organization is not democratic."

A detailed examination of the composition of the subcommittees that functioned in the framework of Project Renewal demonstrated that most of the committees' chairpersons were loyalists of the local boss. One of the prime examples is that of the chairperson of the community services subcommittee, who was also editor of the local newspaper. This position was of great importance because the local paper was delivered to every family in the neighborhood as well as to the city council, government offices, and to the offices of the city's weekly newspapers. During the local election campaign in 1982 this gave the local boss the opportunity to be interviewed and take up an entire page without allowing any comment from others, even though most of the newspaper's staff members agreed to the interview only on condition that a response from rival candidates would also be published.

This monopoly over local power positions, which arose against the background of a specific historical situation, put the boss at the intersection of contacts between the neighborhood and the state, with his role being a double one. On the one hand, he served as a local advocate, representing the interests and needs of the neighborhood residents to the state and seeing to the delivery of resources and services to his constituents. On the other hand, he served as the designated representative of the political apparatus—the Mapai-Labor party, the Histadrut labor federation, and the local authority—acting to advance their goals in the neighborhood. Much like the boss in the American city, his place at the intersection of contacts between the neighborhood and the state, and the positions of power he controlled, helped allot resources to the local population: housing, building permits, business permits, scholarships, and employment. And this eased the absorption of the immigrants. Yet his action was fraught with tensions and problems. The central tension was that, alongside a modern system that strove for universalism in the provision of services and in political-social activity, there developed a particularist system with traditional characteristics that was based on personal connections, the solution of individual problems, the distribution of benefits, loyalty, and social dependence. This tension was expressed both in the relations with the local environment and in the system of relations with the political-institutional system.

From the point of view of communication between the state and the neighborhood, the local boss system had a narrow channel of communication between the center (the party, the Histadrut, and the municipality) and the periphery (the neighborhood), in which the residents were cut off from decision-making processes, from establishing priorities, and from allocating resources. The role of the local boss as a mediator had no formal basis, but was supported by the state, which strengthened his position in the neighborhood. This informal relation required the boss to be loyal to the state agents, to maintain harmonious relations with them, and to refrain from acting outside the political system. While the boss took a confrontational approach from time to time, it was always for a short period, controlled, and meant to serve as a means of applying pressure and not as a goal in and of itself. Thus, for instance, the neighborhood boss threatened to bring the Project Renewal Program to a standstill, and proposed, to work out the existing problems, that the deputy mayor be appointed to head the local steering committee. At base, the relationships between the neighborhood boss and the state were founded on mutual loyalty and obligation, as the boss noted:

> If I go out today, even as a neighborhood leader, and help the mayor Teddy Kollek, I have no doubt that the mayor will remain obligated to me for a full four years. His door will be open to me, he knows that he has a leader who is his man . . . it's impossible to separate the political and the public factor, they go together.

Such a centralization of power in the hands of the local boss was not exceptional among Jerusalem neighborhoods. In the housing projects of the Katamonim, for example, the local boss held the position of chairperson of the neighborhood council and served in the following capacities as well: chairperson of the directorate of the Gonen community center, coordinator of the Katamonim chapter of the Labor party, secretary-general of the Kurdish community organization, and a member of the city council during the years 1969–1978.

To defend their power positions against the protest movements of the second generation, the local bosses, aided by the state, assumed all sorts of opposition tactics. In the Katamonim housing projects, the local boss refused to recognize the neighborhood committee, the Katamon Higher Committee, and worked to dismantle it; in Shmuel Hanavi the local boss opposed the neighborhood Ohel movement; and in Musrara the local boss opposed the activities of the Dai movement. In Ir Ganim a number of attempts were made in the late 1970s and early 1980s to reform the neighborhood power structure, to topple the local boss, and to function independent of him. The local organization which appeared on Iceland Street and dealt with apartment and parking lot expansion, deliberately ignored him, as one of those involved said: "We had no faith in him, the people don't trust him" (interview with a local activist in Iceland Street). The boss considered these attempts as competition designed to undermine his position, and they were therefore generally aborted in their early stages. An attempt to organize a group of young people of 18 years old and up, made up of unemployed young people with criminal records, was frustrated by creating friction between the members of the group through differential job promotion of a number of them, which in the end led to the dissolution of the group.

A community worker who tried to found a representative neighborhood council was transferred out of the area. An attempt by Ohalim movement activists to set up an "Ohel" council in the neighborhood was frustrated, and the initial steps of the YFN and ICL were met with forceful opposition. For a long period the local boss refused to hand over his position as head of the neighborhood steering committee to the newly elected chairperson of YFN and continued to control local power positions. The opposition to local paternalism reached its peak with the creation of YFN and ICL, as described in Chapters 2 and 3. From a geographic perspective, these organizations wished to create a different, more democratic environment in which the people would take an active part in shaping their surroundings. These organizations opposed the kind of political relations fostered by the state and its local agents; relations that turned the residents into passive figures in local affairs, without political responsibility and cut off from political influence.

In retrospect, however, it would be too simplistic to interpret the neighborhood boss as no more than an expression of political manipulation and to label this expression as a pragmatic denial of ideological-political-universal principles. The local boss grew out of the structural requirements of the political system, but he also came into existence because of the needs of the immigrants themselves. The need for a mediator is common among immigrants in a city, groups that need a liaison with the local bureaucracy and assistance in obtaining resources, especially at the initial phase of absorption. Against this background, the neighborhood bosses rightly argued that their activity was at base a service to the community through which they displayed social sensitivity and a sense of duty toward their fellow immigrants, thus facilitating their absorption (Azmon, 1985). The patronage system of the local boss reached its height in the 1950s and 1960s. Yet, during the mid-1970s, this method, in its original version, began to lose its hold. The development of universal welfare services, the weakening of the party structures as the professional bureaucracy gained power, processes of socioeconomic mobility, as well as the increasing knowledge of individuals about the political-bureaucratic system reduced dependence on the services of the local boss. Indeed, the end of overt paternalism and bossism in the Israeli city bear close resemblance to processes that took place in the American city in the 1920s.

The birth of the social reform movement in American cities, which brought about the consolidation of a welfare policy with universal principles, reduced people's dependence on local bosses and undermined their political power. Moreover, the benefits and sense of friendship that the local bosses gave lost much of their importance once the immigrants began to be absorbed into society and as their incomes increased. Voters, who in times of need could apply to a professional social worker and receive unemployment compensation and social security or welfare payments for the children and elderly who were their dependents, needed little help from the local bosses (Banfield and Wilson, 1967, p. 121). The diminution of dependence on the local boss was apparent in Israel from the beginning of the 1970s. The declining power of the political parties, the increasing power of a bureaucracy with a universalist approach, and the mobility of the immigrants, all mitigated the importance of the local boss in Israel as well.

These processes were experienced with special intensity by the younger generation and created much tension between them and the boss. In the eyes of the younger generation, organized into protest movements, the local boss had become a symbol of the social problem and of the parties' political manipulation. Their activity was directed against this social problem and against the organizational model that represented it. For this reason, it is not surprising that the social protest that developed in the younger, second generation in the immigrant housing projects was directed not only against general problems, but also against the boss system, which on the local level became a symbol of unequal relations, paternalism, and control.

Confrontation and Repression

The rise of urban movements in immigrant neighborhoods has sent a shock wave through the Israeli system, affecting both society and government. For the first time in the short history of the state, the central myths and ethos of gathering in the exiles, narrowing social gaps, and building up a democratic-socialist society were called into question, and the issue of poverty was openly raised on the public agenda. Consequently, some serious cracks appeared in the Israeli self-image of social consensus and exemplary society. From a historical perspective the appearance of the militant urban social movements like the Black Panthers and the Ohalim movement was an immense innovation that challenged the existing set of national priorities and posited a great challenge to the existing procedures of welfare distribution. The basic belief that poverty was a nonissue was shattered, and the priority given to defense and security needs was seriously questioned.

The protest also hit the traditional power centers of the central and municipal government, inasmuch as it criticized the paternalistic relations fostered by state agents and undermined the position of the loyalist bosses. Many of the bosses were associated with the Labor party of Mapai, with the Histadrut, and with the municipal list of the city mayor, Teddy Kollek. Indeed, Kollek's electoral victory in 1965 and his long incumbency have been attributed to the close connections he maintained and to the mutual trust he developed with the local bosses in immigrant and poverty neighborhoods. Now, all these networks of friendship and mutual support, developed over the years, were put into risk by the rise of a new generation of leaders, whose loyalty and political inclination were still unknown.

Hostile Response

It is no wonder, then, that when the first movements, the Black Panthers (1971) and Ohel Yosef (1973), appeared, the state was not ready to respond positively and constructively to this challenge. Moreover, throughout its initial contacts with the movements, the state had no appropriate structures for coping with the rise of radical leadership and therefore found it difficult in the short run to respond positively to the radical demands originating from below. In such situations, Huntington (1968) argues, when the system does not succeed in making its position more flexible, the protest tends to become more radical and violent. This was indeed the case in the short run with the Black Panthers and the Ohalim movement. As a result, members of the two movements radicalized their interpretations and became engaged in a series of violent demonstrations and squatters' protests (see Chapter 3). True, certain elements in the state supported the movements for ideological or power reasons and even gave them secret support (Sprinzak, 1986). But these supporters generally came from the periphery or semiperiphery of the state. In contrast, key figures in the state saw the radical protest as a threat to the central system of values and a challenge to the existing order, and therefore they tried to hold it back and neutralize its leaders.

Golda Meir, prime minister in the period of the Black Panthers, reacted to their activities with much hostility: "There is no greater disaster than a division within the nation. Nothing will succeed if we let this poison penetrate us" (Speech by Golda Meir to activists of the Moroccan immigrants' association, following the 10 May 1971 demonstration). One of the senior politicians in the Jerusalem municipality defined the activists of the Ohalim movement as "human dregs . . . the generation of the wilderness . . . wild African tribes that received independence." On the practical level the government's hostile reaction revealed itself in different ways: repression, delegitimization, individualization, blockage of expansion, and neutralization of supportive professionals.

Repression of the Movements. This kind of response entailed a deliberate attempt on the part of the government to either eliminate the organization or to reduce its impact. The Katamon Higher Committee is a striking example of this process. The Katamon Higher Committee appeared shortly before a municipal elections campaign of 1981, a period in which the leading party in the local authority was working hard to foster its loyalists among old-time vote enlisters—the local bosses—in the neighborhoods. The committee's campaign against the local boss was interpreted, under these conditions, as a campaign against the leading municipal party and a challenge to its political position in the Katamonim region. The politicians in city hall did not have a clear picture of the nature of the new local organization and its direction, even though some of the representatives on the Katamon Higher Committee were identified with the leading municipal party.

At first there was an attempt to plant the local boss in the committee, and he claimed that it was his right as chairperson of the local community center to participate in the committee's meetings. This position was not approved by members of the newly established organization, who basically sought to broaden the participation of the residents beyond what was acceptable to the local boss. Hence, they decided not to invite the local boss to the founding meeting of the committee, and they insisted that he not attend the committee's meetings. However, in the social exchange developed with the agents of the local authorities, members of the committee were told that the neighborhood's problems should be raised through the neighborhood boss.

When government attempts to maintain its power position failed, and the committee managed to develop its own contacts with different municipal departments, government offices, and the media, there was another attempt to dismantle the Katamon

Higher Committee from the inside and the outside. This was done from the inside by urging supporters of the leading municipal party on the committee to leave it; from outside it was done by cutting the committee off from the resources of the local community center and professional personnel. The director of the community center received orders not to cooperate with the Katamon Higher Committee, and when he refused was fired; the local community worker was also told to cease her work with the committee. The response of the remaining portion of the committee, that is, the representatives remaining after the supporters of the leading municipal party left, was a radicalization of orientation and action. The committee's spokesperson said:

> What the chairperson of the community center wants to establish is, in fact, a political cell for Teddy Kollek. He wants to advance his own people while throwing others to the dogs . . . he decides whom to help and whom not to help, and all in accordance with a party key. (*Kol Yerushalaim*, 13 May 1983)

In the course of the conflict with the neighborhood boss there was an attempt to set fire to the community center. Local residents also staged a demonstration in front of the municipal building. The local boss received the full support of the local authority and was described by the deputy mayor, Yosef Gadish, who also held the neighborhoods portfolio, as follows:

> This is a public figure who is highly aware of what goes on in Katamon. I or any other person could be chairperson of the community center, but because of our acquaintance with him we offered him the position. It is a great privilege that he accepted our offer and took upon himself this difficult job. (*Kol Yerushalaim*, 13 May 1983)

At a certain point the municipality also tried to undermine the position of Ohel Yosef. The chairperson of the organization was deposed by the mayor from his influential position as head of the Neighborhood Steering Committee, a committee that headed the local Project Renewal Program. An establishment loyalist was appointed in his place. A similar development occurred with the Dai movement. In the elections to the neighborhood council held in 1982 the movement won seven of the thirteen seats on the council. But, despite their success in the elections, members of the movement were not recognized by the municipality as local leaders and subsequently received no authority in the local institutions financed by the city, such as the community center, the steering committee of the Project Renewal Program, and the housing subcommittee. The leader of the movement summed up: "Not much came of it. They're laughing at us. Getting around the law. They don't recognize us."

In a historical perspective, these attempts to cut off the protest movements from political-economic resources were part of a continued effort made by the government to create politically moderate and pragmatic organizations that would function in the framework of the existing system.

Delegitimization of the Leaders of the Movements. The leaders of the Black Panthers were delegitimized by pointing to their connections with radical groups from the Left, such as Matzpen (a Trotskyist group) and Siah (the Israeli New Left). The leaders of the Ohalim movement were delegitimized by citing their criminal past.

Individualization of Macrosocial Problems. This means seeking individual solutions to collective problems. The typical response to the movements' demands quite often has been a genuine attempt by conservative politicians to solve problems on an individual basis; in contrast with the movements' objectives, which aimed at dealing with problems in a qualitative and collective manner. Thus, for example, jobs and housing were offered to prominent activists with the intention of absorbing them into the system and moderating their influence.

Blockage of Socioterritorial Expansion to Other Neighborhoods. At the macrosocial level a series of measures was taken designed to hinder the movements' activities. At first, the conservative politicians refused to cooperate with the new organizations and recognize them as representatives of their communities; in certain instances resources were withheld from the movements (interviews with activists in Ohel Yosef, YFN, and Dai). Another means adopted to curtail the movements' expansion was to exert influence on local neighborhood organizations, to deter them from joining the movements' activities (minutes of the Association of Neighborhood Councils, Activists, and Ohalim Councils, 1 March 1981).

Neutralization of Community Workers Who Supported the Movements. The politicians who were hostile to the movements invested considerable effort in neutralizing the effects of the professionals who assisted the movements and attained influential positions in neighborhoods affiliated with the movements. In 1971, while the Black Panthers and their supporters took out to the streets, a fierce conflict emerged within the municipality between Rabbi Menachem Porush, the deputy mayor who was also in charge of the Department of Social Welfare, and the community workers in the department. In a letter addressed to Mayor Teddy Kollek, Rabbi Porush complained that community workers cooperated with radical groups, like Matzpen, and assisted them in establishing connections with unattached groups (which formed the core of the Black Panthers) in poor neighborhoods. The main target of Porush's accusation was the Community Work Division in the municipality (letter by Menachem Porush to the Mayor Teddy Kollek, 17 February 1971). Despite the firm denial of this accusation by the head of the department, the mayor accepted the major tenets of Porush's complaint. Consequently, the Community Work Division was separated from the Department of Social Welfare and, in line with Porush's recommendation, was attached to the Department of Education. Even today, twenty years later, the Community Work Division is still separate from the Department of Social Welfare.

It appears that Teddy Kollek, then relatively a new mayor, was shocked, like many other traditional politicians, by the rise of the Black Panthers and the undeniable fact that the movement was assisted and to some extent, even guided, by members of Matzpen and Siah. Consenquently, the community workers, who ran social clubs in the slums (including the neighborhood of Musrara, where the Black Panthers appeared) were held responsible for the rise of the movement and were neutralized. Such a neutralization quite often started with a warning, followed by professional scrutiny, and ultimately ended in removal from the office or the area. The politicians even resorted to blocking the professional advancement of senior community workers. For example, in an attempt to foster control of neighborhoods from above, primarily through modern community centers, which in Jerusalem are conceived as the modern rivals of the older social clubs, promotions were held up for senior professionals who stressed field work in the streets and youth houses and who cooperated with the urban movements. The Ohalim movement protested this measure in a letter to the mayor of Jerusalem, which said, among other things:

> We consider this to be an obviously discriminatory act, a continuation of your policy of deprivation in the neighborhoods.

> . . . Why, then, did you prefer someone with no affinity whatsoever for the neighborhoods, for the position of department director? It appears that you were none too happy with the fact that there is finally a department in the country that has absorbed hundreds of young people from the neighborhoods for educational and guidance work. This apparently offended you. (Letter from the Ohalim movement to the mayor of Jerusalem, 25 August 1981)

The conservative political response was reinforced by mainstream social and community workers. These professionals openly rejected any cooperation with criminal and unattached groups, and they were dismayed by the movements' conflict strategy. One senior professional claimed that "violence arouses opposition." The conflict approach sharply contrasted with traditional views, which supported "cooperation" between the state and the neighborhoods. Such "cooperation," as described by another senior official, was directed toward the following objectives: (1) "positive channeling of existing neighborhood energies"; (2) obtaining "administrative benefit" (through feedback from the neighborhood to establishment activities); (3) "serving neighborhood interests." For mainstream professionals, the conflict strategy adopted by the movements constituted a challenge to conventional methods, which were based primarily on conflict resolution, harmony, and consensus. Moreover, urban social groups operating from below and supported by some professionals and politicians posed a radical challenge to the professional legitimacy of mainstream workers. The response of this group was, therefore, one of countercriticism, in which those professionals who supported the movements were accused of negative activities, agitating against the local government, politicization that exceeded the bounds of professional ethics, constructing a local empire, and creating a negative public image of the neighborhood (interviews with community workers).

Apparently, the conservative elements in the Israeli government viewed with suspicion the rise of protest movements, interpreting them as a subversive force that could, in Golda Meir's words, poison the existing social fabric. Such an hostile attitude toward protest movements is quite widespread among conservative politicians and appointed officials. The conservative group, whether in Israel or in any other place, thus tended to interpret the movements as a symptom of social disintegration and anomie and assumed, overtly or covertly, that they were an expression of irrational behavior undertaken by marginal groups in society

(Smelser, 1968; Banfield, 1974). For the conservatives, these movements express a deep crisis of Western society. The signs of this crisis, according to Bell (1978), are a rise in the level of expectations, which brings in its wake growing demands from various groups. Against the background of these demands, the state appears unable to satisfy all the groups, which causes a crisis of legitimacy (Habermas, 1975). According to the conservative school, the growth in expectations and demands is opposed to the ascetic work ethic, and signifies the growing secularism of modern society and the loss of its basic ethical values. Accordingly, politicians and appointed officials in Israel often warned against the *magi'a li* (I am entitled to state allowances and benefits) argument, raised by some members of the movements and viewed it as a sort of parasitic demand that has no socio-moral justification.

It would be a mistake, though, to assume that all state activities were directed against the urban movements. Indeed certain elements within the state supported the movements' activities.

Supportive Response

Elected and appointed officials in the central and local government lend their support in certain occasions to the protest movements. Three types of supporters can be identified: progressive community workers; elected officials at the local level; and elected officials at the central level. Each group of supporters had its own goals and interests, and relied upon different sets of strategies to advance its goals.

Progressive Community Workers. This group included community workers, employed by the municipality, who identified with the objectives of the movements and aspired to reformist changes in the local and overall national power structure. Their criticism was directed at the political and appointed levels in both the local and central state. They criticized the central state for its social and housing policies toward the new immigrants. In their view, the two levels of government failed to consider human beings in their entirety, ignored their needs and aspirations, and did not secure human basic needs (Paran, 1982). They claimed that the state's policies led to the destruction of the traditional-Oriental community, all because of manipulative efforts to obtain a local political power base. This, they contended, caused the collapse of the internal support system, prevented the rise of social consciousness, and subsequently led to deviance and crime. Project Renewal, for example, was conceived by progressive professionals as a mask for the government's manipulative political intentions (Amiel, 1982). The progressive community workers also criticized their traditional colleagues. A progressive community worker who played an important role in organizing the Black Panthers and the Ohalim movement claimed that

> the problem is rooted in social work, which develops client dependence; it leads the clients not to attempt to overcome problems on their own. . . . Consequently, neighborhood young people who aspire to master their own destiny seek to get rid of the social workers. . . . There is a clearly discernible feeling that social workers and people like me are on two opposing sides. (Paran, 1982, p. 32)

Another progressive community worker challenged his traditional colleagues and stated that "regular activities do not solve the problem in a fundamental manner. You have to supply something more radical . . . they [the traditional professionals] have not proven themselves; over the years, they have only granted welfare and charity. Residents do not consider them as the address to turn to. They do not believe that they possess any political power."

This social conception and critique led certain community workers to identify with the movements' critique and demands. Already in the early 1970s, as outlined in Chapter 2, the community workers developed new social programs designed to serve unattached and juvenile groups like those found in Musrara and Katamon Tet. It was within this context of involving the unattached and juvenile delinquents groups in local-social activities that the Israeli Black Panthers movement appeared. And it was the proximity of the events that led the deputy mayor and perhaps the mayor himself to draw a link between the activities of the community workers and the rise of the movement. In retrospect, it seems that the activity of the progressive community workers was intended to socialize marginal groups in slum areas, such as Musrara, and improve their social and physical conditions. But things moved out of their control when a link was formed between the local group of unattached youth and members of Matzpen and Siah. In the organizational dynamics that followed, the progressive community workers supported the movement's activities, served as its spokespersons, and, as illustrated previously, some of them paid with their careers.

Following the rise of the Black Panthers, the Division of Community Work was separated from the Department of Social Work, but the conception of cooperation with unattached and delinquent youth, even when it clashes with the conception of the authorities, has become part of the professional norms. These norms, which place accountability to clients above loyalty to employers, surfaced once more in the mid-1970s with the rise of Ohel Yosef and the Ohalim movement. One of the professionals, who played a leading role in setting up the movement, expressed his feelings rather literally: "I hate the establishment that sent me, hate the system." In practical terms, these feelings were expressed in encouraging of grass-roots organization and participation in grass-roots activities.

One of the unique characteristics distinguishing the activities of the progressive community workers while working with these organizations was the involvement of criminal groups; groups that were generally regarded as a deterrent factor and rejected by traditional professionals (interview with local social workers). According to Michael Paran, a community worker who played a leading role in setting up Ohel Yosef and later the Ohalim movement, local crime was a disguised expression of social protest: "They are protesting against society, which has denied them their right to exist." Hence, he saw his role as a progressive professional: "If we open the way toward social protest, they will move out of criminal protest activities." In other words, the progressive professionals sought to sublimate aggression, diverting it from criminal channels to positive social activity. In keeping with this approach, the process of social action from below implied that "a neighborhood must organize from the street. You have to start at the bottom. From there, you cannot go downward, only upward. You have to start with the worst. The worst will rise and take everyone with them" (interview with Michael Paran). This approach was reinforced in the words of a movement leader: "People understood that the power that can change things resides with the criminals . . . when the criminals saw where I was going, they joined me. I helped the 'Yorams' [the noncriminal, mainstream-oriented group] and made sure that the criminals did not interfere."

In contrast to the traditional community workers, the progressives, who assisted Ohel Yosef and the Ohalim movement aspired to bring about change in the system (a conception subject to varying interpretations) through social action from below. One approach emphasized the revival of territorial life through the planning from below of self-help services, representation of all groups in the territory, and independent management of the neighborhoods. Paran claimed:

> The method is to enable people who live with the problems to establish means for dealing with them independently. . . . The initiative for defining and solving the problem and the method of implementing the solution should be left to the local residents. . . . Residents must realize that the neighborhood is their own. From it, they will extract its finest latent powers. (Paran, 1982, p. 34)

This conception called for raising territorial consciousness, "developing neighborhood nationalism," and creating a territorial social conflict in which the movement would achieve local autonomy and subsequent control over vast areas of the urban system. According to this approach, Paran continued,

> Poor people must hang on to their environment; here they know every corner; here, they are free of tension. This explains the attacks on outsiders. It's nationalism. At the first stage, you have to tell these people that all outsiders must go . . . you have to take over the community center, the clinic. Only at stage B can you open windows. First of all [you have to gain] local control . . . since the intention is to create an ideology of territory . . . you become the neighborhood authorities. Everything passes through you. From local control, you have to reach overall municipal control: Katamon to the south, Shmuel Hanavi in the north, and then Nachlaot in the center. You have to set up a federation. The battle objective is expansion, from blocks 101 and 102 to all of Katamonim and from there to other parts of the city.

Another approach prevailing among progressive community workers called for creation of class consciousness and a cognitive link with left-wing parties to promote social change. Avner Amiel defines his method of work as follows: "My function as a community worker is to impart class conceptions . . . to initiate political socialization of all kinds of people, to develop a culture of social struggle." This approach espoused such nonterritorial goals as social justice, equal opportunities, and social legislation concerning universal distribution of welfare services. It supported class conflict through which, it was hoped, the movement would join wider political struggles. "It would be wasteful to work on a neighborhood level," contended Avner Amiel, explaining that the objective is "exploitation of the Ohalim system to create social tension." Nevertheless, he had little optimism regarding the possibility of success in raising class consciousness. "Doing business with a subculture is a difficult problem . . . the subculture somewhat ruins things . . . it is interested in immediate achievements. Their id is also somewhat stronger; Flatto-Sharon gives out money, so they go to work [for him] immediately. You have to wait a little bit, to prepare the background, and then embark upon the struggle" (interview with Avner Amiel).

As far as the Ohalim's goals are concerned, disagreements often emerged among progressive professionals: Paran supported territorial integration and Amiel, class-party integration. Nevertheless, there was often consensus between both sides in terms of means, as the basic strategies of both were based on conflict. In addition to territorial or class consciousness raising, progressive community workers recruited material resources and public support for the movement. They often mediated between the movement and the state and aided in disseminating the movement's message to the neighborhoods.

Supporting the Ohalim movement, the progressive community workers exposed themselves to a new wave of social critique by elected and appointed officials. Paran was officially warned by his superiors and removed from his office in Katamon Tet. But the interesting thing is that some politicians in both the central and local governments supported the movements' demands and at times even its underlying progressive approaches.

Supportive Politicians. The political support lent to the movements was rooted mainly in power conflicts between coalition and opposition parties at the national level and between the central and local governments. Only rarely did the politicians lend their support for ideological reasons. The opposition parties and some politicians in the Jerusalem local authority tended to support the social movements, seeking to create electoral power bases at the neighborhood level. The movements that were supported, either overtly or covertly, were Ohel Yosef, the Ohalim movement, ICL, and Dai. For example, during the 1976 Pat neighborhood protest, which was initiated by Ohel Yosef, the opposition parties on the Right (Likud) and the Left (Sheli and Rakah) both expressed identification with the movement. After the protest, a senior Likud Knesset member visited Katamon Tet and arranged a meeting between residents and the Likud party leader, Menachem Begin, at which local problems were considered (interviews with community workers who participated in the Pat protest and with squatters from Katamon Tet). In 1977, when the Labor party went into opposition, it too supported Ohel Yosef and partially funded the Ohalim movement election campaign for the Tenth Knesset in 1981. This financing was not rooted in ideology, but rather in practical interests, and it was aimed primarily at taking votes away from the Likud, which since the 1960s had been the favored party in the area (interviews with movement–Labor party mediators).

Political interests in recruiting local support also explain the aid offered to the Ohalim movement by the International Sephardic Federation, by Knesset member Flatto-Sharon (a millionaire who set up a one-man party and was elected to the Knesset by buying the votes of poor people), and the Jerusalem municipality. The International Sephardic Federation placed the sum of $200,000 at the disposal of the Ohalim movement and gave it an office (worth some $1,200 in monthly rent), office supplies, and a secretary. In return, it invoked the movement as a means of pressuring the Israeli government on social matters. The status of the federation was thus recognized in the socioethnic field; its president was even invited by the prime minister to mediate between the government and the movement in the Ohel Moreh protest (*Kol Ha'ir*, 6 February 1981). MK Flatto-Sharon, who attempted to acquire votes in distressed areas through support of the movement, underwrote part of the Ohel Moreh protest expenses (purchase of tents, mattresses, a refrigerator, generator, and communication equipment), and even offered places on his Knesset list to movement leaders (*Kol Ha'ir*, 1 August 1980 and 10 April 1981). The Labor-dominated Jerusalem municipal government supplied material aid to the Ohel Moreh protest, which was primarily directed against the Likud government's housing and settlement policy. This support, which was justified as a humanitarian gesture, included a water supply, easing of police tensions, and mediating between the movement and the government (interviews with members of the Ohalim movement and with a senior municipal official; *Kol Ha'ir*, 13 June 1980).

The analysis of responses by the central government indicates the prominent absence of any ideological, value-based supportive orientation. The Labor party and other left-wing political groups that claim to represent the working class were not involved in the movement's activities and avoided ideological-educational work within it. The Sheli party (to the left of Labor) remained detached from the movement, despite support for the party from certain Ohalim activists (who, in the course of the Ninth Knesset elections, even established a group called Young People for Sheli). The Communists (Rakah), then active in Jerusalem neighborhoods through the I Am Israel organization, generally did not cooperate with the Ohalim movement, considering it to be a reformist group vulnerable to state control. As a result, each organization worked separately—with a certain measure of covert competition—in the struggle over community center policy and operation (minutes of the Association of Neighborhood Councils, Activists, and Ohalim Councils, 5 April 1981; interviews with activists and members of I Am Israel; see also Arachim Editorial Board, 1981).

Only rarely was the state supportive for ideological reasons. Such a support was particularly noted in the late 1970s and early 1980s when Ela'ad Peled, assumed the deputy mayor office. Peled endorsed certain aspects of Amiel's social conception, particularly Amiel's inclination to collaborate with new and young forces in the immigrant and poverty neighborhoods (interview with Ela'ad Peled). For Peled, the rise of the new movements attested to "The occurrence of an authentic and quiet revolution in the neighborhoods—one that was liable to become violent." Hence, as he put it, "It is both desirable and necessary to express this protest, which is so often justified. We should therefore cooperate with the movements and aid them, as long as they follow the rules of the game." Peled openly criticized those traditional politicians, whom he called the *conventional* or *orthodox establishment*, claiming that the latter had not learned to identify rising young powers within the neighborhoods, preferring to continue working through old local bosses. Contrary to the orthodox establishment, he contended, "it is far better to work with the rising wave, introducing it into your own game, than to say 'I don't see the waves'." In analyzing Peled's attitude and behavior toward the movements, it becomes extremely difficult to distinguish between ideological orientations and power interests. The Ohalim, for instance, were perceived as representing authentic expression, which should be encouraged, but also as competitors for power and control. As the deputy mayor said:

> They grasped the idea of power; they understood that power means control of resources. You want a summer camp? All right! Give me the money and I [the Ohel council] will organize it. The intention was to develop population dependence upon the Ohel council rather than the system. . . . What Mapai [Labor] dinosaurs realized was that you have to control the tap. Someone [from the Ohalim movement] wants to control all the taps. If you make sure that people receive better housing, then they'll be dependent upon you. If you are the

> channel through which various privileges are determined, then you've got power . . . they want all renewal projects to pass through them.

Peled reacted by saying that "we dare not accord them a monopoly on power," while his value-oriented ideological reaction was "the more universal the services, the more intense the democratic process becomes." This supportive attitude exposed Peled to criticism from his traditional counterparts. Practically speaking, Peled cooperated with Ohel Yosef, Ohel Shmuel, and the Ohalim movement, including the criminal group therein, by participating in ongoing dialogue with the movements' leaders, providing resources for social activities initiated from below, supporting Amiel's social conceptions and defending his position in the face of municipal criticism, promoting the Ohel Moreh campaign, mediating between the Ohalim movement and the central government, and providing individual assistance to movement members by finding them employment or serving as character witnesses.

Peled's support enabled the movements to achieve three objectives: resources for local positive activities; protest activities supported—at time covertly—by part of the local state; and local political legitimation for the activity of progressive community workers, despite opposition from their immediate superiors. Apparently, Peled's orientation was not endorsed by the conservative elements in the local government, and in 1981 he resigned his office and turned to academic life. The deputy mayor office was taken over by Yosef Gadish, who represented a paternalistic cum pragmatic position toward neighborhood affairs.

Indeed, Gadish represented the old, conservative tradition of Mapai, which fostered local loyalists among members of the immigrants' first generation. In the early 1970s, while he was responsible for educational affairs, he refused to support the youth club established by Ohel Yosef and described the movement's leaders as "the generation of the desert" (interview with Yosef Gadish). This dislike for the grass roots was somewhat attenuated in the aftermath of the 1977 political change. The rise of the right-wing Likud party to power led many ideologists and pragmatists in the Labor camp to consider new ways of confronting the Right, especially by penetrating its power bases in immigrant and poverty neighborhoods. Consequently, an attempt was made by both intellectuals and pragmatic politicians from the Left to mobilize new supporters in these neighborhoods, by organizing grass-roots movements that would challenge the Likud housing and settlement policy. Collaboration with such movements became a viable option even for conservative politicians like Gadish. In July 1981 a meeting was held between Gadish and Amiel in which a decision was made to send two liberal-radical community workers to the immigrant neighborhoods of Musrara and Ir Ganim, to establish grass-roots movements that would agitate the local residents against the Likud social and housing policy (the evidence is based on participant observation in the meeting). Later that year, ICL in Ir Ganim and Dai in Musrara were formed with the active intervention of these two community workers (see Chapter 2).

The ambivalent stance of the state toward the urban and neighborhood movements thus resulted in contradictory responses such as opposition, repression, cooptation, encouragement, and support. Essentially, this incoherent response reflected power and ideological struggles between the local and central governments and between politicians and professionals within the local government.

Coproduction and Social Exchange

With time, government agents learned some fundamental lessons and developed flexible systems of response that dealt with greater sophistication with the grass-roots demands. This flexibility was expressed in the incorporation of the new local leadership into the existing system, enlisting them in joint projects, and conceding to those demands that did not challenge the balance of power or endanger it. This is the essence of the coproduction strategy developed during the 1980s and 1990s.

The main path to coproduction was the Project Renewal Program. The program, initiated in 1978, comprised a couple of dozens of neighborhoods all over the country, six of which are located in Jerusalem: Ir Ganim, Stern Street, Katamon Het and Tet, Musrara, Shmuel Hanavi, and Shchunat Habucharim. Protest movements appeared in four of these neighborhoods prior and during the implementation of the program. Although Project Renewal ostensibly represented a positive view of local activity, it was characterized by bureaucratic centralism and a conflict between the implementing agencies and neighborhood residents-recipients. The practical results in the case of the protest movements were that every decision and innovation initiated at the neighborhood level had to be approved by a series of official committees. In other words, local initiative from below was absorbed into the bureaucratic-political system directed from above.

Reacting to this situation the Ohel Yosef's leader during that period (1973–1975) said: "It's the establishment's bear hug . . . it's pollution: controlled local initiative that prevents you from operating according to your own basic inclinations. In principle, it doesn't solve anything." A volunteer from the Hebrew University, who assisted the movement up to 1978, claimed that Project Renewal diminished the process of self-aid services, coopting local residents primarily for physical projects. The Ohalim's leader summed up Project Renewal activities up to 1981 in a similar manner: "The Ohalim movement failed because it was neutralized by Project Renewal activities." Against this background, three Project Renewal employees in Gonen Tet resigned in October 1980, claiming that "the neighborhood staff has neither decision-making authority nor tools for implementation . . . the staff and the residents are simply superfluous. They let us sit in at meetings and make decisions, make us feel important—and then, the Prazot company [the state company charged with the implementation of the program] does whatever it likes" (*Kol Ha'ir*, 10 Oct. 1980). The chairperson of the steering committee claimed that during the three years in which Project Renewal worked in the neighborhood (1978–1980), "there was a retreat from the previous situation, when the Ohel Yosef Council was active in the neighborhood."

It can be concluded that Project Renewal created a substitute for original local initiative and to a great extent led to its neutralization. This process was further accelerated because Project Renewal had at its disposal resources not available to the movement. Consequently, some of the movements' activists and leaders were absorbed into the bureaucratic system and became state employees. This type of coopting was not essentially the result of a conspiracy planned at the top, but rather a consequence of the bureaucratic structure that characterizes the state system. Nevertheless, there are indications that certain bureaucrats did not overlook the possibility of cooptation. A document authored by a senior Prazot official during the early stages of Project Renewal expressed a positive view of the involvement of residents. Nevertheless, the document stated that "it is easier to direct and control the behavior of groups when their representatives are within the focus of decision making, rather than outside it . . . involvement of the population in rehabilitation is likely to impart new behavioral patterns in their contacts with the various services" ("Outline and Guiding Principles for the Project Renewal Program in Distressed Jerusalem Neighborhoods," 27 October 1978). Cooperation, as presented in this report, appears to have a manipulative character (Arenstein, 1969), in which the state aspires to direct and control activity arising from below, imparts new behavioral patterns, and thereby perpetuates existing patterns of dependency and control. Minutes of the movements and interviews with activists indicate that these declarations were not expressed on paper alone. In November 1978, the leader of the Ohalim movement was invited to participate in a course on the subject of Project Renewal; and at the movement's meeting of 3 December 1978, he announced that he would soon be moving out of the neighborhood. He subsequently received aid, moved elsewhere, and became a state employee. In an interview, he conceded that "they bought me but they did not succeed" (minutes of the Ohalim movement, October–December 1978). Obviously, this reactive response took the political sting out of the protest, absorbed the activists into the system, and moderated their influence.

The cooperation between the movements and the government through the joint activity in the Project Renewal Program marked the intensification of social exchange between the two parties. The state supported the organizations by increasing their efficiency in delivering services to the community. Moreover, they were prodded into dealing with well-defined physical and social issues and received financial aid and professional guidance. In addition, their sphere of responsibility was broadened, especially through their participation in physical projects of the Project Renewal Program. The political-economic support extended from above encouraged professionalization and increased the efficiency, but also led to growing dependence on the state. On the one hand, local needs were supplied more efficiently, but on the other hand, there was a gradual decay of local power; the interest in social change disappeared entirely.

These changes occurred slowly, being associated with the system of social exchange that develops between the organization and the government. A detailed study carried on the YFN in Ir Ganim shed more light on the nature of this exchange. In essence, this exchange brought about a retreat of the organization from its original universal orientations and messages. The ideals of the YFN movement, as they were described in Chapter 3, were to solve local problems, to create a sense of belonging, to increase citizen involvement, and to achieve broad, democratic local management and thus to create "a model to be imitated as a trail blazer for the social future of the State of Israel." After the protest dust settled, it became clear that the original goals had been only partially achieved. The explanation of this is rooted in a series of social and political constraints on which a political "exchange deal" was developed—a deal that to a large measure shaped the nature of the organization's activity and its impact on the neighborhood.

From their election to office in 1982, it became evident to the members of the new neighborhood committee that their presence in the neighborhood committee did not guarantee them control of the neighborhood centers of power. A precondition for gaining access to these power positions—the most important of which were membership on the Project Renewal steering committee and the boards of the community center and the center for vocational training—was the approval of the local and central state agents. Yet these agents preferred to work with the local boss, whose loyalty and efficiency had been proven in the past. This political constraint required ongoing negotiations with the state—the local authority, the Jewish Agency, government ministries—and activity within the existing system. The integration into the system was reinforced by the basic orientation of the movement's leadership, which explicitly rejected activity outside the established system.

These constraints, which are nothing but a system of conventions and resources implicated in social behavior, served as a framework within which a system of social exchange developed between the organization and the state. The organization received legitimacy and broadened its control of local centers of power; in exchange it adopted an orientation and strategy acceptable to the state. The exchange was not a planned one. On the contrary, it was entirely the product of a situational-gradual development, during which the state went from ignoring the new committee to coproductive activity with it. In the first stages, for example, the local authority preferred to work with the local boss, who despite having been deposed from his position as chairperson of the neighborhood committee still controlled the important power position at the head of the Project Renewal steering committee. Only gradually, as the newly elected committee proved its adherence to the existing rules, did local centers of power pass into its hands, one by one: leadership of the Project Renewal steering committee, appointed by the mayor; director of the Project Renewal Program, approved by the coordinator for neighborhood rehabilitation and renewal in the Ministry of Housing; responsibility for the community center budget (signing authority and representation on the center's board); partnership in responsibility for the local Histadrut club and membership of the employment committee and the Center for Vocational Training. When this exchange was completed, the YFN had achieved local control while institutionalizing itself along politically acceptable lines.

The general outline of this institutionalization was this: adopting a pragmatic approach and a neighborhood orientation, focusing on basic material needs, a strategy of activity within the established system, and compromise with the local boss (all the chairpersons of the Project Renewal subcommittees were members of the former neighborhood committee).

The YFN's penetration of local power positions, which was conditioned on the consent of the state, brought the organization to adopt a pragmatic approach and a benign view of the state. The social exchange with YFN and the ones that developed with Ohel Yosef and Ohel Shmuel were meant to divert the organizations in the particularistic direction, making them work within the existing political framework. This tendency was supported by the movements' interaction with the local environment, which remained largely traditional, materialist, and fairly uninterested in the political processes associated with local empowerment, democratization, and decentralization (on this matter see the findings of the Project Renewal survey that indicate a similar phenomenon: The Government of Israel and the Jewish Agency, 1984).

Coproduction also entailed the absorption of the leaders and activists of the movements into the existing political and bureaucratic system. The leaders of the protest movements were offered attractive jobs in the central and local governments, and as a result many of them were neutralized. The two leading leaders of the Israeli Black Panthers were recruited by leftist parties; one of them has served for a long time as a Knesset member of the New Communist party (Rakah), and the other served for a short period as a Knesset member of the Peace for Israel (Sheli) party. The leader of the Ohalim movement is now a member of the central committee of the Labor party. The leader of ICL was offered a municipal position by Teddy Kollek: a representative of the neighborhoods in the City Council. The leader of YFN has been appointed special aide to the prime minister.

Conclusion

One of the major arguments advanced in this chapter is that the relationships between the state and protest movements cannot be abstracted from the specific sociohistorical conditions. Within the specific Israeli context these relations were shaped under conditions of mass immigration, socioeconomic dependence of the newcomers on the state, and an unmasked attempt of the leading political parties to enlist the votes of the newcomers and thus maintain the status quo. As a result, at the preliminary stages of immigration, the state tended to foster paternalistic forms of relationships associated with local bossism and control. The rise of protest movements was met at the initial stages with hostile state response, as the state tried to delegitimize the movements, block their expansion, and neutralize their supporters among the community workers. In line with Castells's theoretical arguments, one may convincingly argue that there is a structural, bureaucratic conflict between the Israeli state, accustomed to allocative planning from above (see Chapter 2 and Gradus, 1983), and the urban social movement, which represents the lower class and operates innovatively from below. The state tendency toward bureaucratic centralism (Elazar, 1987; Marx, 1982) and preservation of its power bases contrasts sharply with the movements' demands for devolution of power and decentralization of authority. In time, however, the state assumed more flexible strategies, encouraged cooperation with the movements as long as the latter maintained the rules of the game.

From a historical viewpoint, it seems that social protest and state repression, challenge from below and control from the top are not static relations, as Castells seems to suggest in his dualistic model. Within the Israeli context they represent a transitory phase between the paternalistic strategies of the 1950s and 1960s and the strategy of coproduction, which was adopted in the 1980s, especially through joint activities of Project Renewal. The transition is also evident in the nature of the movements themselves. Whereas the first ones were inclined toward protest and change, those that came later entered into coproductive relations with the state. In time even the more radical movements, like the Black Panthers and the Ohalim movement, assumed coproductive relations. From a historical perspective it is impossible, therefore, to argue that the protest diverged. Although a synchronic examination, as advanced in Chapters 3 and 4, corroborates the diversification argument, a diachronic examination sheds a different light on the process. Basically, it points to the divergence of protest being part of a wider process, wherein the different forms of protest converged into a well-defined pattern of coproduction.

This change in the pattern of relations invokes an interesting theoretical question concerning the relationships between routinization and change, system maintenance and its charismatic challenge (Weber, 1948). From a theoretical point of view, the protest movement marked the rise of a charismatic power that challenged the established system and its conventions and rules. Although in the short run social conflict, confrontation and repression seemed to be unavoidable, and to some extent did occur, things worked out quite differently in the long run. Over time, a complex process of social exchange developed between the state and the movements in the course of which some of the demands and challenges raised by these organizations were accepted, whereas others were rejected. The state made its position more flexible with regard to some of the demands and even began to encourage grass-roots activity, as long as it was restricted to local issues and conducted within the existing frameworks.

This was the nature of the coproduction process that characterized the system of relations between the state and the protest organizations at the end of the period under consideration. Interaction of this type is an elegant way out of the internal contradiction confronting the state while trying to enhance democracy and at the same time uphold power positions. Coproduction allows the state to take economic and symbolic advantage of participation while minimizing the political price. It allows the political system to avoid a comprehensive social reform or genuine sharing of power resources and influence and to argue that it is decentralizing authority. This is the essence of the conflict absorption strategy assumed by the Israeli government.

Coproduction also implied that the intention of creating a new type of place by producing new models of local political activity was realized only partially. The local boss was removed, dependence on the state was reduced, the influence of political parties on local activity was mitigated, and there was an attempt to increase local democracy by decentralizing authority and broadening the involvement of the residents. This activity was supported by Project Renewal, which encouraged citizen participation, a division of labor, and professionalization in the framework of the activity of the subcommittees. Nevertheless, the goal of societal and territorial change was only partly attained. When the dust settled, it became clear that the protest had resulted in organizations that, although they indeed had changed the former situation, still had preserved a large measure of continuity. During the transition from original ideals to pragmatic activity, the organizations became institutionalized in accordance with the prevailing sociopolitical rules.

Theoretically speaking, then, the convergence of protest

seems to provide another example of the routinization of charisma. The critical and utopian force has been institutionalized over time and has become part of the political-bureaucratic system it originally wished to challenge. During this process, the state's institutions and agents and the movements' participants underwent a significant transformation, in the course of which old conventions were modified, new interpretations were given to the existing conditions, and new modes of exchange were adopted. Moreover, several leaders were integrated into the institutional system, turning into government politicians and bureaucrats.

The social exchange between the movements' members and state's agents affected both parties by remolding their norms and developing common conventions, thereby enhancing routinization and even integration. Nevertheless, this routinization and integration should be interpreted carefully because it is by no means an indication of system maintenance. The persistence of structural problems in Israeli society, manifested in deeply rooted social, cultural, and gender conflicts, is undoubtedly rich with conflict potentialities.

The discussion so far has treated the state as if it was a monolithic whole. The empirical evidence, however, does not support such a view. On the contrary, in its relations with the movements the state presented an incoherent response that ranged from neutralization-suppression to support-encouragement. These contradictory responses reflected internal divisions and conflicts within and among different state levels. Fundamentally, they reflected a wide variety of attitudes stemming from the structure of the political system, the internal power struggles taking place therein, the interests of various groups (central and local governments, political parties, and departments involved in the process), and the sets of values upheld by politicians, administrators, and professionals.

The empirical findings clearly corroborate Saunders's theory, as formed in the British context, according to which the division of labor between central and local governments might encourage cooperation between urban movements and the local government. In Jerusalem, however, this well-known division between production and consumption orientations was overloaded with national-political conflicts. The leading municipal list, which is associated, despite its disclaimers, with the Labor party, has lent support and at times actively encouraged several protest movements that challenged the Likud's settlement and housing policy. In other words, the coexistence of a central government headed by the Right and local government headed by a Labor-oriented list made the forging of a coalition between the local level and the grass roots, as invoked in a different context by Bacharach and Lawler (1980), almost inevitable.

The pragmatic-political collaboration between the local government and the grass roots, which emerged at certain occasions, should not be interpreted, however, as a full-fledged endorsement of the goals and interests of these organizations. Within the local government there have been always certain powerful elements that viewed with suspicion and even outright hostility the rise of the movements, whereas other elements tended to identify with them. It seems that power considerations at the local level concerning its steering capacity, coupled with value-related ideological considerations, led to a series of internal conflicts at that level regarding attitudes to the movement. This produced a set of contradictory responses. The two main conflicts identified within the local government were the ideological dispute over the desired sociopolitical and spatial order and the power struggle for dominance and control of the urban space. The ideological conflict was waged between professionals, primarily community workers employed by City Hall, and politicians who supported the movement (henceforth, *progressive professionals and politicians*) and professionals, politicians, officials, social workers, and community workers who opposed it (henceforth, *traditional professionals and politicians*). The power conflict took place among politicians, among professionals, and between politicians and professionals with political aspirations, each group attempting to maximize its own interests through either suppressing or encouraging the movement. It was often difficult to distinguish between the ideological and power conflicts, as they were frequently interrelated. Figure 4 depicts the major participants in the local government's internal conflicts and the coalitions among them.

One of the most interesting features of progressive community work in Jerusalem has been its long tradition of involvement and cooperation with unattached and juvenile delinquents groups; and it was among these groups that the protest movements of the Black Panthers, the Ohalim, Ohel Yosef, and Dai emerged. Representatives of the traditional wing in the local government did not remain indifferent to the rise of the movements and their support by the progressives. Their varied responses included aid to individuals within the movement and support of the movement in its struggle with the central government, but essentially it was intended to preserve the existing power structure. Such a response of maintaining the status quo characterized both the traditional pro-

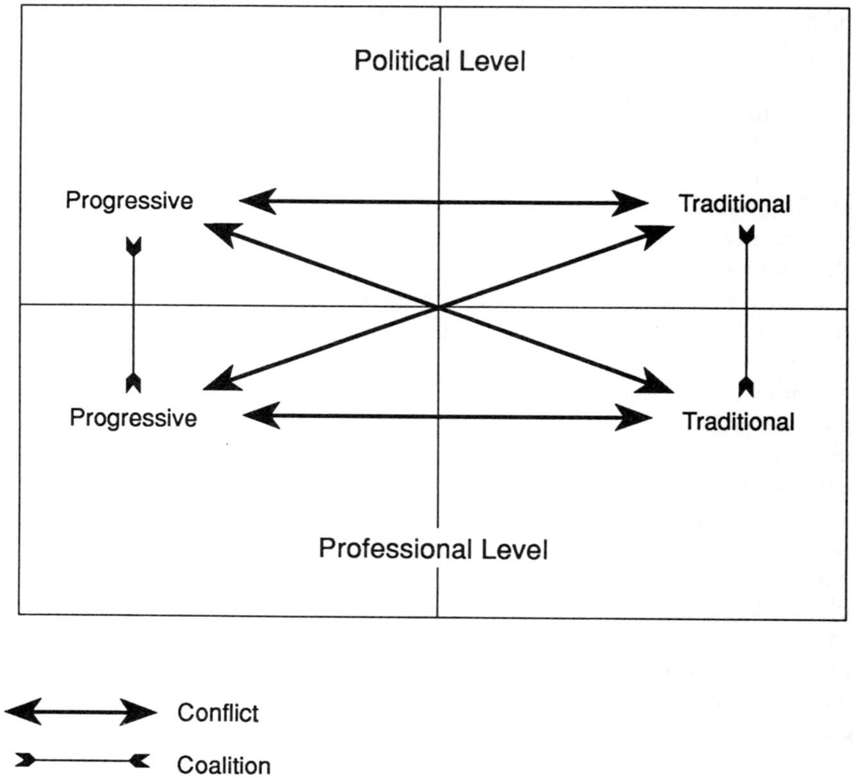

Figure 4. Internal Conflicts Within the Local Government

fessionals, (i.e., administrators, social and community workers) and the traditional politicians.

The ambivalency characterizing the state's response implies that extreme caution must be exercised when approaching the theoretical debate concerning the role of the state with regard to urban social movements. At the risk of oversimplification, it might be argued that the neo-Marxian and neo-Weberian theories complement rather than contradict each other. In terms of pure tendencies, identified through interpretation (Marxist hermeneutics) that goes beyond the empirical facade (Bauman, 1978), it appears that the Marxist theory of antagonistic conflict between the state and urban social movements is correct. At the level of pure tendencies, the state, whether at a central or local level, aimed at controlling local politics, while the urban social movements challenged this goal. These tendencies were deeply rooted in the development of the Israeli political-economic structure discussed in Chapter 2.

However, as one moves from pure tendencies to empirical reality, the politics of neighborhood control becomes much more complicated, lending some support to the neo-Weberian postulates. On the one hand, the movements did not represent a pure tendency of qualitative change. They had a reformist orientation and were partially subject to state penetration. On the other hand, the state appeared not as a monolithic whole, but rather as the scene of struggles between different orientations and between bureaucratic and political agents who represented different social groups and political interests—some seeking to maintain the status quo, that is, state control over the neighborhoods, whereas others were attempting to undermine it. In this way, the geographical-political conflict between the state and the urban social movements became represented in a microform within the state itself. In other words, the state became a focus of sociopolitical and geographical conflicts, hence its diversified responses. Indeed, this point has been recognized by neo-Marxists and neo-Weberians alike who, in spite of some fundamental differences in sociopolitical conceptualization, recognize the political-bureaucratic struggles existing within the state and subsequently the possibility for contradictory responses (Poulantzas, 1978).

The dividing line between the two schools lies in their answers to the question on whose terms the state–urban social movements conflict is to be resolved. For neo-Marxists, retaining their basic postulates and avoiding inconsistency requires looking back at the pure tendencies, "transcending" the sophisticated political, empirical analysis and coming up with a tendency-based answer. This creates internal tension between empiricism and deductive theoretical reasoning, which seems to haunt the neo-Marxist school (Duncan and Ley, 1982). On the other hand, focusing on empirical phenomena, neo-Weberians would tend to emphasize such issues as concrete activity, pluralism, cooperation, and interpenetration and to transform these empirical facts into a normative theory. Whereas the neo-Marxists seek to impose the basic normative tendencies on empirical reality, the neo-Weberians seem to quite prefer the opposite; namely, transforming empirical interpretation into a normative theory. In doing so, neo-Weberians ignore the fundamentally different concerns of the neighborhoods and the state as they evolved in the specific historical context. For these reasons, both schools can be regarded as complementary and at the same time inadequate. The answer to the question on whose terms the issue of divided polity is to be decided cannot be given in the abstract by resorting to pure historical-political-economic tendencies. Nor can it be provided by transforming the empirical reality of interpenetration into a normative theory that justifies the status quo. It has to be answered theoretically and practically by interpreting the balance of power, locating internal conflicts within the state, forming coalitions, and widening political divisions.

6

Theoretical, Practical, and Ethical Reflections

Theoretical Aspects

The Main Features of Social Protest

Faced with the mass immigration of Holocaust survivors and refugees from the Moslem world, the State of Israel assumed a leading role in immigrant absorption. One outcome was that the production of space during the 1950s and 1960s—the establishment of new towns, immigrant neighborhoods, and rural settlements—was carried out by state agents. Guided by the state's goal of settling peripheral areas, these agents determined the location of the newcomers, quite often segregating them from the host society. Moreover, operating under low budgets within a centralist-socialist system, these state agents played a leading role in shaping the new places in terms of physical outlines, social composition, and level of services. The new places thus formed differed markedly from the older ones. They were inhabited by lower-class people, many of whom were of Sephardic (Oriental) origin, and consisted of either evacuated Arab neighborhoods or monotonous, low-standard housing projects.

When those European-born immigrants who received reparations from West Germany moved out, they left behind the Sephardic newcomers, both spatially and socially. In this manner, an ethno-class division was translated into a spatial configuration. The middle class, the older working class, and growing numbers of the European newcomers occupied central places, while the new fraction of the working class, made up mostly of Sephardim, lived at the periphery. This sociospatial structure repeated itself at the national and intraurban level. In Jerusalem, on which this study focuses, it was manifested in a series of immigrant neighborhoods and housing projects located along or near the 1948 cease-fire line.

There was nothing in the cultural heritage of the Sephardic newcomers to ensure ideological or political support for the then-dominant Mapai (Labor) party. Yet through the massive intervention in local life, the power elite of the older working class, which had attained political hegemony prior to the establishment of the state, sustained its power positions for a long time. To further tighten its grip over the newly formed neighborhoods and towns, the power elite (Mapai activists, politicians, and bureaucrats) developed a patronage system of local bosses who, as was shown in Chapter 5, served as mediators between the party and the neighborhood residents. Over the years, as Chapter 2 shows, internal class stratification developed within the Sephardic ethnic group, making itself noticeable in differential occupational mobility and variation in ownership of housing. Consequently, relatively privileged and underprivileged groups appeared at the urban outskirts. The grass-roots movements surfaced in the underprivileged housing projects.

Social unrest and political resentment were slow to follow. The Wadi Salib riots occurred as early as 1959, but the Israeli Black Panthers did not appear until 1971. Later, social protest found a relatively massive form of expression in the rise of Tami, an ethnic Sephardic political party. During this entire period, Sephardic people living in disadvantaged areas increasingly distanced themselves from the Labor party, holding it responsible for their social and physical misfortune. In 1977, the Likud, a party of the Right, came to power with massive support from disadvantaged areas. Within this general pattern of social resentment, the grass-roots organization that developed in Jerusalem during the 1970s and 1980s occupied a special position. Although the political protest was essentially negative in character—that is, directed against the so called Ashkenazic establishment, which was held responsible for the social misfortune of the newcomers—the activity of the urban social movements went far beyond this form of negative protest. The urban movements were formed by the younger generation brought up in the housing projects, and this generation sought to intervene in daily life and reshape its social and physical surroundings. As shown in Chapter 3, members of this generation initiated services from below, encouraged citizen participation, challenged old patronage systems, demanded political representation in urban decision making, and defended local traditions and heritage. A new agent thus emerged in underprivileged areas, challenging the awesome bureaucratic-centralist system and bringing back to urban political life a hitherto manipulated and confined social group. The protestors, or more precisely the members of the leadership elite, found themselves involved in a threefold struggle: against the local bosses, against the parties and state, and against the cultural environment, which generally remained conformist, traditional, and primarily concerned with material achievement. The struggle of the protest movements appears against this background as an attempt to deal with double alienation, from both the native and the absorbing societies. Over the course of this confrontation an attempt was made to reshape the local environment and sometimes even the entire urban system.

Another common feature that surfaced throughout the protest was the growing engagement in deciphering the actors' own identities. Metaphorically speaking, the different movements appeared as local theaters in which the participants presented their local, social, or individual identities. Members of each movement related to their predecessors or contemporaries in a critical manner, presenting themselves as unique, innovative, and by far more efficient. The Israeli Black Panthers depicted themselves as a vanguard; the founders of Ohel Yosef criticized the Black Panthers and sought to develop a positive project; YFN criticized the violent actions of both the Black Panthers and the Ohalim movement. In displaying their identities, the conveyors of protest expressed themselves with differing metaphors. "A new intelligentsia" had appeared in the neighborhood, maintained the leader of YFN, whereas the leader of the Ohalim movement likened the ghetto to a center of power. These identities or meanings, attached by the participants to their movements, seemed to go beyond the broad ethnic, class, or housing struggles; they were associated with the people's self-image. In other words, self-assertion became another force in shaping the movement. Touraine's theorization seems to be particularly fruitful in this regard, because it turns precisely on the unique experience of social actors engaged in a process of self-realization. It is true that, although conceptualizing the search for meaning, Touraine focuses primarily on the macroproperties of the societal structure: economy, culture, science, and morality. Yet the search for meaning goes beyond these spheres to embrace the socio-psychological search for meaning that resides at the individual and group levels (Perlman, 1982). This may call for a more elaborate and refined approach to the study of social movements, one that moves beyond collective goals and general ideologies to consider personal motives as well.

The struggle against double alienation and the search for meaning are seemingly rooted in the specific social situation in which the major conveyors of urban protest, that is, the elite groups that lead the movements, found themselves. These groups were situated, I will argue, in a transition process—a rite of passage situation—that in Turner's (1969) terms may be well described as a "liminal situation." He likens those going through the process to tourists passing from one cultural region to another, while all the burdens and roles established by law, customs, and norms are suspended. The leadership groups of the urban social movements of the second generation were in a classic liminal situation: passing between generational units, between party patronage and a great measure of local management, and between Oriental heritage and Western culture. In this situation, those who took part in the process of transition tended to develop a unique kind of community that Buber describes as communion and Turner as communitas. This communitas is made up of members who possess very close ties with each other, emphasizing spontaneity, liberation, self-realization, equality, a low level of institutionalization, and internal dialogue. Members of the communitas find themselves in constant conflict with the social structure, which is characterized by a well-defined system of labor division and social reward. The conflict between the communitas and the social structure is expressed in a series of dichotomies: universalism–particularism, lack of clarity–purposefulness, equality–inequality, lack of institutionalization–full institutionalization. With the completion of the transition process, members of the communitas abandon their original characteristics, the group dissolves, and the members of the organization tend to adopt the characteristics of the social structure, including its instrumental-particular orientation. It is not surprising therefore that in the course of this transition parochial, group-oriented ideologies had been developed that magnified the role of the movement in changing the face of Israeli society. For the Black Panthers this ideology represented the uncompromised struggle of peripheral groups with the powerful establishment; the leaders of the Ohalim portrayed their organization as the cradle of neighborhoods' self-management in Israel, and members of the YFN described themselves as those who helped to remove the social stigma associated with immigrant housing projects. In other words, within the liminal situation new ideologies were formed beside the original ones, and these ideologies later served as a point of reference in describing the movements' achievements and success.

The Social Construction of Protest

Despite the features common to the movements, social protest diverged and was expressed in different forms of organizations: urban social movements, which sought to advance a comprehensive change in society through action outside the established system; neighborhood protest movements, which aspired to produce fundamental changes in the neighborhoods while emphasizing action outside the established system; and coproductive organizations, which wished to bring about limited change in the environment while acting within the established system. What seems to me extremely intriguing about these organizations is the diversified patterns of protest they display despite their common location in the ethno-class, generational, and spatial matrix. The structural approach, presented in Chapter 1, and the societal structures, discussed in Chapter 2, appear in this light as necessary yet insufficient conditions for the emergence of protest movements.

This is by no means to suggest that one should ignore the structural conditions; that is, the constitutive role of the societal context. Within this context, as shown in Table 3, the second generation underwent similar experiences and developed common tendencies to act. Within the general constitutive context, that is, the structural conditions, members of the second generation witnessed sociophysical deprivation and at the same time were exposed to the modern Israeli culture and developed a broad system of expectations from their environment. The massive politicization of the housing space implied frequent encounters with state bureaucrats and the party's local agent. Being exposed to a modern Israeli education, they experienced social mobility that, in certain instances, was accompanied by intergenerational conflict. All these experiences occupied a specific geographic setting, implying in most cases the formation of cohesive local groups, which preceded the development of the movements.

People have, in other words, related to the structural conditions of ethno-class division, state control, generational structure, and spatial segregation through specific experiences taking place within concrete geographic settings. Indeed, it was the concrete experience that informed their generational tendencies to protest. Yet structural conditions, and even specific experiences, do not necessarily imply social protest. They merely denote the fact that the possibility of protest is higher in one place than in another. In Jerusalem, the probability of social protest aspiring to overcome socioethnic deprivation, to remove the patronage system, to de-

Table 3. Structural Conditions, Experiences, and Protest Tendencies

STRUCTURAL CONDITIONS	SHARED EXPERIENCES	PROTEST TENDENCIES
Social (ethno-class structure)	Sociophysical deprivation and ethnic discrimination	Negation of initial conditions: material critique, search for new cultural identity
Political (politicization of space and local patronage)	Local control by bureaucrats and party agents	Democratic self-management, local politics free of state interference
Generational	Social mobility, generational conflict	Advancing post-material needs: political partnership, cultural expression, removal of old bosses
Spatial	Spatiocultural enclosure	Spatial fragmentation of social action; territorial-communal ideologies

mand cultural recognition, and to present a new social identity was higher in the disadvantaged neighborhoods than in the more established ones. To realize the potentialities embedded in the societal structures and concrete experiences, the social actors had to assume an active role in interpreting the context and experiences, in mobilizing the social base and in transforming it into a social force.

The divergence of urban protest, I will argue, did not stem from the structural conditions or from the specific problem associated with these conditions. It was rooted, in my view, in the numerous ways in which different human agents located in varying places realized the potentialities embedded in the social structure. In other words, to account for the differentiation of protest, local interpretations are to be studied in depth. Some of these interpretations, as shown in Chapter 4, turned to deeper structures, whereas others focused on concrete problems. And these interpretations and their combinations created the three distinct types of protest organizations: urban social movements, neighborhood protest organizations, and coproductive organizations. Turning to deeper structures, the urban social movements and the neighborhood protest organizations insisted on the relationships between macrosocial problems and specific microconditions in the housing projects. Hence their expressivist-universalist claim that any genuine solution to local problems requires some fundamental changes in the sociopolitical structure. In striking contrast, the coproductive organizations conceived of the problems they encountered as concrete issues that could be solved through pragmatic action and peaceful relations with state agents; hence, their instrumental orientation and particularistic, neighborhood-oriented action.

Some interesting questions seem to arise at this point. To begin with, what social mechanisms informed these radically different interpretations? Why was a certain interpretation adopted and preferred over another? Was the interpretation static or dynamic over time? One cannot conclude the study of protest (and by extension of any social action) by turning solely to interpretation (whether they are thin or thick). The interpretations themselves have to be subjected to a further inquiry that examines those contingent, place-specific factors that informed them (see Figure 5).

Among these factors are the biographies of individuals and groups, the power resources at their disposal, interaction with different cultural environments, and learning from the experience of other organizations. Through these encounters and interactions, conventions (world-views concerning the center's authority and its values, modes of conduct, aggressive or piecemeal approaches, modes of speech, norms and values) and resources (skills, knowledge, power) are learned and acquired. Conventions and resources are acquired, as shown in Chapter 4, through everyday life experience, for instance by being brought up in a broken or stable family; through group membership, for instance by being a member of a criminal network or a student group at the Habad (Hassidic) school; through interaction with different environments, whether local-traditional or outside-radical ones; and through learning from the experience of other organizations, whether critically or approvingly. Nothing is determinate in these contingencies, and they should be treated as informing specific experiences at the local, everyday level.

The construction of meaning is also affected by the power relations among the participants and by the resources they possess. As the case of the Ohalim movement clearly shows (see Chapter 2), two different conventions intervened in the structuring of the movement, one oriented toward the center (the dominant authority and its norms and values) and the other toward the periphery. The differences themselves varied with the social groupings involved, and their individual and collective biographies. The struggle between the two interpretations was resolved by the use of resources; that is, the power of the former gang in terms of strong leadership, authority over people, social cohesiveness, and intellectual support provided from outside. Counting on its power resources, the elite group, whether in the urban social movements or in the coproductive organization, dominated the constitution of meaning. Other groups either followed the interpretations, and subsequently the orientations, suggested, or left.

Obviously, the construction of the movements' meaning covers only one aspect in the construction of the organizations. The interpretation given by human beings to the constitutive context of which they are part, and to their specific experiences, is only a starting point. To move from meaning to action, the actors employed the resources at their disposal to mobilize the local base, obtain resources, and negotiate with other social and political actors. In the specific case represented here, forces from the outside, especially progressive community workers, and the local elite brought in their skills, knowledge, power, and contacts to affect the specific form of action taken. Moreover, the interpretation given to the societal context, affected as it is by varying factors, does not lead directly to social action. There is, in other words, no complete correspondence between the interpretation and practical activity. Making reality meaningful through interpretation directs action, especially in its first stage; but the social action itself is in constant tension between original interpretation and reality, between the subjective world-view of the group, as expressed in the interpretation given to the context, and the objective conditions that exist at the time of action. It would be idealistic and naive to assume consistency between interpretation or the way the context is read and the activity carried out in reality. The transition from interpretation to practical activity is fraught with much tension, stemming from the transition from an abstract orientation to concrete interaction with the sociopolitical environment with its contingencies and constraints. Over the course of the interaction with the sociopolitical environment, as shown in Chapters 3 and 5, the organization may radicalize or moderate its positions and eventually may develop new patterns of activity and interpretations. This point has been vividly illustrated by the trajectory of the Katamon Higher Committee, where meaning and action were constantly modified as a result of social interaction with other actors. Originally, members of the Katamon Higher Committee developed an empirical interpretation, a particularistic orientation, and a strategy based on activity within the system. Yet when they were faced with the local authority's attempt to disband the organization and protect the local boss, the leaders of the movement moved toward a structural interpretation and universal orientation, blaming the political machine for perpetuating the patronage system. Moreover, the attempt to burn down the community center, where the local boss served as board chairperson, may indicate a move toward a strategy of action outside the system.

It is apparent, then, that the original interpretation leads to action, shows a preliminary direction, but from here on out the path is not straight and winds along the lines of the social relationships developing between the organization and the environment. Touraine (1981) indeed emphasized this point while insisting that the actors are located in a "field of action" wherein they encounter other forces and within which they may change their perspective. This means that the "data processing" of the societal context, alluded to by Mannheim (1965), is a continuing process associated closely not only to factors that were active in the past (i.e., before the rise of the movement), but also to the ongoing interaction with other forces that takes place in the present. The constitutive social structure, schemes of meaning, resource mobilization, and social interaction are some of the generic principles of protest construction that I have tried to abstract and theorize in Figure 5.

It would be imprudent to go beyond these principles and generalize any social phenomena from the specific case of Jerusalem. Although the Jerusalem examples show that universalist movements were formed around street gangs whereas mainstream groups turned to coproductive activity, there is no reason to assume at this point that this might be the case in the future or in other places in the present. To avoid ethnocentrism, one should avoid generalizations of types of movements and their social correlates and instead focus on the generic principles of social construction of the movements' meaning.

To sum up, in Chapters 1 and 2, I presented a number of theoretical approaches (the collective behavior and the resource mobilization theories) to the study of social movements, approaches that disagree as to the importance of structural conditions and the role of human agency in shaping the movements. Inspired by Giddens's structuration theory (Giddens, 1984), I have argued through the study that, although the role of the structural conditions should

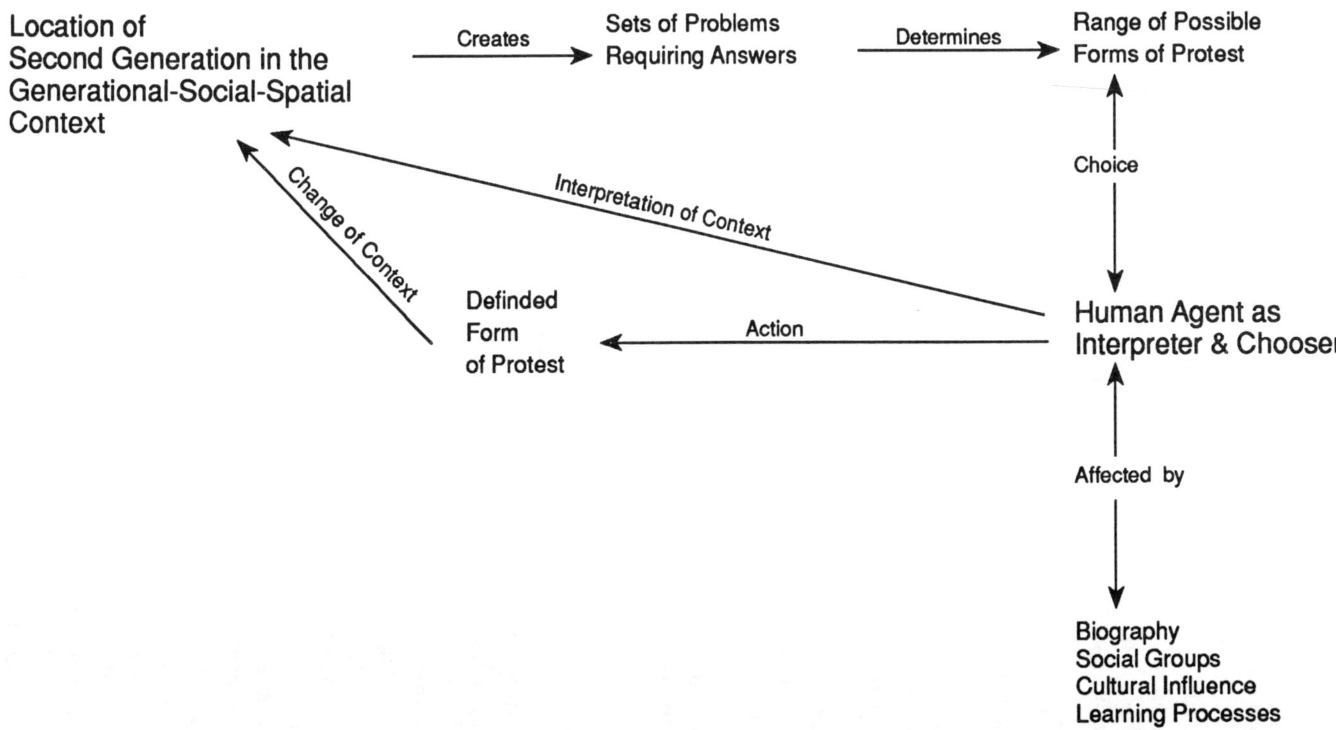

Figure 5. The Relationships Between Context and Human Agency

not be overlooked, it would be rather simplistic to treat the movements as if they were an outcome of a given context that presumably dictates their meaning. Social movements cannot be treated as mere outcomes of superorganic forces, such as modes of production, class structure, socioethnic stratification, or ecological systems, inasmuch as they are also affected, as shown in Chapters 3, 4, and 5, by the actors' schemes of meanings, the specific contingencies wherein these schemes are shaped, and the social exchange and interaction with the sociopolitical system.

Having said this, I by no means wish to argue that urban social movements are the culmination of an interpretive project carried out in isolation from the structural conditions. More often than not, the movements' members may be affected by unacknowledged conditions (in this study, for instance, by social and housing class structures) of which they might be unaware; and their activity may lead to unintended consequences, such as socialization, routinization, and cooptation.

The analytical project of exposing the societal structures may tell us quite a lot about the social and spatial probabilities in which protest will appear (e.g., in disadvantaged areas inhabited by Oriental immigrants of the lower social class). But, in itself, this analytical insight does not tell us precisely where and how the social protest is to occur. The collective behavior approach and the structural Marxist theory, which primarily engage the macrosocietal conditions, tend in fact to substitute the when and how for the question of what. And although such insightful lists of structures and factors as those provided by Smelser (1968), Castells (1983), Pickvance (1985), and Lowe (1986), are most necessary, these authors tend, despite the remarkable differences among them, to emphasize the regularities of social action. There is also a certain risk in this of reification, where structures seem to be endowed with a power to work and influence. To avoid this risk, both Castells and Lowe resorted to empirical studies, but so far they have not developed any theoretical links between the construction of social protest by human agents and the structural forces.

Instead of a one-sided approach that focuses either on how structure determines protest or how a sequence of actions leads to protest, I have tried to show how human agents engaged in specific experiences rooted in a constitutive context realized the potentialities inherent in this context to create different forms of protest. In doing so, I shifted from a static position, whether of context or agency, to a dynamic one that shows that there is no smooth and simple transition from one position to the other. Intervening between the two positions are some intermediate factors associated with the actors' conventions, biographies, everyday life experience, sociology of knowledge, schemes of interpretation, choice, social interaction and exchange processes, modification of interpretations, remolding of conventions, and routinization. Herein lies my argument that one-sided approaches, whether structural-analytic or agency-interpretive, should be replaced by a theorization that engages experience and interpretation within the framework of local contingencies and general constitutive conditions.

The Routinization of Protest

The common pattern of social change, identified in this study, was toward socialization and routinization of the grass roots: the movements increasingly adopted empirical interpretations, particularistic and instrumental orientations, and strategies of working within the established system. Through participation in the Project Renewal Program, Ohel Yosef became a particularistic organization functioning within the existing system; the leader of ICL was elected to the city council as a member of the governing party's slate. The Ohalim and Black Panther movements remained but symbols, while particularistic organizations continued to function in the neighborhoods in cooperation and coordination with the state. The emphasis was shifted from universal and expressivist protest to "solid, drab, and quiet activity," utilizing professional expertise and concentrating on well-defined neighborhood territories.

This social transformation of poor peoples' movements from protest vanguards, that pursue universal ideologies to pragmatic organizations that engage local and ad hoc issues is not unique to Israel. A similar process was identified by Perlman among neighborhood organizations in American cities. She claims that the organizations that characterized the 1960s, which she calls *self-help alternative institutions*, transformed into *issue-oriented direct action organizations*, the type that became dominant in the 1970s. In her view, the organizations of the 1960s devoted themselves more to protest, whereas those of the 1970s focused on defined issues and displayed a higher level of sophistication. Others, such as Heskin, accept this distinction, but tend to be less enthusiastic about it. According to Heskin (private communication), the transformation described reflects the loss of interest in universal issues; that is, the equal distribution of power in society in the face of growing sophistication of the state. The argument is that, in confronting the problem of citizen participation and maintenance of power positions, the state found the comfortable solution of increasing citizen participation while neutralizing them politically.

The question that arises, then, is whether the intensification of particularistic activity in cooperation with the state is evidence of increased democracy in local politics or whether the opposite is true, as this process marks the increased power of the bureaucracy in the existing sociopolitical system. Perhaps, one might ask, the process described is simply the story of spontaneous collective action with universal tendencies that, during its development, confronts economic, political, and organizational forces and, in the end, without intending it, is absorbed into the existing system. Assuming this line of thought, one may argue that the universal protest evaporated into ad hoc pragmatism, whereas the power of bureaucratic control and political centralization has grown, even though, on the face of it, things seem otherwise.

In my view, the answer to the social process outlined in this study is much more complex and has to be drawn against the background of the constitutive context and the social construction of protest. The protest organizations in Jerusalem essentially signified a popular attempt to expand civil, social, and political rights; hence, the Black Panthers' critique of ethnic discrimination, and the Ohalim critique of the repudiation of the basic principles of Israel's Declaration of Independence. In presenting their demands, the movements' participants confronted political institutions (sets of rules, resources, and practices) and state actors that lacked a well-established tradition of defending and expanding civil, social, and political rights. Israel is a young nation without a written constitution. In my view, however, the absence of tradition in this field—that is, a set of social and moral codes and practical precedents that form and sanction social behavior—is by far more important than the absence of a constitution. The protest demands may be interpreted in this context as a force that contributes to the development of such a tradition by introducing new norms and practical precedents. As shown in Chapter 5, the meeting between the movements' activists and some of the state actors led to some significant changes in institutional rules. The existence of poverty and an ethnic gap was recognized, the need for social change and retreat from patronage systems was admitted, new models of citizen participation were devised jointly, protest movements were allowed to pursue their activities, concrete plans for rehabilitating marginal youth and clearing slums were launched, and massive injections of resources were directed to the disadvantaged neighborhoods via the Project Renewal Program. In this way, many of the innovative conceptions, interpretations, and demands raised by members of the second generation seeped into the institutional system and became part of the conventions employed by the state actors. In other words, a new social tradition was informally formed without necessarily being recognized as such by the social actors.

Today, as I have shown elsewhere (Hasson, 1989), it is the politicians and senior administrators in the Jerusalem municipal authority who seek to promote self-management and local democracy. The social protest of the 1970s and 1980s reshaped, in my view, the basic properties of the existing institutions and in so doing lost its significance as its original messages turned into cliches. Self-management, participatory democracy, local elections, local planning, supply of services from below, and leadership development today are the rule rather than the exception. Does this imply that urban social movements have become redundant? Not at all. Gregory's critique of Giddens's tendency to emphasize routinization (i.e., reproduction of conventions) at the expense of social change, and Giddens's unwillingness to relinquish his position, in my view, trace the dialectical process of institution building, a process in which protest and routinization play an equally important role (Gregory, 1989; Giddens, 1989). The process of expanding human rights (whether civil, social, or political) seems to have an oscillating dynamic, where innovative rules raised outside the system penetrate and restructure the system. Paralleling this process, the conveyors of protest recreate and modify their own conceptions, interpretations, orientations, and strategies of action to match them with the social changes of which they are part. This may explain why the pragmatism of the 1980s is layered on the radicalism of the 1960s and 1970s.

The answer to the question of whether urban social movements have become redundant can be found, then, not by turning to old movements that have exhausted their messages, but by looking at the incessant struggle of human beings to expand their rights. Because this struggle is, in essence, as Touraine (1981) rightly contends, a neverending one, I suspect that urban movements are bound to reappear, although perhaps in different forms and places and under different leaderships. To put it another way, routinization tells us nothing about the conditions of human beings, about social inequality, gender exploitation, immigrants' painful conditions, or socioethnic discrimination. As long as these conditions prevail, new movements are bound to emerge. The unequal conditions prevailing in Jerusalem for Arabs and Jews, the ultraorthodox and secular groups, the poor and the affluent, the old timers and the recently arrived Russian immigrants are fraught with tensions and potentialities for urban unrest. The process of routinization indicated in this study should not then be equated (nor would Giddens seem to suggest that it should be) with integration and system maintenance.

Practical Significance—Problems and Lessons

Today organizations like Ohel Yosef, Ohel Shmuel, Dai, ICL, and YFN continue to exist, but as organizations with a particularistic character, acting in cooperation with the state and having only minor, if any, impact on society as a whole. Over the course of their political institutionalization, a large part of their protest energy was discharged as a large part of their material demands were satisfied (a solution to the housing problem, the development of infrastructure, the extension of social services). Cooperation with the state also reduced the protest energy of the leading elite, energy that was originally directed, at least in part, to the satisfaction of postmaterial needs. Participation in joint activities, and especially in the Project Renewal Program of renovating and revitalizing the disadvantaged neighborhoods, diverted the protest of the social movements to citizen participation and led to their routinization.

In addition, several other macrosocietal factors moderated the protest. One was the political success of the right-wing Likud party, whose populist line, culminating in Project Renewal, emphasized its obligation to its voters in disadvantaged areas. Other such factors were the economic downturn, unemployment, the war in Lebanon, the national debate over the future of the occupied territories, and most recently the uprising (Intifada) in the occupied territories. All these diverted attention from the consumption problems of poor people in the city and, to a large extent, lowered expectations in disadvantaged areas. Some of the leaders who led the protest have despaired, at this point, of the possibility of creating social change from below through urban movements and have joined existing parties, especially the Labor party. Only time will tell if the parties will become the major field of action for these absorbed elites or whether after experiencing the party from the inside they will return to their turfs to reorganize the dormant movements. True, in the wake of mass immigration from the Soviet Union in 1990, which comprised about 200,000 people, the summer of that year saw a growing discontent in the immigrant slums and housing projects. Hundreds of families took to the streets and established tent camps to protest the soaring housing rents and the inadequate government housing policy. But as in the past the numerous organizations formed in the streets and in the squatters' camps remained isolated one from the other and pursued their goals separately.

The question that remains unanswered is why the protest organizations that developed over the last twenty years have not combined forces to exert greater pressure for social change, why they have not become "the live schools," in Castells's words, "where the new social movements of our emerging society are taking place" (Castells, 1983, p. 331). If anything, they failed to develop long-standing connections with alternative movements like the feminist movement, Peace Now, the alternative media, and Palestinian national groups (although short-lived links with Peace Now and the Palestinians were established).

The foregoing analysis has provided a number of macrosocietal responses to these questions, associated with changes in Israeli society and with the swiftness with which grass-roots innovations became part of the institutional system. But beyond these macrosocietal explanations, some fundamental problems seem to be associated with the structure and activity of the movements themselves.

One structural problem diagnosed in the movements was their confinement to a narrow class stratum within the Sephardic (Oriental) community. Even the organizations like the Black Panthers and the Ohalim movement never enlisted Sephardic supporters other than members of the lower classes. Upper-class Orientals (i.e., professionals, managers, intellectuals, and private-sector entrepreneurs) kept their distance from these movements and from their radical activities and developed two alternative paths. One was the establishment of particularistic and pragmatic organizations that acted within the established system (YFN, the Katamon Higher Committee); the second was individual mobility.

The different paths of action and mobility testify to the existence of different problems, conceptions, and needs among the members of the Oriental community, whose sources were rooted in different class positions and cultural attitudes and interests. In other words, members of the Oriental community who had witnessed upward mobility did not wish to become involved in social struggles pursued by movements made up of members of the lower classes. For this reason I doubt whether an ethnic message, as radical as it might be, can overcome the diverging class-based interests and attitudes within the Sephardic community and unify these strata. The social split within the Sephardic ethnic group is too fundamental and basic to be forced into an ethnic (whether scientific or popular) mold.

In my opinion, there is no need for such unification of forces for pursuing material struggle. Each group must, on this level, look after its own interests. On the other hand, there is room for a coalition on a higher level of needs, such as defining identity and achieving cultural and political representation, but such a coalition will be limited by nature, at least in the short run, to the social elites.

The second problem faced by the movements, especially those with a universalist orientation, is that the "redemption" they sought was not meant for all of society, but for a certain segment of it. Unlike social movements of the middle class (the feminist, Peace Now, and civil rights movements), they did not create a general ideal of an alternative city and an alternative society. They remained primarily engaged in redistribution of material resources and, as such, were the offspring of older social movements. As long as these movements restrict themselves to the needs of the lower classes and to neighborhood interests, their contribution to society will be limited, even if their message is worded in universal terms. On this point, then, I support Castells's claim (1983, p. 323) and argue that without links to the new social movements, the protest organizations I have surveyed will make only a minor impact on society. But the opposite is also true: if the new social movements do not create links to the urban movements, they will remain detached and alienated from the needs and problems of a large segment of Israeli society.

The proposal to link up with movements of the middle class is not without problems, and it is liable to increase the already-existing tension within the movements between the elite and the periphery. Here, a third structural problem arises: the division within the movements between the elites with their universal, postmaterial messages and the social-cultural environment with its orientation to material values. The difference is not sharp. The elites are also interested in solving material problems, but they tend to go beyond them and so clash with local traditions and expectations. The result is either accepting the neighborhood's conventions and developing a particularist-pragmatic approach, thus turning into a parochial organization, or conflict with the neighborhood's conventions and detachment from the local base. Perhaps the lesson to be derived is the need to develop two-way messages, material and postmaterial, and the creation of both neighborhood and urban national patterns of action. Such an approach requires cooperation between organizations to create a coalition that can function on the supraneighborhood level and that will leave work in the individual neighborhoods to each constituent organization. In this way, it would be possible to integrate different cultural approaches and satisfy the needs of both the neighborhood base and of the local elite.

A fourth problem found among all the movements is their conservative attitudes as they are revealed in under representation of women and the tendency toward neighborhood bossism. The creation of an "oligarchy" made up of male activists, the patriarchal Oriental tradition that kept women outside the leadership circles, the opposition to the new bossism, and the power struggles that result have weakened the organizations, led to internal divisions, and in the case of the Ohalim movement and the YFN, led to their gradual demise. This was due, to a large extent, to the charismatic nature of these organizations, some of them formed around the personality of a given leader and his ability to mobilize activists and convey messages to the public. Coping with this requires, first and foremost, that the leadership recognize that a problem exists and that processes and models must be created that will allow wider involvement of both women and men. This implies that the movements need a higher level of social consciousness and awarness to human needs, institutionalization, an internal division of labor, and multiple possibilities of self-realization and exposure within the movement. The resource mobilization theory, which emphasizes the importance of symbolic rewarding, can here serve as a helpful way of thinking about the enlistment of activists and the preservation of the vitality of the movements over time.

A fifth problem is associated with the extent of autonomy the organization has with regard to the state. Under conditions of coproduction, the penetration of the movement by the state's norms, values, and even agents is inevitable. The question is at what rate and to what extent this process should occur. The less cohesive the movement is in its structure and behavior, the easier and swifter the state's penetration will be; and it is liable to divert the organization in directions that do not correspond to the original goals. In such circumstances, the spontaneous activity that comes up from the grass roots would become short lived and quickly absorbed into the existing political-bureaucratic system.

Social action in Jerusalem's disadvantaged neighborhoods appears, in this light, like an uncertain journey with an undefined destination and with all the structural weaknesses—internal splits, bossism, parochialism, and the lack of organizational development—being discovered along the way. It is not surprising then, that the leadership response to this set of problems has been a return to individualistic activity, giving up on the movement, and turning to political party activity or parochial organizations. Thus, the leaders of the Black Panthers turned to political activity in parties of the Left (Sheli and the Communists); the leader of the Ohalim movement became a member of the Labor party central committee; the leader of YFN was appointed a special social aide to the prime minister, and the leader of ICL became a member of the city council. Another possibility worth examining is that of an urban social movement that integrates within it a process of collective learning. Such a possibility has been theoretically discussed by Eder (1985), Touraine (1985), and Habermas (1982), but these theorizations seem to require further elaboration to clarify the methods and content of collective learning. In a preliminary way it may be suggested that the material to be discussed can be lessons derived from the history of former organizations, the orientation and activity of protest organizations, the interaction between the movements and the state, and the system of relations between the elite leadership and the neighborhood base. This social learning may benefit from cooperation with members of other social movements, to create bridges between the two groups and strengthen the movements in their negotiations with the state.

It may be further suggested that this learning process should be spontaneous, uninstitutionalized, and based upon creative forces. Social and intellectual training are required, and the universities can play a crucial role here. I do not wish to challenge the well-known fact that the modernization process, with its concomitant division of labor and specialization, requires the training of bureaucrats and technocrats who can coordinate and manage complex political, economic, and technological systems. Yet, in parallel to these processes are societal changes in the opposite direction, such as increasing personal involvement, the expression of feelings, ethical criticism, and the tendency toward a wide political discourse far removed from the bureaucratic and specialized discourse. These changes necessitate, in my view, a different type of training, which is sensitive to social issues, oriented toward communal life; one that reflects on questions of politics and ethics and encourages the development of a sociopolitical dialogue with different groups in society.

Ethical Reflections

The interrelation between scientific work and ethical conduct confronts any social research, the present work included. In studying the behavior of participants in the urban social movements that have emerged in disadvantaged neighborhoods, one has to grapple with the question of whether the participants were merely objects of study or human beings who pose demands and require an active response. This dilemma, though in a different context, is vividly illustrated by Rowles's reflection while standing by the deathbed of one of his research participants:

> Sometimes I experienced anger. "Damn it. You can't die now, I haven't finished my research." Immediately I would be overtaken by feelings of self-revulsion. Did our friendship mean only this? Thus I would engage in a conflict between my human sensibilities and my scholarly purpose. (Rowles, 1978, p. 179)

This is precisely the conflict between science and ethics. Faced with the distancing (alienation) nature of scientific activity, which transforms the participants into objects, the researcher is confronted with another interest, that of overcoming the distance, of taking a position and becoming socially involved in addressing the other.

The problem is how to make science more ethical and ethics more scientifically informed and yet to maintain an analytical distinction between the two projects (for a detailed examination of this issue, see Hasson, 1984; 1985; Hasson and Goldberg, 1987). My argument is twofold. In their pure forms, science and ethics are two distinct projects, whereas at the pragmatic sphere of social interaction with human beings, the tension is bound to be resolved whether one takes an action or not. My attempt has been to show, in taking an action, (1) how the scientific findings, the "what is," are to be employed in informing social conduct, the "what ought to be," and (2) how the social involvement may inform and enrich scientific research. I will discuss each component of this argument in turn.

I find it necessary to emphasize the distinction between science and ethics in the face of growing interest in humanistic approaches in the social sciences and the tendency to equate them sometimes with ethics. Such an equation, I will argue, is highly dubious. Generally speaking, a humanistic approach applied to the study of urban social movements may clarify the actors' purposive actions as expressed in their norms, values, intentions, emotions, thoughts, and their embodiment in interpretations of specific situations. In other words, it may help uncover the meaning of the movement. Such a discovery of meaning may be done in different ways. Assuming a phenomenological approach, the researcher may try to expose, through a hierarchy of reductions and the principle of bracketing, the subjective and intersubjective life-world underlying the constitution of meaningful action by the participants (Bernstein, 1978; Husserl, 1960). Thus, one might reveal, as attempted here, the preintellectual experience of different groups by exposing the basic conventions through which they constitute a meaningful world. The researcher assuming a *verstehen* approach would attempt to reveal the rational thoughts of the participants in their specific cultural context by rethinking the thoughts of the other and by reconstructing what the movement means for them (Weber, 1948).

Penetrating as they may be, these approaches should not be equated with ethics, because they do not provide any goals and guidelines as to the proper conduct of behavior. Confronting the participants' problems, needs, and interests, the researcher may choose to remain passive or become active and support the movement. Whatever the decision may be, it has its origins not in science but in a different sphere. Obviously, a detached phenomenological or *verstehen* stance might be criticized, as Buber does, on moral grounds:

> is it so? Is there [a] here-where, as the philosophers say, pure subject separates itself from the concrete person in order to establish a world for itself—a citadel which rises towering over the life of dialogue, inaccessible to it, in which man-with-himself, the single one, suffers and triumphs in glorious solitude? (Buber, 1971, pp. 44–45)

Against the category of the "single one" advanced by Kierkegaard's existentialism and the method of self-reflection, Buber argues, "we are created along with one another and directed to live with one another . . . if we remove the object, then we have removed the object altogether" (Buber, 1971, p. 75). Buber insists on the need to go beyond "empathy" or the "imagining of the other's act of will" (1957, p. 103), because both imply "the exclusion of one's own concreteness, the extinguishing of the actual situation of life, the absorption in pure aestheticism of the reality in which one participates" (Buber, 1971, p. 75). The humanistic procedures of science, whether phenomenology, existentialism, or *verstehen* appear in this light as pseudo-humanistic or even as deliberate cynicism. To gain insight into the other's experience, needs, and interests and still to remain passive, so Buber seems to argue, is inhuman. The alternative approach, he says, is to take a position by responding to the other's call, to overcome the distance posited by science, that is, to move from the sphere of the I-It to the realm of the I-Thou.

Although I personally sympathize with Buber's critique, it does not change in any way the distinction between science and ethics. Even Buber's demands can be regarded at the most as a plea for moral behavior without being in itself moral conduct. To examine Buber's ethics, one has to transcend his writing, to examine his practical behavior and the way he himself responded to others, be they women, men, or nature itself. Science, in other words, should not be equated with ethics, nor should ethics be equated with a plea—sensitive, incisive, and conclusive as it may be—for ethical conduct. This argument may also hold with regard to Habermas's project of ideal speech situation and its principles of universal pragmatics (Habermas, 1970; 1979). The description of an ideal speech situation, wherein validity claims (relating to objective reality, social conduct, and personal expression) are to be redeemed, may provide accurate criteria against which human behavior in different spheres might be evaluated. In itself, such a description might be true or false, and therefore has very little to do with right or wrong (ethics) and sincerity or insincerity (self-expression).

In the course of my study of the movements, I decided to relate to their needs and take a position. As mentioned before, I felt sympathy for the actors' struggle against the patronage system and for what appeared to be a genuine attempt to improve social and physical conditions and maintain their cultural identity. Taking a position, however, is not an unproblematic issue from an ethical point of view. Suppose, for example, that one studies a fascist movement, like the Kach movement, and understands the motives, aspirations, and needs of the movement's participants. In this particular case, most of us would argue that responding to the movement's aspiration (expulsion of the Palestinian Arabs) would be immoral behavior. We need, in other words, criteria residing outside the sphere of relations and exchange to guide our ethical behavior. Such criteria reside in faith; that is, in our fundamental set of beliefs about society, state, personal development, and nature. It is in light of such considerations that I chose to become a member of the board of the Ohalim movement, of the Moreshet Heritage project of the Black Panthers, and to take part in establishing the Katamon Higher Committee.

Although taking a position has nothing to do with scientific considerations, the two projects may still benefit from each other. The data collected through active participation and the scientific findings thus made may be used to show the social agents some of the unacknowledged conditions and unintended consequences of their actions. On the other hand, social involvement may enrich the existing social knowledge in ways hitherto out of bounds to researchers. This indeed is a genuine process of social learning, where findings about "what is" inform the "what ought to be" and vice versa. Such a process has been alluded to by Friere in his book *The Pedagogy of the Oppressed* (1971). This book captures some of the essential tensions between objectivity and subjectivity in science and ethics.

Friere suggests that the pedagogy of the oppressed (substitute the urban social movements) should be predicated on a continuous dialogue between intellectuals and the oppressed without imposing the former's ideas on the latter. He calls for respect toward the needs, emotions, beliefs, and intentions of the oppressed, yet refuses to accept oppressed subjectivity as the only truth that counts (Friere, 1971, p. 181). Friere also argues for the existence of an objective truth, which might escape the oppressed consciousness and which is to be unveiled through critical analysis. "The subjective aspect exists only in relation to the objective aspect [the concrete reality which is the object of his analysis]. Subjectivity and objectivity thus join in a dialectical unity producing knowledge in solidarity with action, and vice-versa" (1971, p. 22). Practically, such a unity is to be attained, according to Friere, by presenting social reality as a concrete problem to be solved by the oppressed. Once coping with the problem, the participants become aware of the deeper economic, cultural, and political structures with which their visible or local problems are intimately tied. This is not to suggest, however, that concrete, local problems are reducible to structural ones. Rather, this pedagogy aims to show that local issues, around which organizations are formed, are deeply anchored in a larger political, economic, and cultural context. Moreover, the nature of the interaction between local interpretations and societal structures is not analytically given, but must be uncovered continuously as its features tend to change over time and space. Such a learning process avoids dogmatism and at the same time refuses to be relegated to parochial and superficial appearances. It is beset by a tension between deep structure and appearance that practically entails a twofold learning movement. The first is a movement from the abstract to the concrete, posing social reality as a concrete problem; and the second relates to a movement from the concrete to the abstract, coping with the concrete problem and thereby unveiling the structural problems. It thus follows that territorial problems and local consciousness are not pushed aside as a secondary object or treated as an impediment. Rather, they are treated as a crucial object of study and practice, which along with the appropriate guidance, leads toward a genuine understanding of abstract and profound reality.

It is evident that such a learning process poses serious demands on those who seek to develop it. One has first to be in a position to integrate the different epistemologies that form an integral part of the territorial educational process. On the one hand, one is required to *analyze* the sociopolitical structure and, on the other hand, to be capable of *interpreting* the subjective structure of the social actors. Second, because what is objectively analyzed might not correspond with what is subjectively recognized by the organization's members, one should also master the art of communicating with people who think differently. Thus, in addition to being an analyst and interpreter, someone involved in the learning project should be sensitive to human consciousness, endeavoring to establish a genuine dialogue with those with whom one works (Touraine's [1981] idea of the intervention group may play an important role in this regard). In this way, a real understanding would be gained of the needs and beliefs of the organization's members and appropriate measures of consciousness raising will be devised that fit the specific historical-cultural-territorial context. Last, in this delicate process, one should refrain from elevating structural theorization, which is arrived at through an objective analysis, into the status of an absolute truth. Structural explanations, whether functionalist, neo-Weberian, neo-Marxist, or ecological, of urban problems may serve as a source of inspiration and background knowledge, but should not be raised to the status of the last truth, as it merits further examination and critique. It follows, then, that critical analysis cannot be directed at society alone. One involved should also be self-critical by subjecting one's own scientific theorization to critique and refutation through ongoing dialogue. Through a learning process proceeding in this manner, the social participants in the movement enjoy the heightening of their knowledge; on the other hand, the researcher is enriched with new knowledge that reveals broader insights into society and urban life.

Bibliography

Amiel, A. 1982. "Project Renewal: Corruption of Soul and Ethics—And the Alternative." Mimeographed [Hebrew].

Arachim Editorial Board. 1981. "Communist Activities in the Neighborhoods." *Arachim* (Values) 63: 33–57 [Hebrew].

Arenstein, S. R. 1969. "A Ladder of Citizen Participation." *Journal of the American Institute of Planners* 39: 216–224.

Azmon, Y. 1985. "Urban Patronage in Israel." In Cohen and Almagor, eds., *Essays in Honor of S. N. Eisenstadt*, pp. 284–294. Boulder, Colo.: Westview.

Bachi, R. 1977. *The Population of Israel*. Jerusalem: Institute of Contemporary Jewry, The Hebrew University.

Bachrach, S. B., and Lawler, E. J. 1980. *Power and Politics in Organizations*. San Francisco: Jossey-Bass Publishers.

Banfield, E. 1974. *The Unheavenly City Revisited*. Boston: Little, Brown.

——— and Wilson, J. A. 1967. *City Politics*. Cambridge, Mass.: Harvard University Press.

Bauman, Z. 1978. *Hermeneutics and Social Science*. New York: Columbia University Press.

Bell, D. 1978. *The Cultural Contradiction of Capitalism*. New York: Basic Books.

Ben-Ari, E. 1984. "Community Action and Community Care in Present-Day Japan: A Study of Two Communities." Ph.D. dissertation, University of Cambridge.

Berlin, I. 1969. *Four Essays on Liberty*. Oxford: Oxford University Press.

Bernstein, D. 1972. "The Black Panthers." MA thesis, The Hebrew University of Jerusalem.

Bernstein, R. J. 1978. *The Restructuring of Social and Political Theory.* Philadelphia: University of Pennsylvania Press.

Borja, J. 1978. "Urban Movements in Spain." In M. Harloe, ed., *Captive Cities: Studies in the Political Economy of Cities and Regions.* Chichester: John Wiley.

Buber, M. 1957. "Distance and Relation." *Psychiatry* 20: 97–104.

———. 1971. *Between Man and Man.* London: Fontana Library.

Castells, M. 1976. "Theoretical Propositions for an Experimental Study of Urban Social Movements." In C. G. Pickvance, ed., *Urban Sociology: Critical Essays.* London: Tavistock.

———. 1977. *The Urban Question.* New York: Edward Arnold and MIT Press.

———. 1978. *City, Class and Power.* London: Macmillan Press.

———. 1983. *The City and the Grassroots.* London: Edward Arnold.

Choshen, M. 1990. *Elections to the Knesset in Jerusalem.* The Jerusalem Institute for Israel Studies: Jerusalem.

Cloward, R. A., and Ohlin, L. E. 1960. *Delinquency and Opportunity.* New York: The Free Press.

Cohen, E. 1980. "The Black Panthers and Israeli Society." In E. Krausz, ed., *Studies of Israeli Society.* New Brunswick, N.J.: Transaction Books.

Cornwell, E. E. 1964. "Bosses, Machines and Ethnic Groups." *Annals, American Academy of Political and Social Sciences* 353: 27–39.

Coser, L. A. 1957. "Social Conflicts and the Theory of Social Change." *British Journal of Sociology* 8: 197–207.

Cox, W. H. 1976. *Cities: The Public Dimension.* Harmondsworth, Middlesex: Penguin Books.

Deshen, S. 1982. "Social Organization and Politics in Israeli Urban Quarters." *Jerusalem Quarterly* 22: 21–37.

De Tocqueville, A. 1955. *The Old Regime and the French Revolution.* New York: Anchor Books.

Dolev, A. 1976. "The Curse of the Gonens." *Ma'ariv* (daily newspaper) (9 July) [Hebrew].

Duncan, J., and Ley, D. 1982. "Structural Marxism and Human Geography: A Critical Assessment." *Annals, Association of American Geographers* 72: 30–59.

Dunleavy, P. 1977. "Protest and Quiescence in Urban Politics: A Critique of Some Pluralist and Structuralist Myths." *International Journal of Urban and Regional Research* 1: 193–218.

———. 1981. *Urban Political Analysis—The Politics of Collective Consumption.* London: Macmillan Press.

Eder, K. 1985. "The 'New Social Movements': Moral Crusaders, Political Pressure Groups, or Social Movements." *Social Research* 52: 869–890.

Eisenstadt, S. N. 1950. "The Oriental Jews in Israel." *Jewish Social Studies* 12: 199–221.

———. 1967. *Israeli Society.* Jerusalem: Magnes University Press [Hebrew].

Elazar, D. J. 1987. "The Local Dimension of Authority and Politics in Israel." In D. J. Elazar and Kalchaim, eds., *Local Government in Israel.* Jerusalem: Jerusalem Center for Public Affairs.

Enosh, H. 1980. "The Orientals in a Class Perspective." *Values* 62: 3–54 [Hebrew].

Enosh, N., Shacham, Y., and Laslow, A. 1981. *Quality of Life in Poverty Neighborhoods.* Jerusalem: The Hebrew University and the Ministry of Labor and Welfare [Hebrew].

Etzioni-Halevy, E. 1980. "Patterns of Conflict Generation and Conflict 'Absorption': The Cases of Israeli Labor and Ethnic Conflicts." In E. Krauze, ed., *Studies of Israeli Society.* New Brunswick, N.J.: Transaction Books.

Evers, A., and Rodrigues, J. 1978. "Participation and Local Politics in Marxist Theory and Practice." In C. R. Foster, ed., *Comparative Public Policy and Citizen Participation.* New York: Pergamon Press.

Friedland, R. 1982. *Power and Crisis in the City: Corporations, Unions, and Urban Policy.* London: Macmillan.

Friere, P. 1971. *Pedagogy of the Oppressed.* New York: Herder and Herder.

Ganim (the Ir Ganim local newspaper) [Hebrew]. 1982.

Gamson, W. 1975. *The Strategy of Social Protest.* Homewood, Ill.: Irwin-Dorsey.

Geertz, C. 1973. *Interpretation of Cultures*. New York: Basic Books.

Giddens, A. 1971. *Capitalism and Modern Social Theory: An Analysis of the Writings of Marx, Durkheim, and Max Weber*. Cambridge: Cambridge University Press.

———. 1980. *The Class Structure of the Advanced Societies*, 2d ed. London: Hutchinson.

———. 1984. *The Constitution of Society*. Cambridge: Polity Press.

———. 1989. "A Reply to My Critics." In D. Held and J. B. Thompson, eds., *Social Theory of Modern Societies*. Cambridge: Cambridge University Press.

Gilroy, P. 1987. *There Ain't No Black in the Union Jack*. London: Hutchinson.

Gonen, A. 1972. "The Role of High Growth Rates and Public Housing Agencies in Shaping the Spatial Structure of Israeli Towns." *Tijdschrift voor Econ. Geographie* (November–December): 402–410.

———. 1982. "The Geography of the Electoral Competition between the Labor Alignment and the Likud in Jewish Cities of Israel, 1965–81." *State, Government and International Relations* 19–20: 63–87.

——— and Hasson, S. 1983. "The Use of Housing as a Spatiopolitical Measure—The Israeli Case." *Geoforum* 14: 103–109.

Gouldner, A. 1979. *The Future of Intellectuals and the Rise of the New Class*. London: Routledge and Kegan Paul.

The Government of Israel and the Jewish Agency. 1984. *The International Committee for the Evaluation of Project Renewal: Annual Report for 1983*.

Gradus, Y. 1983. "The Role of Politics in Regional Inequality: The Israeli Case." *Annals, Association of American Geographers* 73: 388–403.

Gramsci, A. 1971. *Selections from the Prison Notebooks*, eds. Q. Hoare and G. Nowell-Smith. London: Lawrence and Wishart.

Gregory, D. 1989. "Presences and Absences: Time-Space Relations and Structuration Theory." In D. Held and J. B. Thompson, eds., *Social Theory of Modern Societies*. Cambridge: Cambridge University Press.

Gurr, T. R. 1970. *Why Men Rebel*. Princeton, N.J.: Princeton University Press.

Habermas, J. 1970. *Toward a Rational Society: Student Protest, Science, and Politics*, trans. J. J. Shapiro. Boston: Beacon Press.

———. 1975. *Legitimation Crisis*. London: Heineman.

———. 1979. *Communication and the Evolution of Society*, trans. T. McCarthy. Boston: Beacon Press.

———. 1981. "New Social Movements." *Telos* 49: 33–37.

———. 1982. "A Reply to my Critics." In J. B. Thompson and D. Held, eds., *Habermas: Critical Debates*. Cambridge, Mass.: MIT Press.

———. 1983. Neo-Conservatism in the U.S. and W. Germany." *Telos* 56: 75–89.

Harloe, M. 1977. "Introduction to Captive Cities." In M. Harloe, ed., *Captive Cities: Studies in the Political Economy of Cities and Regions*. Chichester: John Wiley.

Hasson, S. 1977. "Immigrant Housing Projects in the Old Towns of Israel: A Study of Social Differentiation." Unpublished Ph.D. dissertation, The Hebrew University of Jerusalem [Hebrew].

———. 1981. "Social and Spatial Conflicts: The Settlement Process in Israel during the 1950s and the 1960s." *L'Espace Geographique* 3: 169–179.

———. 1984. "Humanistic Geography from the Perspective of Martin Buber's Philosophy." *Professional Geographer* 36: 11–18.

———. 1985. "The Neighborhood Organization as a Pedagogic Project." *Environment and Planning D: Society and Space* 3: 337–355.

———. 1989. *Neighborhood Self-Management: A New Experiment in Jerusalem Politics*. Jerusalem: Jerusalem Institute for Israel Studies [Hebrew].

——— and Goldberg, M. 1987. "Rationalism, Bureaucracy, and Ethics." *Environment and Planning B: Planning and Design* 14: 15–27.

Herberle, R. 1968. "Types and Functions of Social Movements." In D. L. Sills, ed., *The International Encyclopedia of Social Sciences*, vol. 14. New York: Macmillan.

Horowitz, D., and Lissak, M. 1977. *The Origins of the Israeli Policy*. Tel Aviv: Am Oved (Hebrew).

Hunt, L. 1984. "Charles Tilly's Collective Action." In T. Skocpol, ed., *Vision and Method in Historical Sociology*. Cambridge: Cambridge University Press.

Huntington, S. 1968. *Political Order in Changing Societies*. New Haven, Conn.: Yale University Press.

Husserl, E. 1960. *Cartesian Meditations: An Introduction to Phenomenology*. The Hague: Martinus Nijhoff.

Israel Central Bureau of Statistics. 1972. *Housing and Population Census 1972*. Jerusalem: Government Printing Office.

———. 1981. *Statistical Abstract*. Jerusalem: Hamakor Press.

Jerusalem Institute for Israel Studies. 1991. *Statistical Yearbook of Jerusalem, No. 8, 1989*. Jerusalem.

Killian, L. M. 1963. "Social Movements." In R. E. L. Faris, ed., *Handbook of Modern Sociology*. Chicago: Rand McNally.

Kimhi, I. 1970. "Urban Renewal Areas in Jerusalem: Gonen Neighborhood Demonstration." MA thesis, The Hebrew University of Jerusalem.

Kol Ha'ir (local Jerusalem weekly). 1980–1982. Various articles dealing with the Ohalim movement [Hebrew].

Kol Yerushalaim (local Jerusalem weekly). 1983. Various articles dealing with urban social movements [Hebrew].

LaCapra, D. 1983. *Rethinking Intellectual History: Texts, Contexts, Language*. Ithaca, N.Y.: Cornell University Press.

Lavon, Z. 1974. *Shelters*. Tel Aviv: Am Oved [Hebrew].

Lenin, V. I. 1961. "What Is to Be Done?" First published 1901. In *Collected Works of V. I. Lenin*. Moscow: Foreign Languages Publishing House.

Lewis, G. K. 1970. "Protest Among the Immigrants." In B. Crick and W. A. Robson, eds., *Protest and Discontent*. Harmondsworth: Penguin Books.

Lipsky, M. 1972. "Protest as a Political Resource." In E. S. Malecki and H. R. Mahood, eds., *Group Politics—A New Emphasis*. New York: Charles Scribner's.

Lojkine, J. 1976. "Contribution to a Theory of Capitalist Urbanization." In C. G. Pickvance, ed., *Urban Sociology: Critical Essays*. London: Tavistock.

Lowe, S. 1986. *Urban Social Movements: The City After Castells*. London: Macmillan Press.

Lowenstein, J. I. 1980. *Marx Against Marxism*. London: Routledge and Kegan Paul.

McCarthy, J. D., and Zald, N. N. 1977. "Resource Mobilization and Social Movements: A Partial Theory." *American Journal of Sociology* 86: 1212–1241.

Mannheim, K. 1936. *Ideology and Utopia*. New York: Harcourt Press.

———, ed. 1965. *Essays on the Sociology of Knowledge*. London: Routledge and Kegan Paul.

Marris, P. 1980. *Meaning and Action*. Los Angeles: School of Architecture and Urban Planning.

Martin, B. 1981. *A Sociology of Contemporary Cultural Change*. Oxford: Basil Blackwell.

Marx, E. 1982. "Rehabilitation of Slums? The Case of Hatikva Quarter." *The Jerusalem Quarterly* 22: 38–44.

Marx, K., and Engels, F. 1961 edition. "Manifesto of the Communist Party." First published 1848. In K. Marx and F. Engels, *Selected Works I*. Moscow: Progress Publishers.

Maslow, A. H. 1970. *Motivation and Personality*. New York: Harper and Row.

Matras, J. 1973. "Israel's New Frontiers: The Urban Periphery." In M. Curtis and M. S. Chertoff, eds., *Israel: Social Structure and Change*. New Brunswick, N.J.: Transaction Books.

Miller, L. 1973. "Theatre and Community." *Bama: Journal of Art Theatre* 56: 82–88 [Hebrew].

Ministry of Labor, Israel. 1959. *Housing Plan for Five Years: Forecast of Housing Needs, 1960–1965*. Jerusalem [Hebrew].

Minutes of Neighborhood Councils, Activists, and Ohel Councils. 1981. Hebrew.

Minutes of the Katamon Higher Committee. 1981 [Hebrew].

Minutes of the Ohalim Movement [Hebrew] 1973–1981.

Minutes of the YFN. 1982–1986 [Hebrew].

Nahon, Y. 1984. "Ethnic Gaps—A Cross-Temporal Description." In Cohen and Ahimeir, eds., *New Directions in the Study of Ethnic Communities*, pp. 23–43. Jerusalem: Jerusalem Institute for Israel Studies.

Oberschall, A. 1973. *Social Conflict and Social Movements*. Englewood Cliffs, N.J.: Prentice-Hall.

Ohalim (journal of the Ohalim movement). 1980. Special edition. (March) [Hebrew].

Olives, J. 1976. "The Struggle Against Urban Renewal in the 'Cite d'Aliarte' (Paris)." In C. G. Pickvance, ed., *Urban Sociology: Critical Essays*. London: Tavistock.

Olson, M. 1965. *The Logic of Collective Action*. Cambridge, Mass.: Harvard University Press.

Paran, M. 1982. "Organization from Below." *Shoresh* (Root) 1: 31–39 [Hebrew].

Peres, Y. 1976. *Ethnic Relations in Israel*. Tel Aviv: Sifriat Poalim [Hebrew].

Perlman, J. 1982. "Seven Voices from One Organization: What Does It Mean?" Unpublished paper.

Pickvance, C. G. 1976. "On the Study of Urban Social Movements." In C. G. Pickvance, ed., *Urban Sociology: Critical Essays*. London: Tavistock.

———. 1977. "From 'Social Base' to 'Social Force': Some Analytical Issues in the Study of Urban Protest." In M. Harloe, ed., *Captive Cities: Studies in the Political Economy of Cities and Regions*. Chichester: John Wiley.

———. 1985. "The Rise and Fall of Urban Movements and the Role of Comparative Analysis." *Environment and Planning D: Society and Space* 3: 31–54.

Piven, F. F., and Cloward, R. A. 1977. *Poor People's Movements*. New York: Pantheon Books.

Poulantzas, N. 1978. "The Capitalist State: A Reply to Miliband and Laclan." *New Left Review* 95: 63–83.

Prazot (governmental-municipal housing company of Jerusalem). 1981. "Project Rehabilitation in Gonen Chet-Tet, Jerusalem" [Hebrew].

Rex, J. A. 1968. "The Sociology of a Zone in Transition." In R. Pahl, ed., *Readings in Urban Sociology*. New York: Pergamon.

——— and Moore, R. 1967. *Race, Community and Conflict*. London: Oxford University Press.

Rich, R. C. A. 1980. "A Political-Economy Approach to the Study of Neighborhood Organizations." *American Journal of Political Science* 24: 559–592.

Roman, M., and Weingrod, A. 1991. *Living Together Separately: Arabs and Jews in Comtemporary Jerusalem*. Princeton, New Jersey: Princeton University Press.

Ross, D. Undated. *Contacts—Individual and Protest Poems*. Jerusalem: Private publication [Hebrew].

Rothman, J. 1974. "Three Models of Community Organization Practice." In F. M. Cox et al., eds., *Strategies of Community Organization*. Itasca, Ill.: Peacock Publishers.

Rowles, G. D. 1978. "Reflections on Experiential Field Work." In D. Ley and M. Samuels, eds., *Humanistic Geography*. London: Croom Helm.

Sait, E. M. 1963. "Machines, Political." *Encyclopedia of the Social Sciences*, vol. 9, pp. 657–661. New York: Macmillan Company, 15th printing.

Saunders, P. 1980. *Urban Politics*. Harmondsworth, Middlesex: Penguin Books.

———. 1987. *Social Theory and the Urban Question*, 2d ed. London: Unwin Hyman.

Shapiro, Y. 1977. *Democracy in Israel*. Ramat Gan: Massada [Hebrew].

Shilhav, J., and Friedman, M. 1989. *Growth and Segregation—The Ultra Orthodox Community of Jerusalem*. Jerusalem: The Jerusalem Institute for Israel Studies.

Shils, E. 1975. *Center and Periphery: Essays in Macrosociology*. Chicago: University of Chicago Press.

Short, J. R. 1982. *An Introduction to Political Geography*. London: Routledge and Kegan Paul.

Skolnick, J. 1969. *The Politics of Protest: Violent Aspects of Protest and Confrontation*. Washington, D.C.: U.S. Government Printing Office.

Smelser, N. 1963. *The Theory of Collective Behavior*. New York: The Free Press.

———. 1968. *Essays in Sociological Explanation*. Englewood Cliffs, N.J.: Prentice-Hall.

Smooha, S. 1978. *Israel: Pluralism and Conflict*. Berkeley: University of California Press.

———. 1984. "Three Approaches in the Sociology of Ethnic Group Relations in Israel." *Megamot* 28: 169–206 [Hebrew].

——— and Peres, Y. 1975. "The Dynamics of Ethnic Inequality: The Case of Israel." *Social Dynamics* 1: 63–79.

Sprinzak, E. 1986. *Illegalism in Israeli Society*. Tel Aviv: Sifriat Poalim and the Jerusalem Institute for Israel Studies.

Susskind, L., and Elliot, M. 1984. "Paternalism, Conflict and Coproduction: Learning from Citizen Action and Citizen Participation in Western Europe." In D. Soen, F. A. Lazin, and Y. Neumann, eds, *Cities, Communities and Planning In the 1980s*. Aldershot: Gower.

Suttles, G. D. 1972. *The Social Construction of Communities*. Chicago: University of Chicago Press.

Thompson, J. B. 1984. *Studies in the Theory of Ideology*. Cambridge: Polity Press.

Tilly, C., Tilly, L., and Tilly, R. 1975. *The Rebellious Century, 1830–1930*. Cambridge, Mass.: Harvard University Press.

Touraine, A. 1981. *The Voice and the Eye*. Cambridge: Cambridge University Press.

———. 1985. "An Introduction to the Study of Social Movements." *Social Research* 52: 749–787.

Turner, R., and Killian, L. 1972. *Collective Behavior*, 2d ed. Englewood Cliffs, N.J.: Prentice-Hall.

Turner, V. 1969. *The Ritual Process*. Chicago: Aldine.

Weber, M. 1948. *From Max Weber: Essays in Sociology*, trans. and ed. by H. H. Gerth and C. Wright Mills. New York: Oxford University Press.

Wiengrod, A. 1963. "Moroccan Jewry in Transition." *Megamot* 10: 2–12.

———. 1980. "The State of the Art: A Review and Overview." In E. Krausz, ed., *Studies of Israeli Society*. New Brunswick, N.J.: Transaction Books.

Weinshal, D. 1976. "Land Policy." Jerusalem: Institute of Land Use Research [Hebrew].

Yin, R. 1984. *Case Study Research: Design and Method*. Beverly Hills, Calif.: Sage Publications.

Yishai, Y. 1982. "Israel's Right-Wing Jewish Proletariat." *Jewish Journal of Sociology* 24: 87–98.

Zaslavsky, D. 1954. *Immigrant Housing in Israel, 1950–1953*. Tel Aviv: Am Oved [Hebrew].

Index

Activists, 11, 45, 60, 64, 130, 143, 145, 165
  students from South and North America, 102
Actors
  appointed officials, 116
  community leaders of 1st and 2nd generation immigrants, 116
  elected politicians, 116
  social, 158, 176
  state, 165, 166
Amidar (state housing agency), 33
Amiel, Avner (head of Community Work Division in Jerusalem Municipality Department of Social Work), 47, 49–50, 136–137, 139–141
Arabs, relations between Jews and, 2–3, 22, 23, 27, 105, 107, 166, 174
Ashdod, 42, 73
Ashkenazic (plural Ashkenazim) Jews, 23–25, 32, 43, 44, 67, 99, 100, 153
Asia and Africa, 23
Azulai, Akiva (deputy mayor and chairman of Moroccan community in Jerusalem), 119
Baka, 29, 31, 46
Be'ersheva, 29, 42, 73
Begin, Menachem (Likud party leader), 137
Bezalel Art Academy, 94, 95, 99
Black Panthers, Israeli, 12, 13, 25, 26, 31–32, 34, 37–38, 40–42, 44–47, 58–59, 64, 67, 71, 73–74, 76, 81–84, 90, 93–95, 100, 102–103, 105, 107–109, 126–128, 130, 131, 134, 145, 146, 149, 154–156, 164–165, 168, 170, 175
Broken families, 58

asablanca, 98, 117
enter-oriented group. *See* COG
harismatic
  nature of organizations, 170
  routinization of, 148, 170
Classes
  capitalist, 54
  housing, 11, 19, 33, 34, 51
  lower, 2, 3, 26, 33, 51, 96, 115, 153, 163, 168, 169
  managerial, 23
  middle, 28, 32, 153, 169
  petit bourgeoisie, 23, 24
  production, 11
  ruling, 113

Classes (*continued*)
small capitalists, 23
upper, 2, 96, 168
working, 23–24, 33, 53–54, 153–154
lower, 28, 51
new, 24, 26, 153
upper, 28
COG (Center-oriented group), 44–45, 48–49, 65
Collective behavior. *See* Urban social movements, Theories of
Collective consumption, 53–54
Communitas, 156
conflict with social structure, 156
Community centers, 74, 122, 124, 128–131, 139, 144
Community theater, 76, 77
Community workers, 11, 39, 46–51, 58, 77, 78, 97, 101, 102, 104, 106, 125, 129, 131–136, 140, 146, 149, 160
Compulsory Education Act (1953), 35
Conflict
absorption, 114
between science and ethics, 172–177
cultural, between ultraorthodox and secular Jews, 2
class, 136
power, 137, 149
socioethnic, between upper- and lower-class social groups, 2, 24, 49, 90, 91, 113
Consciousness
class, creation of, 136
raising, 48–49, 137, 176
territorial, 65, 136
Context of meaning, 89, 94, 159, 161
Crime, 44, 77
Criminal
groups, 94, 135, 159
records, 33, 40, 125
Dai (Enough—Protest organization), 12, 13, 25, 26, 32, 34, 39, 46, 61, 67, 76–90, 93, 95–96, 98–99, 103, 105, 124, 129, 130, 137, 141, 149, 167
Decision-making, 1, 63, 72, 122, 123
citizen involvement, 36, 65, 165, 167
Democratic values, fostering, 62
Demonstrations, 69, 71, 74, 80, 81, 93, 103, 104, 127, 129
Dimona, 29
Disadvantaged neighborhoods, 11, 12, 37, 50, 64, 91, 99, 103–105, 154, 158, 163, 165–167, 170, 172
Drugs, 41

Education, 29, 42, 74, 77
educational level, 33, 35
educational services, 43
higher, 94–95
Ein-Kerem (Jerusalem neighborhood), 29
Elite
cultural, 23, 103, 106
leadership, 60, 155–156, 160, 167
local, 60, 170
political, 23
power, 23, 24, 154
Employment, 27, 29
Environment
internal, 101
outside, 101
Equal opportunities, 136
Establishment (Israeli)
cooperation with, 45,
"orthodox establishment," 139
Ashkenazic, 154
Ethnic
discrimination, 12, 91
discrimination and social deprivation, 68
disparities, 2, 11, 165

inequality, 24, 82
traditions, 59
Ethnic Coalition of North African Immigrants, 12
Ethnic deprivation, 25, 42, 43
Ethnoclass
gaps, 11, 21, 153
division, 27, 35, 50, 51
Ethnopolitical expression, 43
European Jews. *See* Ashkenazim

Flatto-Sharon (member of Tenth Knesset), 138
Frustration, ethnocultural, 2, 42, 63

Gadish, Yosef (Labor-oriented Jerusalem deputy mayor), 50, 129, 134, 140–141
Gangs, 40, 52, 64, 65, 78, 94, 95, 97, 160, 161
Givat Masuah. *See* "ICL Elit"
Gonen. *See* Katamon
Government reaction to protest movements
blockage of socioterritorial expansion, 128, 130
delegitimization, 128, 130
individualization of macrosocial problems, 130
repression, 128, 130, 146, 147
neutralization of supportive professionals, 128, 130–131
neutralization-repression, 148
support-encouragement, 148
Grass roots
activity, 49, 61, 78, 154
organization, 115, 135, 164
relationship with local government, 140, 149
relationship with the state, 114, 116, 170

Habad (Hassidic movement), 41, 58, 98, 159
Hadera, 73
Haifa, 12
Hava'ad Hale'umi (The National Committee), 23
Hebrew University, organizers from, 48, 50, 78, 98, 142
Heritage
ethnic or historical local, 1
(Moreshet) project, 13, 175
Hirch, Katherine, 67
Histadrut labor federation, 23, 119, 121, 123, 127, 144
elections, 74
Housing
for young couples, 74, 75, 78–79, 80, 122
dilapidated, 2, 74, 82
projects, 2, 3, 11, 27, 30, 56, 76, 82, 126, 159
shortage of, 39
state policy, 11, 21, 27, 31, 79, 133, 141
Human agents, 11, 51
Human rights, 166
Humanistic approach to study of urban social movements
existentialism, 174
ideal speech, 174
phenomenological, 173–174
verstehen, 173–174

ICL (Improvement of Community Life), 12, 13, 34, 39, 46, 49, 50, 61, 67, 76, 77, 79–80, 90, 93, 95, 96, 102, 103, 107, 109, 125, 137, 141, 145, 164, 167, 171
"ICL Elit" settlement on Givat Masuah, 80, 103, 106
Ideologies
class interpretation, 48
ethnic, 44, 48
group-oriented, 156
housing-territorial, 48
nationalist, 44
religious, 44
Immigrant absorption, 2, 22, 27, 117

Immigrant neighborhoods, 3, 12, 57, 126, 127, 140, 154
  shaping of, 2
Improvement of Community Life. *See* ICL
Institutionalization, 145, 167
Integration
  class-party, 137
  sociopolitical, 2
  territorial, 137
International Sephardic Federation, 25, 77, 138
Interpretation of institutional system
  hostile, 98
  positive, 98
Intifada (uprising in occupied territories), 167
Ir Ganim (Jerusalem neighborhood), 12, 13, 28, 29, 31, 33, 34, 41, 43, 49, 50, 61, 76, 79–80, 91, 98, 106, 107, 117, 119, 121, 124, 141, 143
  Iceland Street, 124
Iraqis, 24
Issue-oriented direct action organizations, 164

Jaffa, 29
Jerusalem municipality (city council), 77, 80–82, 121, 123, 129, 131, 133, 138, 164, 166
  elections, 93, 128
  Department of Education, 131
  Department of Social Work, 131
    Community Work Division, 47, 131, 134–135
Jewish Agency, 23, 117, 144
Juvenile delinquents, 44, 46, 51, 58, 72, 134, 149

Kach movement, 174
Katamon (Gonen)
  Alef through Vav, 28, 32, 33, 43
  Daled, 12
  France (organization founded at Sorbonne by Jewish scholars), 77
  Gimel, 12, 82
  Hey, 12
  Het, 32, 33, 141
Katamon Higher Committee, 12, 13, 25, 32, 34, 36, 39, 61, 67, 80, 81, 91, 93, 94, 95, 109–110, 124, 128–129, 160–161, 168, 175
Katamon Tet, 13, 26, 28, 32–34, 38, 41–43, 59, 64, 76, 77, 91, 97, 134, 137, 141, 142
  Bar-Yochai Street, 33, 41, 42, 97
Katamonim (singular Katamon), 12, 29, 31–33, 41, 124, 136
Kibbutz (pl. kibbutzim), 99, 100
Kiriat Menachem (Jerusalem neighborhood), 34, 50, 95, 106
Kiryat Hayovel (Jerusalem neighborhood), 12, 46
Knesset (Israel parliament), 43, 64, 74, 138
  members, 106, 122, 145
Kollek, Teddy (Mayor of Jerusalem), 47, 81, 108, 121, 124, 127, 129, 131, 144, 145
Kurdish community, 24, 25, 124

Labor party (Mapai), 23, 26–27, 43, 44, 49–50, 101, 117, 119–121, 123, 124, 127, 137–140, 145, 148, 153, 154, 167, 171
Labor unions, 54
Lebanon, war in, 167
Leftist parties (Israel), 44, 47, 136, 145
  leftist university students, 102
Likud party, 38, 39, 43, 50, 137, 140, 148, 154, 167
Liminal situation, 35, 156
Local
  democracy, 50, 68, 147, 166

leaders, 11, 20, 39, 40, 51, 61, 116, 145, 166
management, 36, 135, 166
citizen participation in, 63, 122
newspaper, 122
nucleus, 40
politics, 27, 83
representation, 76
Local bosses (bossism), 60, 64, 66, 68, 118–129, 139, 144–147, 154, 161, 170, 171
internal bossism, 65, 67, 98, 115, 117
neighborhood bossism in the American city, 120
Local problems, methods of interpretation: empirical, 91, 92, 100, 107, 109, 158, 161, 164
instrumental, 107, 164
particular, 93, 94, 95, 100, 123, 161, 164, 167
structural, 92, 96, 109, 161
Lod, 29

Ma'abara (pl. ma'abarot—transit camps), 29, 31, 117
Ma'aleh Adumim, 77
Mapai party. *See* Labor party
Mapam (United Labor Party), 49, 102–103
Marciano, Sa'adia (Black Panther leader), 40
Matzpen (Israeli Leftist-Trotskyist organization), 47, 102, 130, 131, 134
Media, 19, 51, 69, 128
alternative, 168
Mediators, 116–120, 123, 125, 154
Meir, Golda (Israeli Prime Minister), 127, 132
Mekor Haim (Jerusalem residential district), 76
Ministry of Housing, 50, 77, 80, 93, 122, 144
Modernization, 21, 35, 36
Morocco
immigrants from, 12, 24, 25, 31, 105, 117, 119
Casablanca, 98, 117
Moroccan Jewish Association, 25
Mukhtar (local governor of Oriental Jews in Palestine), 118
Musrara (Jerusalem neighborhood), 12, 13, 29, 31, 34, 38, 41–43, 46, 61, 64, 76–80, 91, 99, 107, 124, 131, 134, 141
Ayin Chet Street, 32

Naggid (local governor in North Africa), 118
Nahla'ot (Jerusalem neighborhood), 12, 136
National Insurance Act (1953), 35
Neighborhood
clubs, 47, 131
nationalism, developing of, 136
Nicanor (section of Katamon), 80

Oded (Left-wing organization of Oriental intellectuals), 102
Ofakim, 29
Ofek (student faction associated with Labor party), 106
Ohalim
movement, 12, 13, 25, 26, 34, 41, 42, 47, 58, 59, 64, 65, 67, 71–76, 81–82, 90, 93–100, 102, 103, 105, 107–109, 124–128, 130, 131, 134–135, 137–140, 143, 146, 149, 155, 156, 159, 164, 165, 168, 170, 171, 175
party, 64
Ohel
Baka, 42
councils, 13, 42, 45, 64, 65, 125
Moreh, 74–75, 138, 140
Nahla'ot, 42
Shmuel, 34, 42, 65, 67, 80–81, 93, 94, 95, 110, 140, 145, 167

Ohel (*continued*)
Stern, 42
Yosef, 12, 25, 26, 34, 38–39, 41, 42, 44, 46, 59, 64, 67, 76–77, 80, 90, 93, 95, 96, 97, 100, 102, 107, 108, 127, 129, 130, 135, 137–138, 140–142, 145, 149, 155, 164, 167
Olswanger (Jerusalem neighborhood), 46
Opportunity theory, 42
Oriental Jews. *See* Sephardic
Orientation
class, 109
ethnic, 109
local, 102
social, 109, 169
universal 71 (Fig. 2), 102, 126, 161, 169

Paran, Michael, 47–48, 135–137
Parochialism, 171
Pat housing project (Jerusalem neighborhood), 12, 59, 74, 80, 104, 137
Paternalistic relationships, 127, 146
Patron-client relations, 119
Patronage system, 125, 157, 161, 165, 174
Peace Now movement, 50, 93, 103, 105, 106, 168
Peled, Ela'ad (Jerusalem deputy mayor), 139–140
Physical and social disadvantage, 58
POG (Periphery-oriented group), 44–45, 48–49, 65
Poland, Jews from, 38
Political
bureaucratic system, 120
control, 36, 151
democratization, 122
expression, outlet for, 2
influence, 68
machine, 121
participation in, 36
parties, 93
power, 126
representation, 79, 82
response, 132
support, 137
Politicians
progressive, 149
traditional, 149–150
Politics
of consumption and wealth distribution, 114
of production and wealth creation, 114
Poor neighborhoods, 40, 127
Porush, Rabbi Menachem (Jerusalem deputy mayor), 131
Poverty belt, 32
Power, centers of, 63, 64, 113, 127, 144, 155
social, 65
concentration of, 66, 124
positions of, 80, 115, 123
relations, between the state and newcomers, 115
relations and strategies of action, 115
source of, 108, 122
structure, 149
will for, 118
Prazot (public housing company), 78, 142
Pressure groups, 19
Prime Minister's Committee for Youth in Distress, 76
Professionals, progressive, 149
traditional, 149–150
Project Renewal Program, 38, 39, 61, 64, 77, 78, 81, 99, 122, 124, 133–134, 141–143, 145, 146, 164, 166, 167
local involvement: steering committee, 39, 122, 124, 125, 129, 130, 142, 144, 147
council, 39, 95, 125

Protest
consumption sphere, 56
cultural sphere, 56
differences between (Table 2), 84
divergence of, 68, 70 (Fig. 1)
organizations, rise of, 2
poem, 105
political sphere, 56
radical and violent, 127
social conflict, 56
songs, 49
theaters, 38, 49, 155

Rakah (New Communist party), 137, 138, 145, 171
I Am Israel organization, 139
Ramla, 29
Rashbag (section of Katamon neighborhood), 12, 80
Rehavia (Jerusalem residential district), 79
Religious revivalism, 43
Resource mobilization. *See* Urban social movements, Theories of
Resources
financial, 49
material, 169
political-economic, 130
social and physical, 1
Romania (Jews from), 38
Routinization, 148, 163, 164, 166, 167

Search for identity. *See* Urban social movements, Theories of
Secular groups, 167
Secularization, 133
Self
self-assertion, 155
self-help alternative institutions, 164
self-identity, 54–55
self-image, 155
self-realization, 155
Sephardic (plural: Sephardim) Jews (Oriental or Asian, Middle Eastern, and North African born), 12, 21, 23–26, 29, 31, 33–35, 38, 43, 51, 67, 72, 90, 100, 105, 118–119, 133, 153, 154, 163, 168, 169
Services
development of, 77
public, 63, 74, 82
self-help, 12, 45, 135, 142, 165
Settlement policy, Israel Government's, 50, 138
in occupied territories, 75, 77, 90, 103, 167
Shahak (Improvement of Community Life). *See* ICL
Shalvi, Professor Alice, 67
Shas (ultraorthodox Sephardi party), 43
Shchunat Habucharim (Jerusalem neighborhood), 141
Sheli (Peace for Israel—leftist party), 137, 138, 145, 171
Young People for Sheli, 138
Shmuel Hanavi (Jerusalem neighborhood), 12, 28, 29, 31, 34, 41, 43, 61, 124, 136, 141
Siah (The Israeli New Left), 47, 103, 130, 131, 134
Slum areas, 56, 168
slum-dwellers, 38, 39, 47, 115
Social
action, 60, 81, 87–89, 92, 135, 160, 163
behavior, 37, 165
belonging, 36
change, 82, 113, 136, 165, 166, 167
conflict, 24, 55, 56, 147
deprivation, 1, 2
disintegration, 132

Social (*continued*)
  enclosure, 50, 52
  force, 49
  identity, 60, 158
  interaction, 161
  justice, 136
  legislation, 136
  liberation, 82
  organizers, 40, 46, 64
  planning, 29
  protest, 1, 29, 38, 40, 50, 110–111, 126, 135, 146, 163
  relationships, reproduction of, 88
  resentment, 38
  services, delivery of, 1, 9
    lack of, 2
    provision of, 27, 32, 34, 78
    system of, 74
  structure, 10, 161
  struggle, 54
  trends, 82–83
  unrest, 50, 154
  values, 37, 72, 115
  wage, 53
Social movements, 3
  civil rights, 169
  control, 54, 69
  ecological, 54
  feminist, 54, 168, 169
  genuine urban, 54
  reform, 54, 69, 126
  student, 54
Social movements, ideal types
  particularism and activity outside the system, 69
  particularism and activity within the system, 69
  universalism and activity outside the system, 69
  universalism and activity within the system, 69
Socialization, 163, 164
Social Welfare Act (1958), 35
Sociocultural identity, 62
  characteristics, 94, 109
Socioeconomic disparity, 30
  mobility, 58, 125
  reforms, 72
  stratification, 33
  weakness, 117
Sociogeographic conditions, 89, 94, 121
Sociopolitical
  change, 82
  criticism, 36, 98
  discourse, 60
  expectations, 36
  pluralism, 113
  policy, 72
  relations, 62
Sociospatial disparities, 31
  relationship, 29
  structure, 31, 153
  system, 30
Soviet Jewry, 38, 39, 40, 167
Spatial enclosure, 21
Spatial planning, 29
Spatial polarization, 51
Spatial segregation, 50
Squatters
  campaigns, 74, 81
  Lifta "settlements," 74
  movements, 9
  protest squat, 49, 59, 69, 71, 104, 127, 168
State
  agencies, 33
  cooperation with neighborhoods, objectives of, 132, 142
  involvement, dependency on, 68, 83
  relationships with urban social movements, 11, 113, 115, 143, 146, 147, 150–151, 164
Stern Street (Jerusalem neighborhood), 12, 141
Strategy
  conflict, 114, 132, 147
  confrontation-repression, 11, 81, 95, 115, 116, 147
  cooptation, 115, 142, 161
  coproduction, 11, 92, 114–116, 141, 145–147

economic, 11
exchange, 116, 143, 144, 147
of action, 11, 69, 70 (Fig. 1), 81, 88, 110, 114, 145
paternalism and control, 11, 114, 116–118, 146
Strategy-orientation classification, 91, 92 (Fig. 3)
development of social classes, 51
Structural
changes, 21, 51
strains, 21, 114
Structural Marxist and neo-Marxist approach. *See* Urban social movements, Theories of
Supraneighborhood action, 170

Talpiot educational institution, 74
Tami (ethnic Sephardic political party), 154
Tel Aviv, 42, 73
Tent-protest encampments, 39, 168
Tsalash (Youth for the Neighborhood movement). *See* YFN

Ultraorthodox Jews, 2, 3, 167
Unemployment, 26, 32, 39, 41, 58, 94, 95, 125, 167
Universal-expressive orientation, 68, 71, 102
Urban social movements, 3
application of social control, 17
consumption, 9
coordinated group, 17
development, 4–6
generalized beliefs, 16
modernization, 21
precipitating factors, 17, 22
relation to societal structures
capitalist mode of production, 18
industrial mode of development, 18
information mode of development, 18
state power, 18
relative deprivation, 16, 21
social mobility, 21, 22, 30, 34–36, 42, 115
social mobilization, 22, 37
structural changes, 21
structural conduciveness, 16
structural conflict with state, 146
structural strains, 16, 21, 114
theories of
collective behavior, 7, 9, 15, 17, 18, 19, 46, 50, 161, 163
resource mobilization, 7, 9, 19, 20, 46, 50, 51, 77, 161, 170
relative deprivation approach, 16
search for identity, 7, 8, 9, 62
structural-Marxist, 7, 9, 17, 51, 55, 57, 163
neo-Marxist, 50, 113, 150–151, 176
Weberian, 18, 51, 114
neo-Weberian, 18, 35, 50, 113, 114, 150–151, 176
types of
citizen, 56, 68, 87
community, 56, 68, 87
coproductive organization (control), 83, 87, 94, 95, 96, 161
trade unionism, 56, 68, 87
urban social movement (genuine), 83, 87, 95, 96
neighborhood protest (reform), 83, 87, 95, 96
Urban unrest, 167
USSR. *See* Soviet Jewry

Vocational training, 122, 144
Volunteers, 11, 13, 51, 63, 65, 66, 77

Wadi Salib, 12, 29, 46, 154
War, 1973 (Yom Kippur), 38

Weberian and neo-Weberian schools. *See* Urban social movements, Theories of
Welfare, 29, 32, 36, 58, 127
  policy 35, 114
  services, 125, 136
West Bank (of Jordan River—refers to territories occupied by Israel). *See* Settlement policy
Women, position of in protest movements, 67, 170
World Sephardic Federation. *See* International Sephardic Federation
Yemenites, 24
Yeruham, 29
YFN (Youth for the Neighborhood movement), 12, 13, 34, 39, 41, 58, 59, 61, 62, 65, 66, 70, 80, 81, 82, 91, 93, 94, 97–98, 101–102, 107, 109, 125, 130, 143, 144, 145, 155, 156, 167, 168, 170, 171
'Yorams' (conforming to mainstream group), 135
Youth clubs, 99